# HOW TO DESIGN AND WRITE WEB PAGES TODAY

Second Edition

## Karl Stolley

GREENWOOD™

An Imprint of ABC-CLIO, LLC

Santa Barbara, California • Denver, Colorado

**Library of Congress Cataloging-in-Publication Data**

Names: Stolley, Karl, author.
Title: How to design and write web pages today / Karl Stolley.
Description: Second edition. | Santa Barbara, California : Greenwood,
    [2017] | Includes bibliographical references and index.
Identifiers: LCCN 2016054208 (print) | LCCN 2016056124 (ebook) |
    ISBN 9781440843136 (hardback : alk. paper) | ISBN 9781440857423
    (pbk. : alk. paper) | ISBN 9781440843143 (ebook)
Subjects: LCSH: Web sites—Design.
Classification: LCC TK5105.888 .S76 2017 (print) | LCC TK5105.888
    (ebook) | DDC 006.7—dc23
LC record available at https://lccn.loc.gov/2016054208

ISBN: 978-1-4408-4313-6 (hardcover)
ISBN: 978-1-4408-5742-3 (paperback)
EISBN: 978-1-4408-4314-3

21  20  19  18  17     1  2  3  4  5

This book is also available as an eBook.

Greenwood
An Imprint of ABC-CLIO, LLC

ABC-CLIO, LLC
130 Cremona Drive, P.O. Box 1911
Santa Barbara, California 93116-1911
www.abc-clio.com

This book is printed on acid-free paper ∞
Manufactured in the United States of America

# CONTENTS

**PART IV. PROBLEMS AND SOLUTIONS**

# PREFACE

The arts are made great, not by those who are without scruple in boasting about them, but by those who are able to discover all of the resources which each art affords.

*—Isocrates, ca. 390 BCE*

The web is unique among all forms of digital communication, in that top to bottom, the web is language. Language that you can learn to read and write. The visual designs of your pages, the structure of their content, the rich interactions that enhance your pages, and even the web servers that deliver your pages to readers—all are nothing more than the products of language. And those who wish to be rhetorically successful on the web must command its languages and their driving concepts in order to best communicate with the unique audience for any given website.

The ability to write and design and communicate effectively on the web is not determined by how much money you have, the software you can afford to buy, or the whims of any particular computer company. It is determined instead by how well you can command the languages of the web to best communicate with the audience you are hoping to reach, while being sensitive to the range of devices and abilities that in turn empower and constrain any potential visitor to your site.

# RHETORIC AND TECHNOLOGY

The web has become a commonplace technology, so deeply embedded in day-to-day experience that it's easy to forget that it's even there. It powers your favorite smartphone app. It delivers movies to your home on demand. It gives you instant access not only to news around the globe but also to what your friends are up to on whatever social networking sites you participate in.

When you sit down and write for the web yourself, it's tempting to think that nothing you've learned previously about writing and communicating will have much benefit. But the challenges of writing for the web are just a recent development in the more than 2,500-year-old tradition known as the art of rhetoric. And it is rhetoric, in tandem with a rhetorical understanding of users and technology, that has informed the web writing and design principles in this book.

You may be more familiar with the word *rhetoric* in its popular, negative usage: politicians in particular routinely attack one another for spouting "empty rhetoric" or "heated rhetoric." My PhD is in rhetoric, and I like to joke that it's the dirtiest word with its own PhD. While the popular usage of the word *rhetoric* is unfortunate and derived from some interesting history that I won't cover here, there are still positive meanings of the word, and that's what you will find in this book.

Rhetoric, in its better sense, is a productive, generative art of communicating with other human beings, using some kind of symbols: speech, writing, images, design, and even computer code. The art of rhetoric enables people to discover, as it is expressed in Aristotle's *Rhetoric*, the available means for developing something to say, and for supporting what it is that they have to say. Rhetoric also suggests how to establish the best form in which to say something, and to deliver it appropriately for a particular audience in a specific setting, sensitive to the context of the audience's values and beliefs.

All of these issues—development, form, audience, and context—are central to the affordances, or available means, of web communication. And all of the web's affordances are derived from language: the language of the content that you post to the web (your text, images, media files, and page design), of course. But the web also has its own languages, including Hypertext Markup Language (HTML), Cascading

Style Sheets (CSS), and ECMAScript, better known as JavaScript. Languages are also used to control the behavior of different web servers, from the old standby Apache server to newer upstarts like Nginx (pronounced "engine-ex"). A JavaScript runtime environment called Node.js lets you install and run your own short-lived web server to test your web writing and design as you work, without exposing your struggles to the open web. And there will be struggles. This is a challenging book that will guide you in practices typically reserved for professional web designers and developers.

Writing and designing a technically impressive site for the web is a worthy goal. But it's not enough. Anyone can post a site, and perhaps even draw people to it once. To go further and provide an experience that merits return visits (or job offers, or admission to schools, or more customers for a business or members in a club) is a matter of good content, good design, and thoughtful use of the technologies that make up the web. It's all, in other words, a matter of good rhetoric.

And that is what I think makes this book unique. Learning technologies apart from rhetoric will gain you nothing more than technical proficiency. Learning rhetoric apart from the technologies and languages will leave you at the mercy of whatever technology you can afford, or person you can afford to hire to build websites for you.

The techniques and approaches that this book covers are grounded in a particular view of human relationships to technology: one that asks you to work differently with web technologies in order to deepen your understanding of them. Building a website is a good goal. Changing how you think, learn, and talk about building a website is a far more challenging goal. But it is a goal that will reward you over the long term.

## KNOWLEDGE AND VOCABULARY

One thing you will notice about this book is that it does not shy away from the technical knowledge and vocabulary of web writing and design. There is a very good reason for this: more than any other form of digital writing, writing for the web is a community activity. People work together to establish new practices and technologies for communicating on the web. Sometimes, as in Ethan Marcotte's term *responsive web design*, which is covered at length in Chapter 14, community members combine a certain set of technologies to achieve a particular effect, described in language that helps to spread the practice.

But in order to benefit from the knowledge of any community—whether photographers, hockey players, or web designers—you have to know or be willing to learn the words that each community uses. And that's in addition to actually practicing the activity at the center of the community. Think for a moment about your hobbies, your college major, or a class you have taken: in each of those areas, you have acquired specialized knowledge and words to talk in a more sophisticated way about different subjects than someone on the outside.

Writing for the web is no different. Technical terms have an especially bad reputation, but they are no more difficult than those from any other specialized subject or domain of knowledge. Web design and development is just another domain. This book does not expect that you already know the terms used in web design, but it will help you learn them, search the web and read documentation for them, and encourage you to use them when collaborating with others on web projects.

## ESSENTIAL TOOLS AND TECHNOLOGY

In addition to knowledge and vocabulary, you need to learn the community's tools: in the web's case, the tools are the languages—HTML, CSS, and JavaScript—that people use to write for the web. They do so using a few generic pieces of software: a text editor, a search engine, and a web browser. More sophisticated writers also use a version-control system and some kind of runtime environment to test their work away from the open web. This book will address those more sophisticated technologies, too.

However, this book does not teach web writing according to one particular piece of software, and it outright discourages the use of what-you-see-is-what-you-get (WYSIWYG) software packages and similar hosted services, because WYSIWYGs fail at three important things:

- First, WYSIWYGs fail to support revision to sites and pages. Writing must always be revised. It never comes out right the first time. On the web, content other than text will need to be revised, including the HTML, CSS, and JavaScript that structures, styles, and enhances text and media content. Those kinds of revisions are not easily accomplished in a WYSIWYG editor. Web page creation is relatively easy; web page revision is not.

- Second, WYSIWYGs fail to prepare their users for forms of web writing that have no visual component. Accessing open data APIs (application programming interface) to dynamically load external content into a website, for example, has no visual equivalent. Neither do the kinds of rich, semantic structures that make for a more accessible web for all people, including those with low vision.

- Third, WYSIWYGs fail at doing the one job they promise: offering an honest and accurate view of a web page as it's being written. Screen sizes and pixel densities vary greatly across a growing range and variety of devices. The interface style of WYSIWYGs was developed in the age of print, when one-to-one correspondence between screen and printed page mattered greatly, and was actually achievable. But there is no one-to-one correspondence between one screen and another in digital work. Accounting for all of the different sizes of screens is a delicate balance between the content you wish to deliver and a design that works in support of your content, not the arbitrary screen widths of a select group of popular phones, tablets, and desktops.

It was exactly those three problems that I encountered in my own web design work and teaching that led me to research, develop, and refine the methods presented in this book.

If you know or are willing to learn the languages of the web, then you will always know how to build web pages, regardless of what software you have available. Learning the languages of the web, coupled with the concepts for thinking and talking about them, will make it even easier for you to pick up other languages, or changes to existing ones, in the future.

# ORGANIZATION OF THIS BOOK

This book is a complete approach to web writing and design: it takes you from learning to read the web like a writer and designer, up through posting a complete, responsive, customized web design. The book itself is organized into a few broad sections:

- "What Am I Writing?" considers the rhetorical situation of the web, including why a web presence that you develop and control is an essential counterpart to social media profiles that you might maintain. This section of the book sets up some important concepts behind the practice of web writing and design. It also introduces a technology called version control that can have a wide-ranging impact on how you build all kinds of digital work, not just websites.

- "Issues and Challenges" presents accessibility, usability, and sustainability as three guiding principles for making informed decisions about every component of your site. All three principles are key to building a site that reaches the widest possible audience, while giving you the foundation to revise and improve your site over time.

- "Strategies for Success" covers essential techniques and strategies that you need to write and design individual web pages. Because a website is basically a collection of pages, any successful site depends on the solid construction of each page.

- "Problems and Solutions" moves to the challenges of constructing and maintaining entire websites. This section outlines site architecture and various tools that enhance website construction. It also describes methods for extending your web presence to the social web.

- And finally, "Resources for the Future" provides a topical list of additional publications to consult to expand your knowledge of writing and designing for the web.

Because this book is a technical treatment of web design, it will necessarily cover many technical topics and terms. A glossary is provided near the end of the book to help you manage the book's many technical terms and concepts.

The book also has a companion site, at http://webpg.es/, with additional source code and live examples that cannot be reproduced usefully in print. I have also created a Rapid Prototyping Kit (RPK) that is available as a free download on the companion site. The RPK will help you start building your site and its pages with confidence, while still giving you plenty of flexibility to meet the specific needs of your audience.

## REFERENCES

Aristotle. 1984. *The Rhetoric and Poetics of Aristotle*, trans. W. R. Roberts. New York: Modern Library.

Isocrates. 1929. "Against the Sophists." In vol. 2 of *Isocrates*, trans. G. Nordlin. Loeb Classical Library. Cambridge, MA: Harvard University Press.

# PART I

# WHAT AM I WRITING?

You can begin writing for the web immediately, even before tackling HTML, CSS, JavaScript and the other technical material that comes later. As with all other parts of this book, you will stand to benefit most if you read with a computer or mobile device nearby so you can try some things out and learn in a hands-on way.

On the web, we write to be found and connect with other people—an idea the first chapter explores along with simple things you can do to immediately begin establishing or improving your web presence. The second chapter offers approaches and tools for reading the web with a writer/designer mindset that will inspire and improve your own work.

The remainder of Part I covers content preparation for sites built according to standards-based, mobile-first responsive web design. Chapter 4 provides a brief history of how web pages were made in the past, and how they are made now. Understanding your work in the context of the web's history will help you avoid the mistakes of the past.

Finally, this section concludes with two chapters that cover best practices for setting up your own custom environment to write, design, and test your pages. Chapter 6 describes the use of a version control system called Git. Building great web pages is more than what any one piece of software can do. Some of the best software you can download for building web pages is freely and legally available on the internet, thanks to many thousands of volunteers who devote their time and effort to develop quality free and open-source software.

# CHAPTER 1

# Why Write for the Web?

When you write for the web, you write for every web-connected device on the planet. No other digital format is so widely accessible, with the possible exception of email. But email has nowhere near the expressive range for content and design that the web does. Web pages written according to the proper standards and best techniques are equally accessible on the latest-model smartphone and a 15-year-old computer, and all imaginable devices in between. The web provides incredible reach and the promise of equal access, even to people with disabilities.

## WRITING TO BE FOUND

Whether you are building a website for yourself, or for a business or organization, there is no more important reason to write for the web than to build a stable, custom online identity that you control. It is no secret that many web platforms, including popular social media sites, exist to make money. If they cease to make money, they cease to exist. Your identity should not evaporate with them.

It is also no secret that schools and employers search the web for their applicants' names as part of their admissions or hiring process. And yet for many people, the results that show up in Google and other search engines fail to convey an accurate, well-rounded identity.

Do a Google search for your name right now. Be sure and try variations on your name, too. If your name is Jennifer, for example, but you sometimes go by Jenny, search for both along with your last name. You might even want to search for alternate spellings of your name: in

Jennifer's case, Jenny, Jennie, and Jenni. Be sure to search for different permutations for how your name might be listed. In my case, I search for:

- `Karl Stolley`
- `"Karl Stolley"` (with quotation marks, to search first and last names appearing in sequence)
- `"Stolley, Karl"` (with quotes, to search last name first, as some pages list names that way)

What kinds of results appear for your name? People with common names, like Jim Smith, may see results for dozens, even hundreds of other people with the same name.

If that's the case for you, you'll want to whittle down the results. Try adding to your name the city where you live, your employer, job title, occupation or professional field, or perhaps the school you attend. For example, I will search for these variations:

- `Dr Stolley Chicago`
- `Professor Stolley Illinois Institute of Technology`

Even for people with uncommon names, the search results may not be encouraging. There may be no results for your name at all. And if there are results, they may be scattered, confusing, and downright goofy: perhaps you were quoted in a story for a school or local newspaper. You might find yourself on a missing classmates page in the alumni area of a college or university website. Or perhaps you used your real name when replying to an online forum about troubles with the type of car you drive. You might even find that some well-meaning relative tagged you in an unflattering photograph on Facebook, and made it public.

In all of those cases, the search results do not point positively to one page or another that fully and accurately represents you. As you look at the list appearing with your name, ask yourself: "What would a potential employer, or a potential college or graduate school think of these results?" If you're working on a website for a business or a club, and searching the web for its name, ask yourself what potential customers or members would think.

Scattered, random results are frustrating. And if you have your own website already, it might be even more frustrating to discover that it does not appear as the number-one search ranking for your name, or even in the top 10.

## STAYING SAFE ONLINE

Everyone's heard news stories of identity theft, stalking surveillance, and other dangers lurking on the web. There's no need to recount them here, or to let them act as a deterrent for building a web presence. But there are some simple things you should do to establish an online presence while keeping yourself safe:

- Don't post any text or media containing sensitive personal information about yourself or others.
- Don't unwittingly reveal location-based information about yourself or others that could endanger you, your family, or your property. That includes location-based check-ins as well as photos and posts that embed geotagging information.
- Transmit passwords, social security numbers, and other sensitive information only over secure, encrypted channels. Email and most messaging apps are not properly encrypted for those purposes.

Many sites require you to set up security questions to aid you in accessing your account should you forget your username or password. Be very careful about choosing questions whose answers are available online. If you have listed your hometown or high school in an online profile, avoid security questions like "What is your city of birth?" or "What was your high school mascot?" If a site allows you to write your own security questions, choose that option, and keep them obscure: "What was your family's word for milk?" or "Where do you think you lost your favorite toy in third grade?" Better yet, use a password manager to record the questions and nonsense answers.

Visit the National Cyber Security Alliance site `https://stay safeonline.org` and the Electronic Frontier Foundation's Surveillance Self-Defense program `https://ssd.eff.org` to learn more about computer safety and privacy.

The methods for web writing and design presented in this book will help you to establish your web presence and, in the process, likely improve your site's ranking in Google and other search engines.

## WRITING TO ESTABLISH AN ONLINE IDENTITY

Whether or not you have a website, one simple step for establishing an online identity is to begin microblogging. There are numerous social sites and apps that encourage brief posts, although perhaps the most

---

### STRONG PASSWORDS

The best way to maintain strong, secure passwords is to use a password manager, which can generate and store completely random passwords for you, protected under one *very* long master password. The securest password is one that you don't know at all.

If you don't want to invest in a password manager, you need at the very least to use strong passwords on all of your accounts. It's now conventional wisdom to avoid using dictionary words, the username itself, or an all-number password. Here is a strategy for creating rock-solid passwords:

- Create a string of letters derived from song lyrics, a line in a poem, or some other phrase that you'll remember easily. "Yankee Doodle came to town, riding on a pony" becomes `ydcttroap`.
- Unlike usernames, which I prefer to keep all lowercase, mix in some uppercase letters (make all nouns uppercase, so they're scattered throughout the password); "Yankee Doodle" has uppercase built in: `YDctTroaP`.
- Swap out lowercase letters with numbers and symbols (note that some services disallow certain characters; adjust your password accordingly). `YDctTroaP` might become `YDc+Tr0aP`, with plus signs replacing the lowercase t, and a zero replacing the lowercase o.
- If you have no other non-alphanumeric symbols, throw in an exclamation mark somewhere: `YD!ctTr0aP`.

The song will make the password easier to remember, but only time and your own consistency (e.g., treating letter Os as zeros) will make number- and symbol-swapping memorable. Remember that the longer the password, the better.

popular is Twitter. You can post to Twitter and most other similar services via their websites, apps on your phone or tablet, or stand-alone clients for your desktop computer.

Registration on Twitter is quick and free (see the "Controlling Your Name" sidebar for help choosing a Twitter username). But Twitter might seem ridiculous to those who haven't tried it: What possible good can 140-character microblog posts do for establishing an online identity? The answer lies in many little lessons that Twitter and similar services teach about web writing in general:

- **Be interesting.** Yes, you can announce that you're eating a sandwich or walking the dog. But that's not terribly interesting. It's much better to post your perspective on issues you care about, or to share unusual details about your professional work or interests.
- **Get to the point, because no one has time.** Brevity is key to web writing. No one has time, so maximum rhetorical impact must be achieved in a few words. Frequent use of Twitter will help you learn the art of minimal expression.
- **Frequent activity is essential to any web presence.** Pages that appear not to have been updated for some time are suspect to web audiences and might seem to have been abandoned. With Twitter's 140-character limit, it is easy to update often and without the extended efforts required of full-on blogs or websites.
- **Write once, publish (just about) everywhere and often.** Some people use their Twitter account to update their Facebook status, and many others use Twitter's API and widgets to publish their latest Tweets to their own websites. Updating Twitter, in other words, causes multiple sites to update simultaneously.
- **There is more to connecting on the web than linking to pages.** An essential part of Twitter is following others' tweets and, by posting interesting things, others following yours. Building networks of connections with other humans is an essential part of being found on the web and establishing an identity that is not an island unto itself. Well-crafted websites become easy to share on social media, too (see Chapter 25).

## CONTROLLING YOUR NAME

Control as many accounts and register as many domain names of your name or your organization's name as possible, even if they go unused. Sites like `http://namechk.com` let you check the availability of usernames over hundreds of sites and services all at once.

Of course, if your name is common enough, it may not be available. Consider these alternatives with the example name of Laura Amy Smith:

- `laura-smith` (addition of a hyphen)
- `laura-a-smith` (middle initial plus hyphens to improve readability, and avoid the double-a of `lauraasmith`, which looks like a typo)
- `laura-amy-smith` (middle name plus hyphens)

Here are other guidelines for registering usernames:

- Don't add numbers or dates corresponding to your birthday, birth month, or birth year.
- Don't include the place where you live (people do move, after all).
- Don't truncate your name in ways that make it look like a typo, e.g., `laurasmit`, with the h dropped.
- For some, professions or job titles might make sense (e.g., `chef-laura-smith`), but career changes are commonplace, too.

Whatever variation or addition you make on your name, keep it readable and memorable.

Beyond microblogging, there are other general categories of social sites where you can begin to establish your online presence by registering and using an account:

- Social bookmarking, such as Pinterest, for sharing bookmarks to things you find on the web
- Professionally oriented networking, such as LinkedIn, in addition to Twitter and Facebook
- Photo sharing, such as Instagram and Flickr
- Video sharing, such as YouTube and Vimeo

## DO UNTO OTHERS . . .

Simply stated, **Don't use your website or any social media account to harm or attack others.** Even more simply stated, don't be a bully or a troll.

Once you begin to write and design for the web, you may find yourself wanting to mention friends and colleagues by name. I have a simple rule about this: never refer by full name to someone who does not have a presence on the web or the service where you're writing, or who is not a public figure or published author. If someone blogs or Tweets under an alias, refer to her by her alias, not her full name.

It is also good practice to avoid referring to conflicts or sensitive situations within your family, school, or workplace, even if you withhold names. My own preference is to avoid referring to family, school, and workplaces entirely.

## WRITING TO CONNECT WITH PEOPLE

A central idea in this book is that you should write and design for the web because, done properly, web writing is a universally accessible form of digital expression. You can reach just about anyone, provided they can find your work. But being found requires more than good search rankings. You need to go out and find others, too. Twitter, Facebook, and other social sites and apps allow you to do this through direct follow or friend relationships.

There are less-structured ways of connecting with others, too. Just as you searched for your own name in Google and other search engines above, you can search for the names of your friends, peers, and colleagues, too. Some of them may have websites and blogs. Finding new people is as simple as searching for interests, professions, or careers and the words *professional website* or *blog*.

Once you have your own website, regularly linking to others' sites or blog posts and portfolio items helps you to develop even more connections with other people. Chapter 25 goes into greater depth on how to establish your site as part of the social web.

## NEXT STEPS

On the web, we write to be found. Twitter is a great first step to establishing an online presence, as are other social media sites that allow you to connect with other people. But such sites are just a start. A custom website that you control is the central component to a well-rounded web identity. The next chapter will address the important rhetorical skill of reading the web, which will help you see how others have worked to establish an identity for themselves. It will also help you develop a better sense of how other sites have been constructed.

# CHAPTER 2

# Reading the Web

Every view of the web is unique. Someone accessing a website on an iPhone with the Safari web browser will see a very different view of a web page compared to someone on a desktop computer running Windows 10 and the Microsoft Edge browser. Someone using an Android tablet to access the web will see still another view. And a person with low vision might not even see the web, but will hear it read aloud instead.

For new and seasoned web writers and designers alike, this is the most important lesson to learn: every view of the web is unique, and every view of the web *should* be unique. That is not a failure of the web, but one of its strengths. The goal of every website should be to anticipate and build upon the differences and needs of a wide range of readers to make each unique view as great as possible. That means abandoning any attempts at uniformity across all experiences of a website. It's not only impossible, but the pursuit of uniformity can actually diminish the experience for a significant number of users.

This book contains guidance for writing and designing to the diversity and differences among different views of the web. The purpose of this chapter is to help you learn to read the web not as a casual user, but as a writer and designer. It is important that web writers and designers appreciate just how differently a page may appear under different circumstances across different platforms and devices. Understanding and appreciating those differences from a reader's perspective will help you become more effective at creating pages that work optimally in many different browsing environments.

## READING WITH MULTIPLE BROWSERS AND DEVICES

Some people access the web using the browser that came installed on their computers: for Windows users, this means Microsoft Internet Explorer or Edge; for macOS users, Safari. Some might have downloaded and installed Google Chrome or Mozilla Firefox. Web writers and designers need to go beyond their own habitual browser use and look at the web in many different ways, using multiple browsers and devices (see the sidebar "A Web-Reading Toolkit").

Try using a different browser every day for a week or so. Rotate through Mozilla Firefox, Google Chrome, Opera, and Vivaldi, particularly with sites you visit every day. Also see if you can install a different

## A WEB-READING TOOLKIT

These free browsers and tools offer many different views of the web for use in your reading and testing. Links are also available on the book's companion site, `http://webpg.es/`:

- Mozilla Firefox (`http://www.mozilla.com/firefox`)
- Firefox Developer Edition (`https://www.mozilla.org/en-US/firefox/developer/`)
- Chris Pederick's Web Developer Add-on for Firefox (`https://addons.mozilla.org/firefox/addon/60`)
- Google Chrome (`http://www.google.com/chrome/`)
- Chris Pederick's Web Developer Add-on for Chrome (`https://chrome.google.com/webstore/detail/web-developer/bfbameneiokkgbdmiekhjnmfkcnldhhm?hl=en-US`)
- Opera (`http://www.opera.com/`)
- Vivaldi (`https://vivaldi.com/`)
- Lynx, a text-only browser (search Google to learn how to install it on your operating system)

If you are not able to install software, try a Google search for "browser emulator" to find sites that offer approximations of the views provided by different browsers.

browser than the one that came with your phone or tablet, if you have one. Install ad-blockers wherever possible, and note sites that disallow access until the blocker is disabled.

You might find that different browsers are better suited to different purposes. On Windows computers, I prefer Chrome for most daily use. On macOS, I prefer Safari. And on all computers, I rely on Firefox Developer Edition for web design and development. Firefox and Chrome both have long-standing support for third-party add-ons, such as Chris Pederick's Web Developer Add-on.

## Many Browsers, Few Engines, One Web

There are dozens of web browsers available: Mozilla Firefox and Opera are two browsers that can be used on Windows, macOS, and Linux operating systems. Mozilla Firefox is also what is known as an open-source browser: Firefox's source code is openly available to everyone. It is also developed and tested by a large group of volunteers and a smaller group of paid individuals working for the Mozilla Foundation. Opera, like Microsoft's Edge browser and Apple's Safari, is a proprietary browser, meaning that most of its code is kept secret and is developed almost exclusively by company employees.

The good news for adventurous readers of the web is even better news for web designers: most web browsers use one of three rendering engines: Mozilla's Gecko engine, the KHTML engine (forked as Web-Kit for Safari, and Blink in Chrome), or Microsoft's EdgeHTML engine, a fork of the Trident engine that was used in Internet Explorer. In many respects, browsers based on Gecko and WebKit display web pages similarly. Firefox and Chrome, for example, tend to display pages the same way, although depending on the operating system (Windows, macOS, Linux), each browser will have access to different fonts (see Chapter 17). But all engines are being developed constantly, so sites like CanIUse.com maintain accurate, up-to-date information on standards and feature support across all major browsers.

If you regularly change up your browser use, you will see that some websites take a hostile approach to readers who aren't using a specific browser. It's not uncommon to encounter websites ranging from banking sites to university and corporate intranet/web portals that demand that visitors use a specific web browser. People attempting to view the site with the "wrong" browser, or with the "wrong" configuration like an ad-blocker, may be greeted with nothing more than a message stating, "Your browser is not supported." Gee, thanks.

I also refuse to install the Flash extension on my primary browsers, and it's amazing to see how many sites still require Flash, especially local news outlets, even though Flash is dead (Hern 2015). The approaches to web design in this book emphasize designing in a browser-neutral, plugin-free way. The technology and standards exist for browser-neutral design (see Chapter 4), but it is an eye-opening experience to see just how many websites, even relatively new ones, are still designed to work only on specific browsers and devices.

## ASSESSING PURPOSE AND CONTEXT

Like any other piece of writing or design, well-built websites have some type of general, controlling purpose. The purpose of a portfolio website, for example, is to promote its creator's work. A collaboratively written blog may have the purpose of advancing views on a particular topic.

Yet as obvious as a site's controlling purpose might be, there are often other purposes at work. The controlling purpose of the Gmail site is to enable people to access and read their email accounts. But Gmail also has the purpose of generating ad revenue and alerting users of other Google services. A personal blog may have the controlling purpose of offering its author a platform for expressing her views, but it also, through links to blogs that she reads, has the purpose of establishing her affiliation with a specific community on the web.

A site's purpose is always situated in many contexts: a charitable organization's website is situated in a broad context of interested supporters and of other websites maintained by similar organizations. Sometimes a site's authors deliberately inject their site into a particular context, even through design. For example, if a local charity supports high school athletes from underprivileged backgrounds, it might favor a design that looks something like ESPN.com. That design choice would help to put the organization in the context of sports and sport websites. (Whether that design choice would increase donations is another matter. An overly lavish website design could conceivably hurt a charitable organization if it appears that donations are all spent on web design!)

When reading a website, challenge yourself to identify its purpose and context. Sometimes the purpose is expressed in the site's content: writing, images, and other media. Design also plays a role in conveying purpose and context, as does the performance of the site. Rather than prescriptively describe good or bad sites, the next sections offer lists of questions for you to consider as you read the web according to site content, design, and performance.

## KEEPING A DESIGN JOURNAL

It's a good idea to maintain a record of sites that you've visited and found to be instructive and inspiring. Design ideas and inspiration can come from many places. Magazines, billboards, even title sequences to movies and television shows can all be sources of design ideas. Consider keeping one or more of the following kinds of design journals as you read and, later, as you design and write:

- **A blank, bound sketchbook.** These can be found for cheap at most bookstores or online. They're very useful for cutting and pasting ideas from printed matter, sketching out your own ideas, and keeping notes about designs that you find.
- **Pinterest or another social bookmarking service.** This is great for keeping track of inspiring sites. For services that offer tagging, a *design-inspiration* tag can help keep things organized. Many services also allow you to write short notes with the items you save, so you can remind yourself why you added the site in the first place.
- **An electronic notebook app.** I never post negative comments about people's sites on Pinterest, but I'm brutally honest in the Evernote notebook I use for tracking sites. A digital notebook helps you keep notes about ideas that didn't work, including screenshots and clickable links back to the site, when that is helpful. Some apps, like Evernote, include browser extensions for easily clipping portions or entire pages of interesting things you find on the web.

## Reading for Content

Reading for content is the most obvious way to read the web. It's probably how you read it already. Content is the most important aspect of any site. Readers may tolerate poorly designed websites if the site's content is still useful. Here are some more specific questions to guide you in thinking about the effectiveness of site content:

- **Text:** How long are the chunks of text on the site? Does the site make use of headings and bulleted or numbered lists? Are the sentences punchy and direct, long and complex, or some mixture of the two? Does the site offer contextual links in its text? Are the links to other places on the site? Or to external sites?

- **Photographs:** What kinds of photographs or other images are presented on the site? Do the photographs appear to be part of the site's content? Or are they part of the overall design? If the photographs are meant as content, are they presented in a way that makes their content clear or interesting? Do the photographs have an appropriate amount of detail and clarity for the subject matter that they convey? Is any text run over the top of the images still readable?

- **Video and Media:** If a site includes video or animations and other media, consider the same questions as for the photographs above. Also, does the video or animation run smoothly, or does it appear choppy? Is it paced in such a way that it can be read (if it includes text) or comprehended? If the media includes sound, does the sound sync with the moving image? Is the sound too loud or too soft? Distorted or crystal clear?

- **Controls:** Do the site's navigation labels accurately describe the pages they link to? Are the functions of other page controls, such as those for sharing or emailing the page, made clear? Does the site use icons or text for controls, or both?

- **Layout and Design:** Layout and design are a kind of content, too. Are text, photos, and media arranged in a way that makes sense for the site's purpose and context? What impressions do the site's colors convey? Does the design seem to support the content of the site—or to contradict it? Does the design affect how credible you believe its creator to be?

## Reading for Design

Effective websites carefully knit their designs and content together. On such sites, the design is clearly much more than a simple container for holding content. Rather, it reinforces or adds interest to the site's content. Users might tolerate sites with solid content but poor design, but they will love well-designed sites with great content.

Of course, websites that look great on a desktop browser might be nearly impossible to use on a mobile phone. Sites built according to responsive web design may intentionally look different across different screen sizes (see Chapter 4). So in evaluating a design, be sure to either look at the same site on different devices or resize your desktop browser's viewport.

- **Text:** Are pieces of text presented in a way that is inviting, that makes you want to read? Are fonts sized and colored appropriately to keep the text readable? Does the text stretch across large areas of the screen? Or is it contained in narrower columns? Is text treated differently depending on the size of the window or viewport viewing the site?
- **Photographs:** Are photographs and other art part of the site's design? Do they compete for attention with the rest of the site's content? Are the photographs presented in true-to-life color? Or are they monochromatic? Do colors in the photographs appear in other site design elements—font colors, borders, shaded areas? Do the photographs resize with the layout? Do they still look crisp and clear even on high-density displays?
- **Video and Media:** Have the edges of video and media been integrated with the design of the site? Or are they simply placed on the page with a stark border between the video/media content and the page design? Are there controls for pausing/playing the media? Do they match the rest of the site design in terms of their shape and color? Like photographs, do videos resize with the layout?

- **Controls:** What is it about the site's controls that make them clear (or not) as navigation? Do the site's controls stand out from the rest of the design and content, or are they integrated? If there are icons or buttons on the site, do their colors, shape, and texture seem to fit with the rest of the design?
- **Layout and Design:** Is the design inviting? Does it encourage you to explore the site's other content? Would you estimate that the design is original or a template taken from somewhere else? Does it seem like the site's designer had content in mind while making the design? If the design appears to be custom, do you think that its creator spent a great deal of time on it?

## Reading for Performance

Some sites are striking to gaze at on the screen. But where they reveal their weaknesses is often in performance: pages and/or images that take a long time to load, navigation and other controls that behave unpredictably, or slow-moving animations that seem to stop time itself and make the whole site feel like it's made of molasses. Perhaps the site stutters as you scroll, especially on a phone. High performance rarely reveals itself the way poor performance does, simply because readers expect pages to load quickly, text to be readable, and so on.

When you're reading for performance, be sure to resize the browser window or use the Firefox Responsive Design Mode to see how the page performs at different sizes (see Chapter 14). Many sites will start to disappear behind the right-hand edge of the browser window. Other sites will respond seamlessly to changes in the viewport, and appear designed specifically for whatever size the browser window is.

- **Text:** Is the text readable, both in its line length and vertical spacing? Has the text been overstyled with bold, italic, and underline all at once? Are there typos or plain old bad writing that slows down your reading? Do contextual links take you to misleading places? Or are links put on text that provides no context for what is being linked to, like *this* or *here*? If you resize the text, usually by holding down the Ctrl or Command key on your keyboard and the + key, does the layout change to accommodate the larger text?

- **Photographs:** Are photographs sized appropriately? Are they worth the download time? Does the site have physically small photographs that seem to take forever to load? Are there whole-page background images that take a while to load? Are they highly compressed? Pixelated? Distorted? If you're looking at the images on a high-density display, do the images appear blurry? Do small, thumbnail-sized photographs link to larger versions of the same image? Do images resize as you change the size of the browser?

- **Video and Media:** Do video and media elements stream? Or must you wait for the whole file to download before it begins to play? On mobile devices, are there image placeholders for videos, so they don't begin to stream or download automatically? Are there any media elements that play automatically when you load a page? Are there controls for starting, stopping, or skipping any media elements? Does the presence of media elements make other actions, like scrolling down the page, seem choppy or slow? Do videos resize as you change the size of the browser?

- **Controls:** Do site navigation controls behave predictably? If any motion or pop-ups are involved, is it easy to control them with your mouse? How about with your finger on a phone or tablet? Do you find the motion or pop-ups distracting? Or do they clarify events that are happening as you use the site? Do links open up in new windows or tabs, or the same window? What do you think about that decision being made for you? Do gestures that work on your phone or tablet on other websites, like tapping the top of the address bar in Safari to scroll instantly back to the top of the page, also work on the site you're looking at? On touchscreens, can you comfortably and accurately activate links and other controls with your fingers?

- **Layout and Design:** How quickly does the page content appear with its full layout? As the page loads, do items appear one place on the screen, and then jump into place elsewhere? As you move from one page to another in the same site, does it take a long time for the page to be redrawn, or does the design appear to be preloaded, with only the content changing?

## Reading by Breaking

In addition to looking at sites in modern, graphical browsers like Firefox, Safari, and Chrome, it is instructive to view sites in the Lynx browser or a Lynx emulator, which provides text-only views of a site. Viewing a site as only text will give you a sense of what will be read aloud to low-vision users, and in what order, when they visit a site. Lynx will also reveal what some older mobile phone browsers may render. It also reveals the content that search engines will reliably index.

For a more nuanced way of looking at a site with certain features disabled, install the Web Developer Add-on for Firefox or Chrome. With it, you can choose to disable any JavaScript on a site, disable the display of images, and even disable the page's CSS.

"Breaking" a page in those ways gives you more than a view similar to users without JavaScript, image display, or CSS. It also gives you hints as to how a page has been made: if you turn off CSS, for example, and the page's design barely changes, it means the page's author used outdated, HTML-based methods for designing the pages. With CSS off, there should be no design other than default browser styles. If JavaScript is disabled and content disappears, or the site no longer functions, the site's author probably used JavaScript to generate content rather than placing the content directly in the HTML where it belongs.

- **Text:** Do the site's headings and lists still appear to be headings and lists in default styling in Lynx or with CSS disabled? Are all contextual links still clickable and usable in the absence of JavaScript? Does the text refer to any missing photographic or media content in a way that makes the site confusing or unusable?
- **Photographs:** Does alternate text appear for missing photographs? Is the text a meaningful alternative, one that would be useful to someone without the ability to view the site's images?

- **Video and Media:** Is there any alternate content offered for video and other media, particularly when the site is viewed in Lynx? Does disabling JavaScript prevent media elements from loading? Are there links to download the media for viewing/listening outside of the browser?
- **Controls:** If JavaScript is disabled, is it still possible to navigate the site? Do any page functions cease to operate in terms of printing, sharing, or copying and pasting? Are image galleries still browsable? If images are disabled, do you see alternate text for buttons or other controls?
- **Layout and Design:** Even in Lynx, are headings, paragraphs, and lists clear? Or does text run together or seem to be spaced in strange ways? When disabling CSS, is a page still useful in terms of the order the content appears in? Is the page readable and navigable on mobile devices?

## NEXT STEPS

There is no single fail-safe way to write a site's content, create its design, or ensure its performance. But reading a variety of websites—the ones you use every day, plus some of the gallery sites suggested on the companion site for this book—will help you to develop a sense of the range of approaches to building websites. Reading a variety of sites for design and performance will also help you get inspired to start working on your own design.

But content is still the most important aspect of a site. The next chapter will look at how you can begin gathering and creating content for your website even while you begin to learn the web technologies covered in Part III, "Strategies for Success."

## REFERENCE

Hern, Alex. 2015. "Flash Is Dead, and YouTube Dealt the Blow." *The Guardian* (January 30). http://www.theguardian.com/technology/2015/jan/30/flash-youtube-nostalgia

# CHAPTER 3

# Creating Web Content

The content for your site is essential to have on hand when designing web pages. Although you can work with dummy content, such as *Lorem ipsum* text, stock photographs, and so on, page design emerges more organically from real content. Page design, in turn, will shape how your content is prepared: if you are designing a site to present small bits of content to be consumed quickly, your writing should reflect that, too.

This chapter is an overview to creating, gathering, and preparing content for the web. More technical aspects of content creation and preparation are covered in greater detail throughout the rest of the book. But the ideas here will help you to start assembling the photographic, audio, and video content for your website immediately, in formats that are accessible across web-connected devices.

## WRITTEN CONTENT

Written content determines how findable and accessible a site is. Even if you are a photographer or visual artist, search engines index and enable people to search the writing of your page. Most image searches aren't image searches at all, but searches on captions, descriptions, and other contextual information. Written content can also be read aloud or presented as Braille, making it accessible to readers requiring assistive technologies. That is why all media elements must have text equivalents and other supporting written content (see Chapter 19).

Web audiences typically expect a website's written content to be direct and concise, with plenty of headings and lists to make the content navigable. Posting to Twitter is a great way to learn to write more directly: How expressive can you be in 140 characters or fewer? In addition to a direct style, written content should contain terms and vocabulary that you think your intended audience might use with search engines. Writing teachers teach students to write with thick, rich description. That approach to writing pays big dividends on the web: it helps your ranking in web searches on key terms, while also helping you to communicate more effectively with your readers.

Although I prefer to compose most web content directly in my text editor, there is nothing wrong with composing your text (but not your HTML or CSS) in a word processor if you're more comfortable writing there. Just be sure that you use the Unicode character set, encoded as UTF-8, in your HTML (see Chapter 10).

Keep in mind the following if you decide to write in your word processor:

---

### OPEN-SOURCE SOFTWARE FOR IMAGES, AUDIO, AND VIDEO

Software for editing photos, audio, and video can cost hundreds or thousands of dollars. But there are many good free and open-source alternatives to expensive software. All of the software listed are available for Windows, macOS, and Linux:

- **Image editing with GIMP:** The unfortunately named GIMP stands for GNU Image Manipulation Program. It is a solid, surprisingly feature-rich, and customizable graphics package. (`http://www.gimp.org/`)
- **Audio editing with Audacity:** A fully featured audio editor. I personally prefer Audacity to all but professional-grade audio products. It requires a plugin to output audio to MP3, but otherwise has everything necessary for preparing audio for the web. (`http://www.audacityteam.org`)
- **Video editing with Blender:** Known for being a 3D creation suite, Blender also supports video editing. (`https://www.blender.org/`)

Check the app store for your mobile devices of choice for phone and tablet possibilities, although note that most apps will cost money.

- **Do not spend time formatting text in the word processor.** You'll be pasting your text directly into HTML, which has no visual properties of its own, so any formatting is going to be lost anyway. And bullets from a word processor's list might get carried over as actual characters in your HTML, which you do not want. An empty line of space between headings, paragraphs, and lists is more than enough formatting.
- **Do not import images into your word processor documents.** Images must be treated in a particular way in responsive web design (see Chapter 19), and are only referenced by file name from HTML. However, if you know of an image you want to accompany your text, you might make a note of it in your word processor file for future reference, so you know just where in your HTML source to write your image tags.
- **Do not post word processor documents on your site or opt to Save as HTML.** If you are creating a portfolio or thinking of posting forms for a small business website, you might be tempted to post and link directly to a word processor document. In most cases, it is better to publish word processor documents in Portable Document Format (PDF), and then post the PDF to your website. But remember that PDFs, like word-processor documents, are formatted for 8.5 × 11-inch paper (or A4, in other countries). They do not at all scale well on mobile devices, and can present additional, significant accessibility problems, depending on how they are prepared. Do not trust your word processor or any other program to generate your HTML.

Regardless of where you write, prefer direct sentences and short paragraphs. Make good use of headings and lists. Headings and lists help readers navigate a page quickly to get a sense of its contents or to locate the specific content returned by a Google search.

## CONTENT IMAGES

Content images, including photographs, scans, and illustrations, can add additional impact to text content. And on the latest generations of screens, they look stunning. Like all media content, images must be prepared for the web in particular ways.

Preparing images for the web is a compromise between the size, in bytes, of an image file and its pixel dimensions and quality. Image quality is determined by the pixel dimensions of an image and in the case of JPEG (.jpg) images, by the amount of image compression, which removes some data from an image to reduce its file size.

## PROFESSIONAL EQUIPMENT

Capturing images and respectable quality audio and video is now possible on most smartphones. To achieve even higher quality media capture, some of the following equipment might be necessary. Check your local library or your school's media center to see if you can get access to professional quality equipment, if you need it.

- **A digital single-lens reflex (DSLR) camera.** The quality that smartphone cameras can deliver is often more than enough for web purposes. If you want to invest in a camera for even higher quality photos, look for DSLR cameras that have a high optical zoom (digital zoom is not terribly useful) and interchangeable lenses.
- **A digital video camera.** Smartphones are also capable of capturing very good video for web purposes. A tripod mount can help up the quality of your videos, just by reducing the amount of camera shake introduced by the human hand.
- **A good quality microphone.** Computers and phones are very good at capturing audio that sounds great, provided you have a quality microphone. Stores that cater to musicians usually have a better selection of microphones available than electronics retailers. For recording the human voice, look into purchasing a condenser microphone that comes with its own power source, usually an onboard battery (just remember to power it off when you're done recording).
- **A scanner.** This is especially necessary if you are working with a lot of print or archival material that you need to digitize. If you only have a few things to scan, try to find a scanner at your school or library.

Always keep copies of your original photographs and scans, at their maximum size with minimal compression. Photographs and images that come off of a digital camera or scanner are almost never web ready; they must be resized, compressed, and otherwise edited first (see Chapter 19). But keep all of the original image files, in case you ever need to re-edit them.

Here are some basic approaches to preparing your images for the web, which should be saved in either JPEG or PNG format (see Chapter 19 for more about loading media onto your pages):

- **Learn to use the crop and resize functions in your image editor.** Most image editors have filters for all sorts of visual effects, and all of them have controls for adjusting the contrast, brightness, and other visual properties of images. But to start, the two most important features you should learn are cropping, which helps you cut off unwanted edges of a photograph or to format a photo in a different aspect ratio, and resizing (sometimes called resampling), which reduces the dimensions of an image to web-appropriate sizes.

- **Images for the web display according to their actual pixel dimensions, so coordinate those with your responsive layouts.** Most image editors have dots per inch (DPI) or pixels per inch (PPI) settings alongside their resize function. But web images display independently of any DPI or PPI setting: 72 dpi or 96 dpi are both common settings for web images, but the setting only has an effect when the image is printed. What matters in the screen display of web images is actual pixel dimensions: an 800-pixel-wide by 600-pixel-tall image will display in a web browser on a standard monitor as 800 by 600 regardless of the file's DPI or PPI setting. However, that same 800 × 600 image will be displayed as 400 × 300 on a high-density display that is pixel-doubled. Chapter 19 covers in greater detail the preparation of pixel-doubled (@2x) and even pixel-tripled (@3x) images.

- **Different photographs will look better at different compression rates.** When you go to save your image, most image editors offer some type of slider that controls the compression of JPEG images. High compression means lighter files and faster downloads, but often at the expense of image quality. And image quality varies under the same compression rate: a picture of the sky, which has a large area of roughly the same color, will get ugly, rectangular splotches at high compression rates. Images with high contrast details, such as naked tree branches against a stark winter sky, will get little "sparklies" and other compression artifacts around high-contrast areas. Get to know your image editor and the way it compresses different images. And always consider the role of your image in your design to figure out where you can get away with cutting corners by introducing a little more compression.

You can find additional examples of image treatment at the book's companion website, `http://webpg.es/`.

## MEDIA CONTENT: AUDIO AND VIDEO

The focus in this book is textual content and images; however, here are some rough guidelines for working with audio and video. See the book's companion site for additional guidance on working with audio and video, as well as the MDN (2016) guide to supported media formats.

### Audio Content

Audio content destined for the web should be prepared in MP3 format. While MP3 is a proprietary file format, it is also widely used in all sorts of desktop and portable digital audio players. It is also supported in all browsers for use with the HTML5 `<audio>` element.

Preparing MP3 audio files is a complex matter, but here are some basic settings that you should use: output your files as 8-bit stereo sound. Perhaps the most important setting on MP3 files is their bit rate; for voice-only files, 64 kilobits per second (kbs) will provide adequate sound quality, although 128 kbs often sounds noticeably better. However, the higher the bit rate, the larger the sound file. Advanced MP3 encoders will also offer variable bit rates that offer different levels of compression based on the complexity of the sound at different points in the file.

Be sure also to record and prepare your MP3 audio at a 44.1 kHz sample rate, simply because that sample rate is supported by most MP3 players, and there are no savings in file size with MP3s when you lower the sample rate.

You can find additional examples of sound treatment and capture at the book's companion website, `http://webpg.es/`.

## Video Content

Video content is the most complicated material to prepare for the web. In addition to shooting and editing your video, it is essential that sound syncs with motion. For most purposes, posting video on YouTube or Vimeo is an acceptable solution (the book's companion site lists other, similar sites for video hosting). First, the videos are stored and transferred from YouTube's servers, not yours. This keeps you from expending large amounts of bandwidth, or the amount of data your server can serve at any one time, on your own server. YouTube also does a respectable job of behind-the-scenes compression and resizing of video, though be sure to consult their documentation on making and posting videos. Finally, maintaining a YouTube account is yet another way to establish your presence on the web. Because YouTube allows you to set up a profile that can include a link to your website, you may be able to attract YouTube users to your site.

The only problem with YouTube is that the code it provides for embedding videos on your website requires the use of `<iframe>` elements, rather than direct access to the `<video>` element in HTML5.

For handling your own native video in HTML5, consult the book's companion website, `http://webpg.es/`.

## NEXT STEPS

The work of writing and designing your pages begins by preparing the actual content of your site. Now that you have some idea of how to prepare content for the web, let's turn to look at what a web page is, the history of how pages have been made, and why it's important to adhere to open standards for web writing and design.

## REFERENCE

MDN. 2016. "Media Formats Supported by the HTML Audio and Video Elements." https://developer.mozilla.org/en-US/docs/Web/HTML/Supported _media_formats

# CHAPTER 4

# Responsive, Standards-Based Web Pages

So far we've looked at reasons for writing on the web and a few approaches to reading the web with a designer/writer mindset. Chapter 3 covered the basics of creating and gathering the content for your site.

This chapter looks at web standards, the guiding principles behind well-built pages that deliver content across the widest possible range of desktop and mobile devices. Web standards are derived from specifications issued by the World Wide Web Consortium (W3C), an international organization of people associated with technology companies and universities. The W3C calls its specifications *recommendations*, not standards, but within the web design community, *standards* is the preferred term. Regardless of the terms used, the W3C's aim is to better ensure consistency in how web languages and protocols are defined. From there, it's up to software developers to correctly implement the specifications in the user agents (UAs) they create. **User agents** is the generic term that describes web browsers and other services and devices that access the web.

On its surface, the idea of standards might seem to contradict an activity as creative as web design. Web standards do not, however, stifle creativity. They actually encourage it. Think for a moment about some of the standards that people rely on. You can buy any kind of electronic device you want—a blender, a television set, a guitar amplifier—and not have to worry that its plug won't work in the socket where you live. That one standard frees you to make mojitos or smoothies, watch trash TV or art films, and play blues or heavy metal.

The design of electrical sockets is standardized, just as are the threads for light bulb fixtures, traffic signals and signage, and the USB connectors on computers and other devices. We also have standardized weights and measures, standards for television and radio signals, and even some standards for spoken and written language: *This is a standard sentence.* But: *Standard this sentence is not, unless Yoda you are.*

The other topic of this chapter is **responsive web design**, a practice for building sites and pages that work across the full range of traditional

## WHAT YOU WON'T LEARN IN THIS BOOK

Here is a brief list of web design practices that you won't learn in this book. These are outdated and should no longer be practiced. Run, don't walk, away from anyone who suggests any of the following:

- **HTML tables to design pages.** Used for their intended purpose, HTML tables are good for one thing: marking up tabular data. Tables for layout present significant accessibility issues and make a page harder to repurpose or redesign later. Instead of HTML tables, use CSS layout techniques (see Chapter 18).
- **Invisible GIF image spacers.** Often used in tandem with HTML tables, invisible GIF spacers are the chewing gum and chicken wire of shoddy web design. Instead of image spacers, again use CSS layout techniques (see Chapter 18).
- **Frames and framesets.** Another accessibility nightmare, frames are artifacts from an era before web servers could easily include content shared over multiple pages, or hold certain content in a fixed position while other content scrolled. Instead of frames, use a preprocessor (see Chapter 22) or position: fixed in your CSS (see Chapters 12 and 18).
- **"Save As HTML . . ."** in a word processor or any other software for authoring content. Just because the option is there doesn't mean it should be used. Word processors are fine for their intended purpose of word processing, but that is it. Write the languages of the web yourself.
- **Adobe Flash.** Flash is dead. Do not use it. Its former top selling points, from video to rich typography to animation, are now all possible using HTML, CSS, and JavaScript (see Chapter 19).
- **Absolute units.** CSS should use relative units, such as em and %, not px (pixel) or any other absolute unit (see Chapters 12, 17, and 18).

and mobile devices that are used to access the web. The term *responsive web design* (RWD) is attributed to Ethan Marcotte (2010), who introduced it in a now-famous article in *A List Apart*. RWD combines three technical approaches—fluid grids, flexible images, and media queries—that are executed over the top of standards-based forms of HTML and CSS.

## WEB PAGES ARE SETS OF INSTRUCTIONS

Like all digital formats, web pages are made up of content and sets of instructions for displaying the content.

However, writers and designers don't often have to think about the instructions that present digital content. When you write a word processor document or even an email, the blank box or page you type in lends itself to the impression that what you write is all that there is to your document. Software dubbed as *what you see is what you get* (WYSIWYG) reinforces that impression.

Below the deceptively simple surface of a blank email or document is an entirely different kind of writing: computer language. That language does things like ensure that the email address in the To: box is where the email is ultimately sent, or that when you hit the bold button in your word processor, the text displays as bold and can be saved and printed that way.

Most of us rarely think about that language beneath the surface. We write our documents, print them out, and hand them off; we send emails or instant messages, or post on social media sites, and never give the underlying code a second thought.

Or at least that's what happens until something goes wrong. And something always goes wrong, eventually.

### Web Design: A Pessimist's View

Everyone has a story about a digital file that gets messed up: a word processor document that mysteriously puts a bullet point next to what ought to be a plain paragraph. An email message whose punctuation appears as question marks or empty boxes. Those errors and thousands like them usually originate in the instructions that get passed to a program that reads the contents of a digital file.

In the case of word processors, email programs, photo editors, and many other kinds of software and the files they generate, there is no hope for a human who wants to fix the file's instructions herself. In many cases, both the software and the document it produces is closed, binary source, meaning that its code cannot be viewed or edited directly by a human being.

By contrast, web pages in HTML and CSS are all open source: go to your favorite web browser and choose View > Source, and you will see the instructions that cause any given page to display and behave the way it does. And not only can you view open source, but you can edit it, too—although obviously your changes will only appear if the page is yours and you have access to the server where it is stored.

### Don't Send a Machine to Do a Human's Work

Unfortunately, choosing View > Source on many web pages is not a comforting, feel-good experience. It's usually just horrifying: miles and miles of unintelligible code appear on even the simplest-looking websites. In most of those cases, however, the code that makes up a site has been generated by a computer, not written directly by a human being. That's why it's a bad idea to use something like "Save as HTML. . ." in software that offers the option.

Computers are tireless. They are the broom in *The Sorcerer's Apprentice*: give computers a set of instructions, and they will continue indefinitely to carry out those instructions without complaint or sign of fatigue. The trouble is, when computers misbehave or do something that someone does not intend (like adding mysterious bullet points to a document), people may have no choice other than to start their projects over from the beginning. The open source in standards-based web design, perhaps with the assistance of a version control system (see Chapter 6), helps you avoid ever having to start over like that.

## DESIGNING ACCORDING TO STANDARDS, NOT BROWSERS OR DEVICES

Many of the bad habits that make for poor web design (see the sidebar "What You Won't Learn in This Book") originated with web designers designing with bad software or to a specific browser. The rest came from designing in an era of limited or nonexistent support for web standards, especially Cascading Style Sheets (CSS). But those bad habits continue because some web designers (and their teachers . . . ahem) are unaware of advances in how the web can now be written and designed. The research-based advice in Part III of this book will help you learn to stay on top of the web's advances yourself.

The most important advances in web design fall under the umbrella term of **web standards**, a term promoted by a grassroots movement formed in 1998 called the Web Standards Project (WaSP, `http://www.webstandards.org`). WaSP, a group of influential web designers who had had enough of browser-based design practices, pressured Netscape and Microsoft to faithfully implement the W3C's specifications for the web's many languages and protocols. The idea behind web standards is that no one company or browser manufacturer controls HTML, CSS, or any other web language. At the same time, all browser manufacturers should support those standards in their browsers (and all modern browsers do, to varying degrees). That means a web page can be authored in a browser-neutral way, and designers can be relatively certain that their pages will display and function acceptably in any browser. Note that "acceptably" is very different from "uniformly," which will be an important distinction to keep in mind when you begin to work with the newer features in HTML, CSS, and JavaScript.

Certain standards have been well supported since the beginning of the web, including the Hypertext Transfer Protocol (HTTP) behind the `http:` string that prefixes all web addresses. Without HTTP, it would be impossible to reliably request a web page from a server and receive it in a web browser. The trouble is that what the WaSP called *standards* are actually issued as *recommendations* by the W3C. In the heated battle between Microsoft and Netscape in the late 1990s known as the "browser wars" (see Berners-Lee 2000, for a history), the term *recommendation* had limited influence. Representatives from both Netscape, the other major browser at the time, and Microsoft served on the committees, called *working groups*, that wrote the W3C recommendations for HTML, CSS, and other key languages and protocols. Yet both companies often ignored the very specifications that their employees had helped to write.

## VALIDATORS AND LINTERS

One of the many benefits to designing your pages according to web standards is that there is an external, nonvisual method of assessing just how compliant your pages are with the standards. The method is known as validation, which subjects your code to a piece of software that compares your work against the rules for the languages you have used, including HTML and CSS. There are two validators that you should use throughout your project's development:

- **The W3C Markup Validation Service** (`http://validator.w3.org/`). This service, offered by the W3C, allows you to validate your HTML either by inputting a URL, uploading an HTML file, or even copying and pasting your HTML directly into the validator. (Writers of HTML5 will be redirected to the "Nu Html Checker" [*sic*]. It does the same thing.)
- **The W3C CSS Validation Service** (`http://jigsaw.w3.org/cssvalidator/`). As with the Markup Validation Service, the CSS Validation Service gives you multiple options for checking your CSS.

In addition to validators, you should also make use of lint tools, which will help you enforce additional style rules on your source code. Chapter 10 and this book's companion site (`http://webpg.es/`) have additional information on selecting and configuring lint tools.

As you are writing and designing, if something strange or unexpected happens when viewing your web pages in a browser, the first thing you should do is validate and lint your HTML, even if you suspect a problem with your CSS. Much of the time, your CSS is probably fine. Broken HTML can do some bizarre things, particularly to CSS-based page layout. If the HTML is valid, then validate and lint the CSS.

---

The tireless activism of WaSP helped leverage support for web standards to end the browser wars. With the stable releases of Internet Explorer 6 (IE6, in 2001) and Netscape Navigator 6 (NN6, in 2002), both leading browsers provided viable support for many W3C specifications. Web designers could begin to design and write web pages in a more browser-neutral way. That is not to say that IE6 and NN6 implemented web standards precisely. Even now, no browser follows all W3C specifications to the letter, although some browsers are more standards compliant than others. But the browsers in 2000 followed the W3C's specifications for HTML and CSS closely enough that browser targeting and browser-specific pages should have become a thing of the past. Should have. Unfortunately, despite improvements in web browsers' standards compliance, some web designers continued to rely on old, outdated practices (see the sidebar "What You Won't Learn in This Book" for examples).

Of course, in internet time, 2002 is ancient history. WaSP's original mission was to persuade the software engineers who build browsers to respect the standards. WaSP is now more concerned with education and outreach, ensuring that new generations of people writing and designing the web continue to respect and follow the standards.

## WEB STANDARDS: A THREE-PART APPROACH

Later in the book, you will learn exactly what the rules of HTML are, and how CSS works to add striking designs to content structured in HTML. But for now, it is only necessary that you understand that standards-based web design consists of three primary components. Web standards guru Jeffrey Zeldman (2007) described these components as structure (HTML), presentation (CSS), and behavior (JavaScript).

A standards-based web page, then, is made up of three separate parts:

- Structured content in HTML (e.g., a hyperlink in a site's navigation)
- Visual design in CSS (e.g., the styling of the hyperlink in the site's navigation)
- Advanced functionality and enhancements in JavaScript (e.g., an AJAX call that only reloads certain portions of the page when a hyperlink is clicked) that do not break the site's core features in JavaScript's absence

The JavaScript component that Zeldman labels *behavior* I prefer to call *performance*. How a web page performs, both with and without JavaScript, is an essential part of accessible web design. Plenty of JavaScript runs and makes modifications without any user interaction, which is what I think of with *behavior*. And page performance includes factors such as user preferences and device capability, which also fall outside of what would normally be considered *behavior*.

## Structure: The XML Recommendation and the Birth of XHTML

In February 1998, the W3C issued the first recommendation for Extensible Markup Language (XML; see W3C 1998 and W3C 2008). But despite being called a language, XML is actually a set of precise rules for creating other markup languages (called *applications* in XML-speak) that enable people and computer applications to share structured content with one another across computer platforms.

The most important XML application for web purposes was XHTML 1.0 (W3C 2002), which first appeared as a W3C recommendation in January 2000. XHTML was the HTML 4.01 language (W3C 1999) rewritten according to XML's rules. In many ways, HTML and XHTML

---

### HTML5, HTML 5.X, HTML: THE LIVING STANDARD

HTML5 (no space before the 5; W3C 2014) is the W3C recommendation for HTML and successor to HTML 4.01 (W3C 1999), which had been neglected by the W3C for 15 years. HTML5's specification originated in 2004 outside of the W3C by a group that dubbed itself the Web Hypertext Application Technology Working Group (or WHATWG). WHATWG was formed in protest to the W3C's plans for a new XHTML specification (*spec* for short), which would have been backward-incompatible with the rest of the web. Eventually, WHATWG's HTML5 spec was adopted and issued by the W3C (2014). Parallel, and sometimes divergent, development continues on HTML: The Living Standard under the auspices of WHATWG (2016). Meanwhile, the W3C released in late 2016 a new proposed recommendation, HTML 5.1 (a space before the 5; 2016) and work at that point had already begun on an HTML 5.2 recommendation.

In this book, you will learn XHTML 1.0 Strict style but write in HTML5, with some references to developments in HTML: The Living Standard (see `https://developers.whatwg.org/`). Ultimately what matters most is not the specs, but what browser-makers have actually implemented from the specs. Documentation at the Mozilla Developer Network (`https://developer.mozilla.org/`) and resources such as Can I Use ... (`http://caniuse.com`) are indispensable guides to actual browser implementations of HTML5 and other web languages and protocols.

are the same language. But XML's rules are simpler and more consistent than SGML's, the language from which Tim Berners-Lee (2000, 91–93) developed HTML originally.

In addition to drawing upon XML's simplicity and consistency, XHTML style also reflects the spirit of XML, which is to provide structured information, free from any visual presentation. Old practices in writing HTML resulted in messes like:

```
<FONT face="Arial, Helvetica, sans-serif"
 color=#cc6600 size=7>
 The World Wide Web
</FONT>
```

Here is the same content, rewritten as HTML5 (W3C 2014) in XHTML-strict style:

```
<h1>
 The World Wide Web
</h1>
```

HTML uses a semantic piece of structure, in this case a heading (`<h1>`) element. The `<FONT>` element is no longer used, as matters of type and typography are handled exclusively in CSS.

This book promotes a well-formed (W3C 2002, under "2. Documents") XHTML 1.0 Strict style, written using the elements in the HTML5 specification. However, in most cases, the book refers to HTML in a generic sense, unless there is something specific to HTML5, XHTML, or HTML: The Living Standard (WHATWG 2016) (see the sidebar, "HTML5, HTML 5.x, HTML: The Living Standard").

HTML is used to do nothing more than provide meaningful structure to all of a page's text content and any media elements such as images, audio, and video. The "Strategies for Success" in Part III of this book offers guidance in building structured content in HTML.

## Presentation: Widespread Browser Support for CSS

Visual design used to be handled in nonstandard HTML "tag soup" as in the `<FONT>` example above. To add the fonts, color, and size from the old tag-soup HTML, web designers now write with the CSS design language, typically in a separate CSS file:

```
h1 {
 color: #C60;
 font-family: Arial, Helvetica, sans-serif;
 font-size: x-large;
}
```

One thing that makes CSS a superior alternative to HTML-based design is that CSS exists in a file separate from the site's HTML. That means CSS can completely change the look of a site without a designer having to touch the site's HTML. The original demonstration of this was the CSS Zen Garden (Shea 2016), a showcase of CSS-based designs that all used the exact same XHTML. The CSS Zen Garden (http://csszengarden.com) lives on as a site that showcases responsive design. Have a look; you'll be amazed.

CSS also controls the look of an entire site from one CSS file. Changes to that file—for example, changing headings to appear in a serif rather than a sans-serif typeface—are instantly reflected across your entire site. Modifying the design of an entire site requires changing only one CSS file. That also makes sites load faster: the CSS instructions only have to be downloaded once and the browser will **cache** the file. That helps web browsers quickly render additional pages on the same website.

But most importantly, changes to the look of a site need not require a revision to the site's content or HTML. That makes content much more portable from device to device, and from design to design as a site improves over time.

CSS can change more than just the visual design of a page on screen: it can also be used to specify how a page looks when printed, removing needless items like site navigation or making visible detailed copyright information. Certain CSS properties can be used for assistive technologies, too. Chapter 12 looks at CSS in depth.

## Performance: JavaScript and the DOM

In standards-based web design, JavaScript works in tandem with the Document Object Model (DOM) to provide interactivity and progressively enhanced features on capable browsers. JavaScript coupled with the DOM is sometimes called *DOM scripting*.

JavaScript is based on a specification called ECMAScript, a standard maintained by Ecma International (formerly the European Computer Manufacturers Association). It's the only prominent web standard not maintained by the W3C. ECMAScript is the specification (Ecma International 2016), and JavaScript is ECMAScript's actual implementation in a web browser. Also, people confuse this point often: *Java* is not a casual way to refer to JavaScript, but an entirely different language. There's a Twitter-famous quip that goes something like this: *Java is to JavaScript what ham is to hamburger.*

Similar to the poor HTML-based design techniques above, there are obsolete ways of calling JavaScript within HTML. Most of these are attributes that begin with **on**, such as onload or onclick:

```
<head>
  <script>
    function doSomething() {
      /* function that does something */
    }
  </script>
</head>
<body onload="doSomething();">
  <!--page content here-->
</body>
```

That can be cleaned up so that the HTML looks like this:

```
<body>
 <!--page content here-->
 <script src="js/site.js"></script>
</body>
```

And then the site.js file would handle the onload event:

```
document.addEventListener("DOMContentLoaded",
  function() {
    doSomething();
  }
);
function doSomething() {
  /* function that does something */
}
```

While that method looks more verbose, it uses progressive enhancement and the `DOMContentLoaded` event to improve the performance of the page. For more about JavaScript and the DOM, see Chapters 13 and 20.

## RESPONSIVE WEB DESIGN

Next to web standards, responsive web design is the most significant development in the history of web design. In Ethan Marcotte's (2010) definition, responsive web design (RWD) has three components, each of which is built by applying web standards in a particular way:

- **Fluid grids**: Fluid grids provide page layouts whose components' widths are expressed in percentages, rather than absolute units like pixels. This is a central topic of Chapter 18.
- **Flexible images** and other visual media: Images must expand and contract to fit their containing HTML element or the viewport. The `srcset` attribute on the `<img />` tag makes it possible to load images of different sizes, based on the size of the viewport. The `<picture>` element provides additional control over which images are loaded under different screen conditions. In turn, CSS is used to ensure that images and visual media, especially video, scale to fit their parent elements. See Chapter 19.
- **Media queries**: Fluid grids and flexible images were technically possible from the earliest version of CSS and HTML. The problem is that a block of text that is readable at 75 percent of the viewport on a small screen quickly gets to be too wide on larger screens: very long lines of text are hard to read. Media queries (W3C 2012) are defined in a module that is part of CSS3. Media queries are a special syntax that applies a group of CSS style declarations only under certain conditions. See Chapter 14.

Taken as a group, the three components of responsive design make it possible to create websites that display appropriately across all screen sizes, but from a single set of HTML and CSS files and from a single URL. That is a better, more sustainable approach than duplicating a site at a special subdomain, like `mobile.example.com`, with its own set of mobile-specific HTML and CSS. RWD is beneficial not only to mobile devices: it accounts for the entire possible range of screen sizes at which a page might be viewed.

Because responsive design is such an important topic, it is discussed in depth in its own chapter (see Chapter 14).

## NEXT STEPS

You should now have a better sense of where web standards came from and why they are necessary for web designers to know when engaging in responsive web design. The next chapter prepares you to write and design by helping you set up a custom writing, design, and development environment that supports your hands-on work creating pages according to web standards.

## REFERENCES

Berners-Lee, Tim, with Mark Fischetti. 2000. "Competition and Consensus," in *Weaving the Web: The Original Design and Ultimate Destiny of the World Wide Web*. New York: HarperBusiness, 103–21.

Ecma International. 2016. "Standard ECMA-262: ECMAScript 2016 Language Specification." http://www.ecma-international.org/publications/standards/Ecma-262.htm

Marcotte, Ethan. 2010. "Responsive Web Design." *A List Apart* (May 25). http://alistapart.com/article/responsive-web-design

Shea, Dave. 2016. *The CSS Zen Garden*. http://csszengarden.com

WHATWG. 2016. "HTML: The Living Standard." https://html.spec.whatwg.org/

W3C. 1998. "Extensible Markup Language (XML) 1.0." https://www.w3.org/TR/1998/REC-xml-19980210/

W3C. 1999. "HTML 4.01 Specification." https://www.w3.org/TR/1999/REC-html401–19991224/

W3C. 2002. "XHTML 1.0: The Extensible HyperText Markup Language (Second Edition)." https://www.w3.org/TR/2002/REC-xhtml1–20020801/

W3C. 2008. "Extensible Markup Language (XML) 1.0 (Fifth Edition)." https://www.w3.org/TR/2008/REC-xml-20081126/

W3C. 2012. "Media Queries." https://www.w3.org/TR/2012/REC-css3-mediaqueries-20120619/

W3C. 2014. "HTML5: A Vocabulary and Associated APIs for HTML and XHTML." https://www.w3.org/TR/2014/REC-html5–20141028/

W3C. 2016. "HTML 5.1." Proposed recommendation. https://www.w3.org/TR/2016/PR-html51–20160915/

Zeldman, Jeffery. 2007. *Designing with Web Standards*, 2nd ed. Berkeley, CA: New Riders.

# CHAPTER 5

# Preparing to Write and Design

There are a few different pieces of software required for web writing and design. This chapter will help you find and install three essentials: a web-friendly text editor, a baseline development browser, and a development-grade web server that you can run from the command line on your operating system of choice. A section near the end of this chapter also looks at purchasing a domain name and hosting for your website. A fourth essential piece of software, a version control system, will be covered in detail in the next chapter.

## SELECTING A WEB-FRIENDLY TEXT EDITOR

A text editor is all that is required to write web content as well as HTML, CSS, JavaScript, and almost any server-side language (Ruby, Python, PHP, etc.). Most operating systems come with a primitive text editor installed, such as macOS's TextEdit or Notepad on Windows. But don't use it. A fuller-featured editor will make your life much easier. Here are features to look for when choosing a web-friendly text editor:

- **Unicode support.** Most editors support the Unicode character set encoded as UTF-8, but it is good to make sure that the editor you select does too. UTF-8 enables you to write directly in your source code typographer's quotes, em-dashes, and other typographical necessities in addition to characters from languages other than English.

- **Unix-style line endings**. Editors on Unix-like systems, such as Linux and macOS, all support Unix-style line endings (line feeds, or LF). Windows editors are less uniform in supporting LF line endings, so Windows users should make sure to configure their editors to use LF.
- **Syntax highlighting** is functionality that recognizes HTML tags and other language features, and colors them according to their purpose. Different editors highlight HTML, CSS, and other languages in different ways, using different color palettes. Some editors may color tag elements orange, while another will color them blue. Still other editors allow you to choose from a variety of color palettes. The colors do not matter, but the coloring does: it makes HTML and CSS easier to read, and much easier to find errors in your code.
- **Line numbering** displays a line number next to each line in your source code. The numbers are not a part of the file. This feature is very useful for correcting errors discovered in HTML and CSS validators, or in the JavaScript console in your development browser, all of which report errors by the line the error appears on.

With those features in mind, here are the free and open-source web editors I recommend to my students:

- **Windows:** Notepad++ makes writing HTML and CSS very simple through syntax highlighting and other features. If you plan to use the lunch hour at work to do web development or if you want to use the program on a public computer, perhaps in a library somewhere, Notepad++ can be run from a USB drive. Be sure to configure Notepad++ to use UTF-8 encoding, without the Byte-Order Mark (BOM). It should also be configured to use Unix-style line endings. (`https://notepad-plus-plus.org`)
- **macOS:** TextWrangler is an excellent free editor, cousin to its for-pay counterpart BBEdit. TextWrangler is available directly from the Bare Bones website. (`http://www.barebones.com/products/textwrangler/`)

You are not limited to these, of course; there are hundreds more that a Google search for *web text editor* will turn up. I also maintain a list of popular editors at this book's companion site. Just keep in mind the features listed above if you choose to use a different one.

## NAMING AND ORGANIZING FILES AND DIRECTORIES

Good file-naming and organization practices will help you avoid many time-consuming problems as you develop your website. Files and directories must be named carefully so that you have memorable, meaningful URLs on your site that are easy to share (see Chapters 21 and 25). *Directories* are the same conceptual container as *folders*, but I prefer *directories* because that is how they are described on the command line and in URLs. Follow these rules to make your files and directories web ready:

- **Show file extensions in your operating system.** This is critical. Most operating systems (Windows, Mac, and Linux) hide file extensions by default. **File extensions** are the identifiers for text files: `screen.css` is a CSS file, using the `.css` extension. And `index.html` uses the `.html` extension. But rather than showing `index.html` listed in your folder, your operating system might list only `index`. You might also think you saved a file as `index.html` from within your text editor, when in reality it was saved as `index.html.txt`, the default extension that many text editors add to files. Do a Google search for *show file extensions* and the name and version of your operating system to learn how to reveal file extensions on your computer. If you work on a Unix-like command line, you will always see file extensions when running the list command, `ls`.
- **Name files only with lowercase letters, numbers, and the hyphen.** Most web servers are case sensitive, meaning that `MyFile.html` and `myfile.html` represent different files. By always using lowercase letters, you and your site visitors never have to guess or remember the capitalization in your site's URLs: there is none. Numbers are safe to use in file names, as

are hyphens. But do not use any other symbols or punctuation in your file names, as almost all of them (?, &, +, =, etc.) have special meaning to web servers and can trigger unexpected behavior.

- **Never use spaces in file and directory names.** All modern operating systems allow spaces in file and directory/folder names. But spaces cause trouble on the web. A file saved as `professional    portfolio.html` on your computer becomes `professional%20portfolio.html` in a URL on the web, through something known as *URL encoding*. And that `%20` is difficult for users to work with, along with making your site look less professional. Instead of spaces, use hyphens: `professional-portflio.html`. Better still, use short, one-word names whenever possible: `portfolio.html`.

- **Make file and directory names as short, direct, and memorable as possible.** `resume.html` is preferable to `my-professional-resume.html` or even `my-resume.htm`. Better still is a directory called `resume` with the actual résumé contained in an `index.html` file, which most web servers will serve automatically at a URL like `http://example.com/resume/` (see Chapter 21). You should be able to tell someone, *My résumé is at example dot com slash resume.*

- **Never use "new," "old," "recent," or other references to time or versions in file names.** `new-photos.html` will one day not be new. And you don't want to have to name the next file `newer-photos.html`. If you must reference time, go with the date: `august-2016-photos.html`.

- **Use numbers with one or more leading zeros.** Serialized file or directory names should begin with one leading zero (e.g., `photo-01.jpg`, `photo-02.jpg`) if you expect fewer than 100 items, or two leading zeros (e.g., `photo-001.jpg`) if you expect fewer than 1,000 items. That helps organize the listing of serialized files in SFTP clients and file-system views on your computer. Of course, a descriptive file name like `photo-of-my-dog.jpg` might be easier to work with, depending on your needs.

- **For HTML files, use the .html or .htm file extension, but not both.** File extensions should be as consistent as any other part of your file-naming practices. I recommend using the `.html` extension on HTML files, but if you opt to use the `.htm` extension for a project, always use `.htm`. You don't want to have to remember whether a URL is `example.com/resume` `.htm` or `example.com/resume.html`. CSS files must all use the `.css` extension, and JavaScript files must all use `.js`. Again, be sure to configure your operating system to show all file extensions.

One shorthand summary for all of those rules: **Name files and directories consistently and as though your keyboard has no shift key or space bar.** Be sure to follow those rules for all of the directories and files you plan to post to the web, including image, audio, and other media files.

## SELECTING A BASELINE DEVELOPMENT BROWSER

The next piece of software in your custom web design setup is a baseline development browser. I recommend Mozilla Firefox Developer Edition (Firefox for short; for the rest of this book, assume that the special Developer Edition is what's being referred to). Because Firefox runs on Windows, macOS, and Linux systems, it is available to everyone. It's not quite as cutting-edge as Google Chrome for implementing certain standards, but it's also not the outlier that Internet Explorer and Edge are. Because Firefox is an open-source web browser, a large developer community has created numerous useful add-ons for Firefox. Many of these add-ons, like Chris Pederick's Web Developer Add-on, are specifically for web development. A list of useful add-ons and their URLs is available on the book's companion site. Firefox Developer Edition is available from `https://www.mozilla.org/firefox/developer/`.

Note that using Firefox as a baseline development browser does not mean designing for only one specific browser. Firefox is just the Goldilocks choice: not too advanced, not too buggy, but just right. Web design and development is a complex activity. Limit early development to one good browser. Once your site is almost ready to post to the web, you will want to have multiple browsers available to check your site. (See the sidebar "A Web-Reading Toolkit" in Chapter 2.)

## SETTING UP A DEVELOPMENT-GRADE WEB SERVER

`http-server` is a basic web server that runs on top of the Node.js JavaScript runtime environment. It's a development-grade web server, meaning that it is perfect for testing your design work on your computer or home network but not for serving pages on the open web. `http-server` runs on Node.js, which you can install by downloading it from `https://nodejs.org/`. It's available for all operating systems (Linux and macOS users should consider installation via a package manager). Once you've installed Node.js, you can open your command-line shell and use Node's package manager, npm, to install the `http-server` package for use anywhere on your file system. Just run `$ npm install http-server -g`

The dollar sign, $, is the conventional indication of the command prompt. Your prompt might not be a dollar sign, but you do not actually type it. Notice also the space followed by a hyphen and the letter g at the end, which means that you're doing a global (system-wide) install of `http-server`. If your web project is in the directory `Projects /website`, you can change into that directory and fire up `http-server` by running these two commands:

```
$ cd Projects/website
$ http-server
Starting up http-server, serving ./
Available on:
   http:127.0.0.1:8080
   http:192.168.1.6:8080
Hit CTRL-C to stop the server
```

The lines that do not have dollar signs represent the output from starting `http-server`. In this case, you can open up the URL `http://127.0.0.1:8080/` in your web browser and see your web project as it will appear on the open web. The special URL `http:// localhost:8080/` should work, too, but it's just `localhost`, not `localhost.com`. Assuming you're behind a firewall (and most networks are), no one outside of your local network can access it. But within your network, the site should be available to any other attached computer or mobile device. On my home network, I can use the second address listed above, `http://192.168.1.6:8080/`, in a browser on my phone or tablet to see how my web project will look on those devices. The address of your machine will probably be different, depending on how your network is configured.

Fuller, up-to-date details on installing Node.js and running `http-server` are available on the companion site for this book at `http://webpg.es/`.

## BUYING A DOMAIN NAME AND WEB HOSTING

Websites that are ready to be shared on the open web require a domain and web hosting. These are two very different things, but they are often confused.

- Your domain name is sort of like a welcome mat for a house. Anyone can go to the hardware store and order a mat that reads "The Johnsons." But throwing it in front of a random door doesn't get you the house, obviously.
- Your web hosting, then, is more like the house. It is the actual server where your files are stored and perhaps where you run blogging software or other server-side scripts. With most web hosts, your site is located at a numeric IP address and often also at an ugly URL created by the hosting company, something like `account123xyz.hostingcompany.example.net`. Neither a numeric address nor a hosting company's URL is memorable or under your control, though, so that is why it's important to buy the domain you want to use to direct people to the server where your website is hosted.

There are numerous domain name registration sites on the web. I will not recommend one particular site over another, but be cautious when choosing a company to register your domain name:

## SCHOOL/BUSINESS WEB ACCOUNTS

Colleges and universities, and even some high schools and businesses, often provide free web accounts to students and employees. Avoid these and buy your own domain and hosting. Here's why:

- **Your web identity should be independent of your school or employer.** People graduate or change schools, and they leave their jobs. When that happens, your identity should no longer be associated with the school or employer. When you own your own domain name and your own hosting, your web identity remains unaffected by school and job changes.
- **Free web accounts rarely have advanced web server features.** You can usually only store a limited amount of HTML, CSS, JavaScript, and media files on free accounts. Most free accounts do not include advanced server-side languages or configuration, nor do they offer the security of encrypted connections and `https` (see the book's companion website for details on serving your pages over an encrypted connection).
- **The URLs are ugly and a pain to work with.** The URLs of free web accounts tend to be structured something like `http://students .example.edu/~username/`. These kinds of URLs make using root-relative paths impossible (see Chapter 21), and oftentimes the tilde (~) gets encoded by other websites or email programs as `%7E`, making the URL even uglier, e.g, `http://students.example .edu/%7Eusername/`.
- **Free-account providers may change the subdomain or URL structure for accounts without notice, or disable certain features.** When you purchase hosting, the host usually wants to keep your business, so those types of unpleasant surprises are almost unheard of. But if your host does do something terrible to you like that, you'll just take your domain and your files, which you'll have kept copies of elsewhere, and move on to a new host.

If you make any use of a free account, limit yourself to posting a nice standards-compliant page linking to the full site that you host at your own domain.

- **Never pay much more than $12 a year** for each of the .com, .org, or .net top-level domains (TLDs) that you buy—and do buy all three of those TLDs together, if they are available and if you can afford to. Pricing on some of the newer, exotic TLDs is wildly unpredictable. Just be careful of promotional registration pricing that goes up substantially the following year.
- **Never opt in to any promises of search engine optimization (SEO) or other services** that registration or hosting companies may offer. Those services are where the registrars make a lot of their money, of course, but they are unnecessary. Register your domain and build a solid, content-rich website. That's the best SEO on the web.
- **Buy your domain name from one company, and your hosting from another.** I cannot stress this point enough. Most web hosting companies invite you to register your domain name with them or to transfer to them the registration for a domain you purchased elsewhere. My suggestion is to avoid this. If you ever get tangled up with a bad web host, or a good web host that gets bought out by a bad company, you do not want them having any control over your domain name. It's routine to point a domain name from your domain registrar to the nameservers that your web host runs (see Chapter 24).

There are also thousands of web hosting companies to choose from. Here are some general things to know as you select a web host:

- **Entry-level hosting generally costs between $5 and $20 a month.** Most reputable hosting will be somewhere within that range. Some hosts will give you a discount if you pay for a year's worth of hosting in advance, but be certain the host is a good one before you commit yourself to a year of service.
- **Large or unlimited file storage is not necessarily a good thing.** A terabyte of storage might sound appealing, but it invites abuse from people posting huge media collections, which may eat up the bandwidth of the server your site is on. Unlimited storage might also be used to deflect customers' attention from

less attractive features of the hosting service. Generally, a few gigabytes of storage is more than sufficient.

- **Unlimited transfer or traffic can also be a bad thing.** Again, it invites abusive customers; 500GB of transfer a month is plenty for most sites. But find out in advance how much the company charges for overage fees beyond your allotted data transfer.

Most web hosts showcase websites that are hosted on their servers. Look through those sites: note how fast they load in particular. While slow-loading pages on one or two of the sites may not necessarily be the host's fault, if all of their featured sites load slowly, look for hosting elsewhere. And of course, search the web for reviews from the host's customers.

Here are some baseline hosting features for the long-term growth of your site:

- **Linux- or Unix-based servers.** That information can be hard to determine for some hosts, so look hard. A Google search for the hosting company's name and "operating system" can often help you discover this information. Most hosts are running some flavor of Linux or Unix. Avoid hosts that run Windows servers.
- **Secure Shell access** (also known as SSH). Some hosts enable this by default, but most require you to request it on your account. Shell access lets you access your server to run certain commands, and is important to have for setting up certain blogging, wiki, or content management system software.
- **SFTP access.** Hosts used to routinely offer file transfer protocol (FTP) access, but FTP transmits your password without any encryption. That is a huge security risk to your site. Better hosts offer SFTP, which stands for "Secure FTP." SFTP is always available from hosts that grant SSH access.

Depending on your needs, you might also consider whether a host offers the following:

- **HTTPS** (Secure HTTP) has long been essential for online retailers, but it really should be enabled on all websites. See the Electronic Frontier Foundation's project, Let's Encrypt (`https://letsencrypt.org`). Let's Encrypt offers free certificates that are trusted by all modern browsers. See if your web host supports Let's Encrypt's certificates, or if you are permitted the level of control over the server that allows you to install certificates yourself.
- **Hosting multiple domain names**, sometimes called virtual hosts, will allow you to host your own website and perhaps another, such as the site for a community organization you belong to.
- **Log files and server statistics** can help you see who's linking to your site, or what search terms they used to find it. They are also generally more respectful of your visitors' privacy than Google Analytics (see Chapter 25).
- **Git.** A host that allows you to interact with Git repositories will help you avoid the pitfalls of SFTP and other file-based access and make site updates far less error prone (see Chapters 6 and 24).

## NEXT STEPS

Once you've set up the basic software and services required for web writing and design, know that you'll discover your own preferences as you work. The great thing about standards-based web design is that switching text editors, baseline development browsers, and even web hosts will not harm your site. Of course, you may have to relearn some things, but that's good too. Finding a setup that works for you and that you're comfortable with is important. But be patient. Give yourself plenty of time to learn all about the setup you choose initially.

The next chapter will look at an optional but extremely useful component to any web design and development environment: version control.

# CHAPTER 6

# Version Control

Since its 1.0 release in December 2005, Git has emerged as a leading open-source program for tracking the development of source code in software projects. Originally written by Linus Torvalds for managing the changes to the Linux kernel, Git now has its own active developer community and is the distributed version control system (DVCS) behind many important open-source software projects.

Some version control systems, including Subversion and CVS, rely on a centralized repository, often on a remote server. That means that there is a single, central repository for any given project, and it usually requires an internet connection in order for someone to interact with it. Git is called a *distributed* VCS because its architecture requires neither a centralized server nor even a centralized repository.

Instead, a Git repository exists in its own directory, .git, inside the directory of the project Git is tracking. It lives right next to your files. If a Git repository is shared—either over multiple computers for a single person, or multiple computers for multiple people—each repository is, in theory, exactly the same as all the others, in that all repositories have the complete history of the project in their own .git directory. Git only has a central repository—such as one hosted on GitHub—when everyone on a project agrees to say, "This is the main repository of the project." That means a central repository is a social arrangement, not a technological one. But all people working on the project still have their own complete copies of the repository, on their own computers.

Web writers and designers, much like programmers, can use Git to manage the changes to a wide range of digital projects. Provided that the contents of a project are primarily plain-text files, Git can maintain and manipulate a complete history of the changes to a project. *Plain-text files* include any files composed in plain text, such as the HTML, CSS, and JavaScript files that make up a website. A plain-text file need not have a .txt extension.

Git can maintain a detailed history for projects whose core files can be edited in any text editor, on any operating system that can run a text editor. That is possible with .html and .css files, but not with the binary .doc or .docx files saved by Microsoft Word. While it is possible to put Word documents, PDFs, images, and other binary files under Git control, Git's full functionality is available only on plain-text files.

## DIFFERENT APPROACHES TO HANDLING CHANGES

In order to understand what Git does and why it is useful, let's first review different approaches that people use to manage changes to digital work, particularly when they need to correct a mistake or recover from a bad choice.

### Undo/Redo: A Limited-Time-Only Approach to Changes

Undo and Redo functions built into most software are the obvious tools for fixing mistakes. Undo/Redo moves through states between changes, typically for a limited amount of time. Some software tracks Undo and Redo only to one step, undoing or redoing the very latest change. Other software tracks a longer chain of changes that can be undone or redone. But in many cases, the cache of changes associated with Undo and Redo is lost when a program or file is closed and sometimes even when a file is saved (even if the file remains open), or when a file is opened in the same program on another computer.

### File > Save As: A Whole-File Approach to Changes

Undo and Redo are useful for sequentially moving between changes shortly after someone has made them. Next to Undo/Redo, another common approach to managing states between changes is to save older, renamed copies of files on a computer's file system. Someone might use `File > Save As` or another means to create a copy of a file: `index.html` becomes `index-old.html` before making changes to `index.html`.

That approach can spiral out of control, leading to a collection of files: `index-old-2.html`, `index-old-2-a.html`, and so on. With the collection comes questions, especially when returning to work on a project after a long period of time. Is `index-old-2-a.html` another version of `index-old-2.html`? Or is it another version of `index.html`? What's the difference between `index-old-2.html` and the `2-a` copy? Might there be a good change in one file that was lost in another, but that should be put back in place? Outside of meticulous, time-consuming record keeping, or perhaps the use of a command-line tool like `diff` that compares one plain-text file's contents with another, there is no way to answer any of those questions reliably.

`File > Save As` presents additional problems in multifile projects where one file refers to another file. For example, consider a set of HTML files referring to a `screen.css` file. If `screen.css` is saved as `screen-old.css`, it becomes difficult to compare newer design changes against older ones by viewing the HTML pages in the web browser. To test `screen-old.css`, `screen.css` might be saved as `screen-new.css`, and `screen-old.css` saved back to `screen.css`. This process not only wastes time, but it also introduces the possibility of losing work in the accidental saving of a file under an incorrect name that overwrites another. That problem only escalates in more complex projects, such as WordPress themes that have numerous interfile dependencies.

But even in single-file projects, saving a file still involves risk for the person making changes. While conventional wisdom might suggest that deletion is the worst thing that can happen to an important file, most operating systems have a trash can or recycle bin from which deleted files can be recovered. There are even software utilities for recovering files after they have been emptied from the trash/recycle bin.

Counterintuitive as it may sound, the worst thing that can happen to a file is for it to be saved, at least in the situation where good work has been changed or deleted within the file.

## Track Changes: A Per-Change Approach to Changes

The system of version control familiar to writers is, of course, the Track Changes feature in Microsoft Word and other word processors. Once enabled, almost every change, no matter how global (reformatting entire pages) or insignificant (fixing typos) is tracked. If document readability, at least in an editing mode, and disk space are to be preserved, any tracked changes must eventually be accepted or rejected. However, at the moment a change is accepted or rejected, the change's history is no longer known or accessible. Acceptance or rejection of a change is as risky to a writer as `File > Save` can be. Tracked changes are also part of the file, making document sanitization a key concern for documents to be shared with audiences unsympathetic to the writing process. Git's presence, by contrast, is undetectable in the files that it tracks.

The Track Changes feature is, of course, only useful for word processor documents, not the plain-text formats that are the focus of this chapter.

## Summary of Common Approaches to Changes

`Undo/Redo` works similarly to the acceptance or rejection of tracked changes, but only within a limited timeframe. In the file system, the basic unit of change is the whole document. In Track Changes, the basic unit of change is the individual change itself, regardless of its size or significance: a corrected typo must be accepted or rejected, as must a major rewrite of a large portion of text.

In the whole-document approach, past changes are accessed by finding a copy of a file. In the individual-change approach, past changes will only be accessible if a tracked change has yet to be accepted or rejected.

# THE GIT APPROACH TO CHANGES

Whenever I present Git in my classes or at conferences, I introduce it through what I call the cat-on-the-keyboard scenario, usually with the HTML file that holds the slides for my presentation. In addition to having the slides up in a browser window, I'll open the slides in my text editor and "accidentally" hit the keyboard combination for selecting all of the file's text. Then I will mimic the typing skills of a cat and enter nonsense garbage that, of course, replaces the contents of the file. Then I hit the keyboard combination for save, followed by the combination for quitting the text editor program entirely. (The imaginary cat has incredible paw dexterity.) I refresh the slides in the browser, showing that they are in fact destroyed. And for added dramatic effect, I might reboot the computer. That sometimes draws actual gasps from people.

But because my slides are under Git control, even after a reboot it only takes a few keystrokes (`git checkout slideshow.html`) to return my slides to their state before the imaginary cat strolled across the keyboard. The point is made for the audience: file deletion isn't irreparably destructive the way that saving is under ordinary circumstances.

Git is a distributed version control system (DVCS; also sometimes called a *concurrent versioning system*, or a *content versioning system*). Git maintains a repository associated with the files that make up a project, which must be saved in a single directory and its subdirectories (otherwise known as folders and subfolders, using the visual metaphors of most operating systems; I will again use *directory* in this chapter). While Git is not the only program in the DVCS software genre, Git's concepts and functionality are similar to those of other DVCSs.

The basic unit of change that Git tracks is the commit. A **commit** is a human-crafted marker in a project's history. The commit captures the state of a project in a specific moment of the project's development. Commits can mark changes in a single file or across many files. And unlike the accept/reject function in Track Changes, Git commits are always "accepted," in that they are just part of the repository's history. "Rejecting" a commit involves rewriting the repository's history. See the book's companion website at `http://webpg.es/` for examples of how to rewrite history in Git.

Travis Swicegood (2012), author of a couple of books that are essential reading for anyone looking to master Git, has suggested a banking metaphor for understanding Git's approach to changes:

You take your valuables—in our case as developers, these valuables are the source code we write—and deposit them in the bank for safekeeping. Each change you mark—or *commit*—is recorded, and you can go back over the history just like you can review your bank statement. (4)

Computer users are accustomed to understanding the file system—the folders/directories where files are stored, the use of `File > Save` commands common to all software—as their "vaults," with optical media, USB drives, and even cloud storage services like Dropbox as additional, backup vaults.

Git complements the file system by creating a repository that serves the dual purpose of a storage mechanism and a bank-statement-like record of the changes to the project. But unlike bank statements, which one can only review for accuracy, the history recorded in a Git repository is mutable. It can be changed. There are Git commands to move forward and backward (and even sideways, through branches) in a project's history.

Git also provides the means to rewrite history. Imagine accidentally overdrawing your checking account. If you owned a time machine, you would have the means to go back in time and make a big deposit so that the overdraft never occurs, even though a big shopping spree still

## INSTALLING AND CONFIGURING GIT

GitHub maintains accurate and usable documentation for installing Git on Microsoft Windows, macOS, and popular Linux distributions, so I will not replicate their specific instructions here. There are links from the book's companion website at `http://webpg.es/`.

Although Git can be enhanced with GUI programs, the fullest range of Git's capabilities are accessible from the command line on Unix-like systems (e.g., Linux, macOS) as well as the DOS-like command line in Microsoft Windows or PowerShell. Msysgit, a distribution of Git for use on Windows, installs Git Bash, which provides commands found on Unix-like systems.

The book's companion site also has details on configuring Git with your email and name, and it also describes some additional configuration options that will simplify your interactions with Git.

happens (or maybe it doesn't; all history in a repository is mutable). Metaphorically speaking, Git is that time machine.

## Interacting with Git

Because Git is a command-line tool, I will be showing examples of input and output on the command line. The commands in this chapter assume a Unix-like command-line shell; see the book's companion site for help if you are on Windows.

The general form of examples showing command-line interaction is that lines beginning with the dollar sign, $, indicate the prompt where a command is typed. Do not type the dollar sign, though. The Enter/Return key needs to be pressed once the command has been typed out. Lines following, without any dollar sign, are the output from the command. So, to indicate running the git version command and its resulting output, the example would look something like:

```
$ git version
git version 2.10.2
```

As a space-saving measure, some examples in this chapter show only partial output from the command line; omitted output is marked with an ellipsis (...). Some Git commands, such as git add, do not respond with any output, unless something has gone wrong.

To those used to the graphical user interfaces (GUIs) common to contemporary software, Git feels like a throwback to more primitive days of computing. The benefits of developing command-line skills through Git are many, but perhaps the most important is that it helps writers become more adept at working with remote servers where websites ultimately reside.

## Creating Git Repositories

Every project that you track in Git has its own repository. To create a Git repository, there must first be some content for Git to track. Git tracks only the contents of files. A directory or subdirectory is not tracked until it contains at least one file.

When a Git repository is created via the `git init` (initialize) command, Git stores the repository in the directory where a project's files are stored. Every file from the project must therefore be saved in a single directory and that directory's subdirectories. That may present an organizational shift for writers in the habit of storing a project's files in different folders across a computer. Git requires organization within a single directory. But then, so do websites.

## EXAMPLE: TRACKING A TO-DO LIST

In this example, Git will track a single plain-text file containing a simple to-do list written in Markdown syntax. Markdown can work like a shorthand for HTML, although here it will just serve to add a little visual structure to the to-do list. See Chapter 22 for more information about Markdown.

It is something of a convention to create in your home directory a directory called `Projects` whose immediate subdirectories will each be a project under Git control. You can create that directory using the GUI for your operating system, or you can create it right on the command line using the `mkdir` (make directory) command. Run `cd` first to make sure that you're in your home directory:

```
$ cd
$ mkdir Projects
```

Inside the `Projects` folder, create a directory called `todo`, which will contain the to-do list text file and Git repository. Again, this can be done from the command line; `cd` (change directory) first into `Projects`:

```
$ cd Projects
$ mkdir todo
```

Using a text editor such as Notepad++ for Windows or TextWrangler for macOS (see Chapter 5), create and save a file called `list.txt` in the `todo` directory. On the command line, you can inspect that the file has been created: first type `cd ~/Projects/todo` (the tilde, ~, is a shortcut to your home directory). Then run the `pwd` (print working directory) command to be certain that the command line is in the directory it should be.

```
$ cd ~/Projects/todo
$ pwd
/Users/someuser/Projects/todo
```

Finally, list the contents of the directory using the `ls` command:

```
$ ls
list.txt
```

Back in the text editor, create the basic structure of a to-do list with Markdown for the headings and list items; for example,

```
# My To-Do List

## Today
* Item

## Tomorrow
* Item
```

Git prefers a blank line of space at the very end of every text file, so hit return one more time after your last line of text content. Save the `list.txt` file again.

Having saved the file, it's time to put Git to work. Run `pwd` again to make sure that your command line is in the right place. If it's not, use the command `cd ~/Projects/todo` to get there, and rerun `pwd` and `ls`:

```
$ pwd
/Users/someuser/Projects/todo
$ ls
list.txt
```

Having confirmed your location on the command line and the existence of the text file, initialize a Git repository:

```
$ git init
Initialized empty Git repository in /Users/someuser
 /Projects/todo/.git/
```

Running `ls -ap` (which lists hidden files and directories, which begin with a dot, `.`, and appends a slash, `/`, on all directories) should confirm the existence of a new `.git/` directory (the `./` and `../` are symbols used in Unix-like systems for traversing directories, and not content that will be tracked by Git):

```
$ ls -ap
./    ../    .git/    list.txt
```

If you are on a Mac and used the macOS Finder GUI to create or view the todo/ directory, it's possible you may see a file called .DS _Store listed; additionally, your text editor may create temporary files such as list.txt~ or list.txt.tmp. You can ignore those files for now, even though git status will list them as untracked files. Instructing Git to ignore certain files is covered later in this chapter.

With Git initialized, it's now possible to run additional Git commands. The first is to check the status of the repository:

```
$ git status
# On branch master
#
# Initial commit
#
# Untracked files:
# (use "git add <file>. . ." to include in what
    will be committed)
#
# list.txt
nothing added to commit but untracked files present
  (use "git add" to track)
```

Git is reporting that it is on the master branch, at the point of awaiting an initial commit to the repository (more on branches on the book's companion site). It reports an untracked file, list.txt. On colorized outputs, list.txt will appear in red text; again, there may be other untracked files, depending on your operating system or text editor, as noted above. There are also instructions for tracking the file using git add. Following Git's instructions from git status, add the skeletal to-do list file to stage it for committing:

```
$ git add list.txt
```

Running git status now reports:

```
$ git status
# On branch master
#
# Initial commit
#
# Changes to be committed:
#   (use "git rm --cached <file>... to unstage)
#
#       new file:    list.txt
#
```

At this point, the list.txt file has been added to Git's index, which behaves as a sort of staging area between a file being saved in, for example, a text editor and it being committed to the repository. No more changes should be made to a file once it has been staged but before it is committed. In more complex changes involving multiple files or portions of files, the index and the git add command are more useful. Once added to the index, the skeletal to-do list can be committed to the repository, using the git commit command with the -m flag followed by a brief message in quotation marks that describes the change:

```
$ git commit -m "Initial commit; skeletal outline
   for my to-do list"
[master (root-commit) 94854eb] Initial commit;
 skeletal outline for my to-do list
1 files changed, 8 insertions(+), 0 deletions(-)
 create mode 100644 list.txt
```

Git provides a large amount of information here; but rather than unpacking all that it outputs in that one-time post-commit message, run git log to see the current history of the repository in a slightly more readable form:

```
$ git log
commit 94854eb0b6ddbe1682f856499e320d9602115f8f
Author: Karl Stolley <karl.stolley@gmail.com>
Date: Thu Jan 1 12:23:33 2016 -0600

    Initial commit; skeletal outline for my to-do list
```

There is a lot of information here as well. The obvious is the author information (in this case, mine), and the date and time of the commit. Git also outputs the brief, one-line commit message.

The commit itself is identified by a 40-digit **hexadecimal** number beginning 94854eb0. Although Git could, like some version control systems, simply number commits 1, 2, 3 as they occur, it instead uses that 40-digit number, known as a SHA-1 hash. A SHA-1 hash is a cryptographic identifier based on the contents of the files in the commit. In fact, every object in Git is identified by a SHA-1 hash (see the chapter "Git Internals" in Chacon and Straub 2014). Although collaboration using Git is outside the scope of this chapter, the SHA-1 hash allows multiple people to work on the same repository, without having to decide which commit is commit 13 or 27. What matters is the content of the commit, not the order in which it occurred.

Back to the current example: now that the skeletal outline version of list.txt has been committed to the repository, running git status again should produce a short and sweet message:

```
$ git status
# On branch master
nothing to commit (working directory clean)
```

That message means that the contents of the working directory match the repository; there are no new changes, in other words, to list.txt to add to the index or commit.

## Telling Git to Ignore Certain Files

But perhaps git status is still listing untracked files. Mac users, for example, might find that Git reports the presence of the little .DS _Store file that macOS uses to track the windows in its Finder GUI:

```
$ git status
# On branch master
# Untracked files:
#   (use "git add <file>. . ." to include in what
    will be committed)
#
#        .DS_Store
```

```
nothing added to commit but untracked files present
 (use "git add" to track)
```

The .DS_Store file has nothing to do with the to-do list project, so it should not be included in the repository. Git should simply ignore it.

There are multiple ways to tell Git to ignore certain files. One is to create a .gitignore file and commit it, like any other file, to the repository you're working on. First, it's necessary to create a text file called .gitignore that specifies which files Git should always ignore. So, to ignore the .DS_Store file, the .gitignore file should contain this line:

```
.DS_Store
```

If your text editor creates temporary files marked by a tilde (~) at the very end of the file name (e.g., list.txt~) or a .tmp extension (list.txt.tmp), there's no need to explicitly list every single file for each and every project. Instead, Git will follow a basic pattern for filenames that should be ignored. Here, the star/asterisk (*) refers to any number of characters in a filename, followed by the tilde or by .tmp:

```
.DS_Store
*~
*.tmp
```

Each pattern or explicit file name to ignore should be written on a separate line. Save this file in your repository directory as .gitignore. Then, add and commit the file to Git:

```
$ git add .gitignore
$ git commit -m "Added Git ignore file"
```

Finally, running git status should demonstrate whether the ignore file is written correctly:

```
$ git status
# On branch master
nothing to commit (working directory clean)
```

If the files you told Git not to track are still appearing with git status, double-check the contents of your .gitignore file. The book's companion site has additional methods for ignoring files in Git.

## Additional Commits

At this point, the to-do list only has a skeletal outline, which has been committed to the Git repository. Now it's time to return to the text editor and add some content to the to-do list for today and tomorrow:

```
# My To-Do List

## Today
* Learn Git
* Finish to-do list for tomorrow

## Tomorrow
* Put everything web-based under Git control
* Update this to-do list
```

Save the file, and run git status:

```
$ git status
# On branch master
# Changes not staged for commit:
# (use "git add <file>. . ." to update what will be
   committed)
# (use "git checkout -- <file>. . ." to discard
   changes in working directory)
#
#     modified: list.txt
#
no changes added to commit (use "git add" and/or
  "git commit -a")
```

Git reports that we're still on the master branch and that the list .txt file has been modified, but those modifications are not yet staged to be committed.

With the list complete for today, it's a perfect time to commit the changes to the repository. But then the phone rings. And a meeting gets called. Then lunch. By the time you've returned to your computer, you have no idea what changes you've made to the file.

In this case, a quick inspection of the file itself might be enough to refresh your memory. But in a text file with hundreds or thousands of lines, with changes made all throughout, specific changes might be less obvious. Conveniently enough, Git includes the `git diff` command, which will explicitly show what has changed—and by extension, what will be committed to the repository when you next run the commands to do so:

```
$ git diff list.txt
  diff --git a/list.txt b/list.txt
  index e324382..4bca1ac 100644
  --- a/list.txt
  +++ b/list.txt
  @@ -1,8 +1,10 @@
    # My To-Do List

    ## Today
  - * Item
  + * Learn Git
  + * Finish to-do list for tomorrow

    ## Tomorrow
  - * Item
  + * Put everything web-based under Git control
  + * Update this to-do list
```

Git is reporting the changes between the latest repository version and the version saved in `list.txt`; lines beginning with a minus (-) are deleted, lines beginning with a plus (+) are inserted. A modified line, then, is reported as deleted and then inserted. Colorization enhances the readability of `git diff` output, with inserted lines appearing in green and deleted lines appearing in red. Unchanged lines are usually white or black, depending on your terminal configuration and preferences.

Having determined the changes to the file, use the `-a` flag shortcut with `git commit` to add the file to the index and commit it with a single command (i.e., without having to run `git add`):

```
$ git commit -am "Added tasks for today and
 tomorrow; Git is on the menu"
[master 6196cc1] Added tasks for today and
 tomorrow; Git is on the menu
1 files changed, 4 insertions(+), 2 deletions(-)
```

Running `git log` again, you can see that the history of the repository includes another commit. Like an archive of blog posts, commits are listed in reverse-chronological order:

```
$ git log
commit 6196cc114a7e24171613f5d6577a40a67c17f110
Author: Karl Stolley <karl.stolley@gmail.com>
Date:   Thu Jan 15 13:51:57 2016 -0600

    Added tasks for today and tomorrow; Git is on
    the menu

commit 3a768acea8b548dd8d6c32fcac339b635b985ae9
Author: Karl Stolley <karl.stolley@gmail.com>
Date:   Thu Jan 15 12:43:33 2016 -0600

    Added Git ignore file

commit 94854eb0b6ddbe1682f856499e320d9602115f8f
Author: Karl Stolley <karl.stolley@gmail.com>
Date:   Thu Jan 15 12:23:33 2016 -0600

    Initial commit; skeletal outline for my to-do
    list
```

That's the default output for `git log`; to get a simpler view of the history, you can pass additional arguments to `git log`. The option `--pretty=oneline` will output a single-line; `--abbrev-commit` will shorten the SHA-1 hash to only its first 7 digits:

```
$ git log --pretty=oneline --abbrev-commit
  6196cc1 Added tasks for today and tomorrow; Git is
          on the menu
  3a768ac Added Git ignore file
  94854eb Initial commit; skeletal outline for my
          to-do list
```

Nice, simple output. See the book's companion site for how to set up aliases for long commands.

## SUMMARY: BASIC GIT WORKFLOWS

Aside from initializing the repository, which happens only once in the entire life of a project, the basic, repeating pattern is: make changes, save the file. Just as you have always done. Once a certain state of the file is reached (either as a goal, a natural stopping-place, or even at the end of the work day), add the file to the index (`git add`), then commit to the repository (`git commit`). The additional commands here—repeatedly changing directories, listing contents, even running `git status`—are not necessary for interacting with Git, but for the purposes of this chapter, they do help show what is happening behind the scenes with the file system and with Git itself. Especially when you're first starting out, it's good to double-check that you are in the correct directory with your project's files, and therefore that the Git commands you write will likely do what you expect them to do.

As demonstrated above, simple single-file commits really do not benefit from the intermediate step of adding the file to the index before committing, so it's possible to run `git commit` with the `-a` flag, which adds all of the changed files (but not, however, any new untracked files) to the index and commits to the repository in one step. Writing also the `-m` flag keeps the message and therefore the entire commit to one line of entry:

```
$ git commit -am "Commit message goes here"
```

The instructional, explanatory nature of this chapter makes Git usage appear far more cumbersome than it actually is in day-to-day use. As a frequent and obsessive Git user, I can report that with time and frequent use, the pattern becomes second nature: change, save, commit. Chapter 24 describes methods for using Git to post your files to the server where you host your live site. To see videos demonstrating Git use in real time, have a look at the book's companion website at http://webpg.es/.

## NEXT STEPS

Now that I have covered Git, in addition to the simpler technologies of the editor, browser, and development-grade server covered in Chapter 5, it's time to look in Part II at the role those technologies play along with web standards in creating more accessible, usable, and sustainable sites. If you'd rather get straight down to the work of building pages, and return to more theoretical matters later, move on to Part III to learn more about writing with source using your new set of production tools.

## REFERENCES

Chacon, Scott, and Ben Straub. 2014. *Pro Git*, 2nd ed. Berkeley, CA: Apress. https://git-scm.com/book/en/v2

Swicegood, Travis. 2012. *Pragmatic Version Control Using Git* (Version P3.0). Dallas, TX: Pragmatic Bookshelf.

# PART II

# ISSUES AND CHALLENGES

Accessibility, usability, and sustainability. Those three interrelated issues are the foundation of a rhetorically successful website. While an accessible, usable, and sustainable site is no guarantee of rhetorical success, an inaccessible, unusable, or unsustainable site is usually a recipe for disaster.

Designers too often delay considering those issues until the completion of a site. At that point, they are matters of assessment: is the site accessible? usable? sustainable? But once a site is complete, it becomes much more difficult to correct its foundational shortcomings.

This book suggests an approach that positions these three issues as instructive guides throughout the process of writing and designing for the web. Accessibility, usability, and sustainability are at the core of a site, but they are achieved through numerous little decisions.

Here is a brief overview of each of the three issues:

- **Accessibility.** Accessibility aims for equitable access for all people, regardless of their physical abilities or means of access. Accessible websites work on fast and slow internet connections and on ultra-high-definition widescreen desktop computers and tiny wearable screens. Accessible websites support interaction via an equally wide range of input devices including keyboards, touchpads, mice, touchscreens, and even voice commands. Sites must also be accessible to search engines and social platforms.

- **Usability.** Usability is often shorthand for **usability testing**, where trained experts observe targeted users interacting with a website. But as a set of principles, usability can also guide site design to conform to user expectations. A site that takes forever to load or otherwise performs poorly makes its use difficult or impossible. If user expectations are not met, as when site navigation has confusing or even misleading buttons, users may become frustrated and leave.
- **Sustainability.** Sustainability aims to keep a site accessible and usable over time. While it is true that digital technologies change quickly and without much notice, there are certain design practices and choices that will help future-proof your website. Sustainability also plans for access and use as a site grows, or scales. Certain writing and design choices may be accessible and usable on a site of only five pages. But what if the site grows to 50 pages? Or 500?

Each of these issues will be covered in greater depth over the next three chapters. Refer to them as you work on the design of your site and as you work through the technical chapters in Part III of the book.

# CHAPTER 7

# Accessibility

Some web designers dislike the word *accessibility*, because they misunderstand it as imposing unacceptable limits on artistic creativity or even promoting a bleeding-heart political agenda. But this chapter reframes accessibility in a much broader scope and shows that accessibility can actually encourage creativity, not limit it. You will also learn that accessibility is not beholden to any political agenda, but rather a rhetorical one: accessibility maximizes the potential size and range of a website's audience.

## WHAT IS ACCESSIBILITY?

The World Wide Web Consortium has a group devoted to accessibility: the Web Accessibility Initiative (WAI). The WAI's introduction to accessibility declares that "web accessibility means that people with disabilities can use the web" (W3C 2005).

That's a very limited definition. And if a web designer believes that disabled people do not use the web, or that disabled people represent such a small minority of users that their needs aren't worth taking the time to design for, odds are that designer will skip over accessibility matters entirely. But the WAI goes further, noting that accessibility "benefits people without disabilities in certain situations, such as people using a slow Internet connection, people with 'temporary disabilities' such as a broken arm, and people with changing abilities due to aging" (W3C 2005). A notable study commissioned by Microsoft (2003) found that some 57 percent of working-age adults in the United

States benefit from accessible technology, and that this percentage is all but certain to increase as the population ages.

Accessible design addresses the needs of people with disabilities, yes, but as a product of serving the needs of all people. The accessibility and accessible design techniques presented below aim to make sites available to all users, "without special adaptation or modification" and regardless of their computer equipment or physical ability (Lidwell, Holden, and Butler 2010, 16)

Accessible design attempts to account for the full range of user-access conditions. User access is determined both by human physiological conditions, such as physical, cognitive, and sensory abilities, as well as technological conditions, such as screen size, network connection speed, and input devices. In certain cases, a particular human condition

## ACCESSIBILITY RESOURCES

Primarily focused on the needs of people with disabilities, each of these resources is worth your time to explore:

- **Web Accessibility Initiative (WAI)** (`https://www.w3.org/WAI/`): The WAI, an organization that publishes a wealth of information on accessibility, is one of the primary advocates for web accessibility.
- **Web Content Accessibility Guidelines (WCAG)** (`https://www.w3.org/TR/WCAG20/`): Released as W3C Recommendation WCAG 2.0 in December 2008, WCAG is a very technical document. Because of this, some members of the web design community have reacted quite negatively to it. See Joe Clark's (2006) article "To Hell with WCAG 2."
- **Section 508** (`https://www.section508.gov/`): Section 508 refers to a 1998 amendment to the Rehabilitation Act of 1973, which was meant to end discrimination based on physical ability within the federal government and federally funded agencies. Section 508 is specifically about information technologies, such as government websites. While Section 508 is not applied as law to nongovernmental websites, the Section 508 guidelines and technical standards (`http://www.access-board.gov/sec508/standards.htm`) should be taken into consideration when building an accessible website.

necessitates a technological condition in the form of an assistive technology. A person with low vision, for example, may require a screen reader to interact with a website.

In almost all cases, conditions of access—both human and technological—are nonnegotiable. They are states. Web designers, no matter how talented, cannot leverage web technologies to transform the device someone uses to access the web, any more than they can change someone's physical or sensory abilities. Access conditions are states that design must account for, but cannot alter.

## ACCESSIBILITY AS UNIVERSAL DESIGN

I prefer to treat accessibility as synonymous with a design approach known as universal design. Universal design attempts to serve the needs of all users through a single design—rather than through multiple designs tailored to different users. The Center for Universal Design's (1997) Universal Design Definition reads: "The design of products and environments to be usable by all people, to the greatest extent possible, without the need for adaptation or specialized design."

One classic example of universal design is a sidewalk that gently slopes into the curb, down to street level. Not only does that design serve the needs of people in scooters and wheelchairs, but also parents pushing strollers, travelers pulling roller luggage, and mail carriers pushing delivery carts.

But sidewalks are a physical medium bound to the limitations of the physical world, where one design is the same for all people. In the digital medium, the web is unrivaled in supporting design techniques that lend themselves to universal design: one single page or one site serves the needs of all users, but it serves each user differently. If the sloping sidewalk example were like a universally designed, responsive website, the sidewalk would automatically change its properties to best accommodate the needs of each pedestrian.

So while you may encounter advice from accessibility advocates who suggest creating separate, specialized versions of web pages that are geared for particular devices, for printing, or for people with specific disabilities, thoughtful practice of standards-based, responsive web design produces pages that maximize the access conditions for any given user.

Universal design challenges web designers to provide the best possible experience under any imaginable set of constraints. If a user cannot perceive images, a site should deliver the best possible image-free experience. If another user has a slow internet connection, a site must be designed to judiciously load only essential data.

## ACCESSIBLE DESIGN APPROACHES BEGIN WITH FILE FORMATS

In its worst uses, the web becomes a catch-all storage system. Any type of file can be stored and accessed via a URL. But just because you can post any type of file to the web does not mean you shouldn't be thoughtful and selective about what you do post.

Postel's Law, or the robustness principle, describes web-appropriate file formats and accessible design more generally: Be liberal in what you accept, and conservative in what you send (Braden 1989).

"Be liberal in what you accept" is a foundational accessibility principle for designing the web: people should be able to visit a site with whatever browser or device they choose, using whatever assistive technology they need, and according to any personal preferences (no JavaScript, running an ad blocker, having text enlarged). The flip side of that is to send content in only a conservative set of file formats that conform to the needs of site visitors.

Specifically, to send conservative and therefore maximally accessible content, build pages with the following:

- **Content structured in semantic HTML.** On the web, text presented in semantically structured HTML is the only content that is reliably accessible, because HTML is the only format that all web browsers, web-connected devices, and assistive technologies can render. Chapters 11, 16, and 19 look in depth at semantic HTML and the accessible delivery of media.
- **Images presented as JPEGs, PNGs, or GIFs.** Most graphics programs can save images in dozens of formats. But there are only three formats that work reliably in all web browsers. JPEG

and PNG images are generally preferable to GIFs, as GIFs are limited to 256 colors. All content images should be prepared and delivered with semantically structured HTML content. See Chapters 3 and 19 for additional information about image formats and accessibility.

That is it for the conservative list, as far as content goes: HTML and images.

What's missing from that list? Plenty, including some very popular formats, such as word processor documents and PDFs, not to mention sound and video files. Any content beyond HTML text and the three common image formats must be treated carefully. The challenge is that no content other than HTML text and common image formats can be viewed directly in most browsers without the use of a plugin (e.g., the now-defunct Flash Player) or other third-party application (e.g., Adobe Acrobat Reader). HTML5 introduced native, plugin-free audio and video to web browsers, but Chapter 19 describes the lingering challenges of delivering audio and video even on a post-Flash, post-plugin web.

PDFs and word processor documents present special challenges on mobile devices. If a mobile phone does not have a word processor application on it, it may be unable to access word processor documents posted to the web. And while most phones are capable of opening PDFs, PDFs are typically formatted to printed-page sizes and therefore difficult or impossible to read on a phone.

If you must post PDFs or word processor documents, be sure to alert users when linking to those kinds of files, perhaps by placing the file format in parentheses: (Word document). You should also include links to download Acrobat Reader or any other software required to view your files. Remember, though, not all users will be able to install software. So keep your crucial content in HTML. Any other format should be considered a last resort and ultimately a bad choice for the web.

## BUILD FROM ACCESSIBILITY, NOT BACK TOWARD IT

One of the mistakes both beginning and advanced web designers make is to delay accessibility considerations until a design is almost completed. I have learned from observing students in my web design classes that this is probably why some designers see accessibility as such a pain: if addressed only after a design is otherwise in place and ready to go, building back toward accessibility only slows you down. In the worst case, it might force you to scrap design components that represent a significant investment of time and effort.

Particularly among web designers who work with JavaScript and DOM scripting (see Chapter 13), there are two related concepts that are instructive for building from accessibility, not back toward it: progressive enhancement and its user counterpart, graceful degradation (Olsson 2007).

- **Progressive enhancement** is the design approach: each component of a web page builds on another. A site begins with well-formed, valid semantic HTML. Then a design component, written in CSS and kept in its own separate `.css` file, leverages the semantically structured HTML to deliver a responsive page design. Unobtrusively loaded JavaScript presents yet another layer for enhancing the interactivity and performance of a page.
- **Graceful degradation** is the corresponding user experience. All browsers render HTML; most render CSS. Users with CSS-enabled browsers have a progressively enhanced experience. But users with HTML-only browsers are not punished by the presence of CSS or JavaScript if the site gracefully degrades to HTML-only presentation. Note that an HTML-only device, such as a screen reader, will not provide what seems to a user to be a degraded experience. Rather, graceful degradation permits an optimal experience for an HTML-only device: the best possible experience under that set of constraints.

Let me share an example of graceful degradation: After redesigning a major online writing lab website, I received an email from a blind student who wished to express her gratitude that the new site contained no design images. (The old site had many, and made it difficult for her to use.) In truth, there were plenty of design images on the site. The difference was that the new site presented them in such a way that they would improve the experience of users who can benefit from a

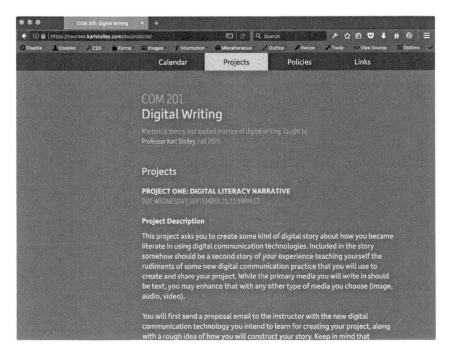

**Figure 7.1.**  A course website of the author's, progressively enhanced with CSS.

graphical display, without punishing users who cannot. That the student thought there were no design images on the site is exactly what she should have thought (content images, however, are a different matter; users must be made aware of those if they cannot view them). Figures 7.1 and 7.2 show how a site progressively enhanced with CSS (Figure 7.1) degrades gracefully for text-only display (Figure 7.2).

Progressive enhancement, then, is how you should design: start with a solid foundation of content marked up in HTML. Add to that a responsive design in CSS and any advanced functionality that your site needs using unobtrusive JavaScript. Progressive enhancement adheres to Postel's Law mentioned earlier section: Be conservative in what you do, be liberal in what you allow others to do. Accessibility represents a conservative design approach. It avoids trendy methods to design pages using a dozen different JavaScript frameworks. But it is a liberal approach in its view of users. Let users access the page in whatever browser or assistive technology they have available, according to whatever needs and preferences they have. In short, stay out of the user's way.

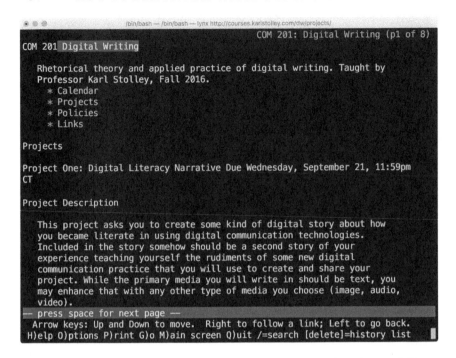

**Figure 7.2.** The same website as in Figure 7.1, without CSS. It degrades gracefully in a CSS-less environment, such as Lynx shown here.

Once you have designed with progressive enhancement in mind, graceful degradation is what you should test for: view your site in Lynx, or in Firefox in Responsive Design Mode with the Web Developer Add-on, which allows you to disable any combination of images, CSS, and JavaScript. Apply the same accessibility tests described in Chapter 2 to your own site. If the site content and controls are still accessible under all of those conditions, congratulations: your site gracefully degrades, and your visitors should have few problems accessing it. Continue to test your site over time, and consider providing your email address or another means for visitors to contact you in case they encounter accessibility problems.

## GOING FURTHER: ACCESSIBLE ENHANCEMENT

So far, this chapter has looked at file formats and a general, somewhat abstract progressive-enhancement approach to design. Later chapters will treat file formats and progressive enhancement more concretely. Here, though, are some additional, concrete features you can add to pages to increase their accessibility: in-page navigation, accessibility attributes in HTML, and accessibility-minded uses of CSS and JavaScript.

## In-Page Navigation

For sighted people, moving through the contents of a web page is usually a simple matter scrolling with a mouse or swiping a touchscreen.

On certain devices and for certain users, such as screen readers and some older mobile phones, scrolling down long pages might be difficult or time consuming. To account for this, it's preferable to design sites to include a short accessible navigation area near the top of each page that allows users to jump to major sections of the page, such as the main content area or the site navigation.

The Rapid Prototyping Kit (RPK, see Chapter 15) includes in its HTML a list item with an `accessibility` class. The link it contains enables a device to jump to the page content using **fragment identifiers**, which point browsers to portions of the HTML assigned a unique `id` attribute (see Chapter 11). Accessible links such as those save users with screen readers from having to listen to all navigation items before being able to access the page's content.

In the RPK, the content area immediately follows the navigation; given that, it might seem silly to have a "Skip to page content" link. However, the idea behind including the link is to inspire confidence in users, whether of assistive or older mobile devices, that they can control their browsing experience and get right to the part of the page that they seek.

CSS can be used to hide the accessible navigation from view on graphical browsers, as described in the comments of the RPK's source code. Sites that use that technique enable assistive technologies to render the contents of the accessible navigation for users who need it, without cluttering up the page for users who do not.

## Accessibility Attributes

The most well-known accessibility attribute in HTML is `alt`, which provides rudimentary alternate text for content images loaded in the image tag, `<img />`. Your HTML will not validate if you do not have an `alt` attribute on all of your images (attributes and other parts of HTML are discussed in Chapter 11). However, `alt` text has been vastly augmented by semantic elements like `<figure>` and `<figcaption>`, which are described in Chapter 19.

There are a few other longstanding attributes in HTML that serve accessibility:

- `title` provides certain additional information, such as the expansion of an abbreviation marked with the abbreviation tag, `<abbr>`. However, most browsers display that information only when a cursor hovers over the element. Chapter 20 walks through an example of progressively enhanced JavaScript that renders the contents of `title` attributes accessibly on touchscreen devices.
- `tabindex` helps set the order in which links and other controls are activated by using the Tab key on the keyboard. Physical keyboards and desktop browsers are generally better than their touchscreen counterparts in responding to `tabindex`, simply because touchscreen browsers do not display a keyboard in the absence of form elements.
- `accesskey` is an attribute that allows someone to use a keyboard combination to activate a particular link, usually in the navigation area. Like `tabindex`, `accesskey` generally works better on physical keyboards. Touchscreen keyboards are limited in accepting simultaneous multikey combinations.

The WAI (2014) published a specification for Accessible Rich Internet Applications, WAI-ARIA, which describes a standard, accessible way to provide "semantic information about widgets, structures, and behaviors, in order to allow assistive technologies to convey appropriate information to persons with disabilities." A large part of the specification is the description of ARIA roles, which can be specified on HTML elements via the `role` attribute.

For example, WAI-ARIA includes a `banner` attribute that is used to mark a portion of the page that "typically includes things such as the logo or identity of the site sponsor, and site-specific search tool." The

HTML5 `<header>` element is a perfect candidate for this role, and can be marked as `<header role="banner">`.

The ARIA `role` attribute is somewhat redundant in that context, however, considering the semantics of the `<header>` tag (see Chapter 16). The WAI has begun work on a new specification, ARIA in HTML (W3C 2017) that will streamline the use of ARIA attributes and require them only on HTML tags whose semantics differ from ARIA roles. For example, at the time of writing, ARIA in HTML discourages the use of `role="banner"` on the `<header>` element shared by all contents of a page.

See the book's companion website at `http://webpg.es/` for up-to-date examples of ARIA attributes written according to the latest ARIA in HTML specification. Subsequent chapters will look more closely at some of the more stable `role` attributes, along with global `aria-*` attributes, such as `aria-labelledby` (see Chapter 19).

## CSS and JavaScript to Enhance Accessibility

CSS and JavaScript do not have to be stumbling blocks to accessibility. Used appropriately in the right circumstances, CSS and JavaScript enhance the accessibility of a web page for users with capable browsers. For example, CSS enables the typography of a page to be more readable than the default styling web browsers apply. And the use of em and other relative units, described in Chapter 12, ensures that your page's text size will respect the preferences of users who may set a larger or smaller default text size in their browsers.

Chapter 20 will demonstrate that JavaScript can be used to add simple, progressively enhanced features for increasing the text size on a page or providing on touchscreens the kinds of functionality that on desktop systems requires a hovering mouse pointer. Of course, a page must still be accessible and functional in the absence of JavaScript.

## NEXT STEPS

Accessibility and universal design form the foundation for a rhetorically successful website, but ensuring equitable access to a site is only the first step. Designers and writers must also be concerned about how and under what conditions users use websites, too. The next chapter will look at usability-driven design approaches for creating more usable sites.

## REFERENCES

Braden, R., ed. 1989. "RFC 1122: Requirements for Internet Hosts—Communication Layers." https://tools.ietf.org/html/rfc1122

Center for Universal Design. 1997. "The Principles of Universal Design." Version 2.0. https://www.ncsu.edu/ncsu/design/cud/about_ud/udprinciplestext.htm

Clark, Joe. 2006. "To Hell with WCAG 2." *A List Apart.* http://alistapart.com/article/tohellwithwcag2

Lidwell, William, Kritina Holden, and Jill Butler. 2010. *Universal Principles of Design*, rev. ed. Beverly, MA: Rockport Publishers.

Microsoft. 2003. "The Market for Accessible Technology—The Wide Range of Abilities and Its Impact on Computer Use." https://www.microsoft.com/enable/research/phase1.aspx

Olsson, Tommy. 2007. "Graceful Degradation & Progressive Enhancement." Accessites.org: The Art of Accessibility. http://accessites.org/site/2007/02/graceful-degradation-progressive-enhancement/

W3C. 2005. "Introduction to Web Accessibility." https://www.w3.org/WAI/intro/accessibility

W3C. 2014. "Accessible Rich Internet Applications (WAI-ARIA) 1.0." https://www.w3.org/TR/wai-aria/

W3C. 2017. "ARIA in HTML." https://www.w3.org/TR/html-aria/

# CHAPTER 8

# Usability

Accessibility is a matter of designing to account for states or conditions of user access, as Chapter 7 argued. By contrast, usability is a matter of designing to account for user behaviors. But it is futile to design for usability if a site is inaccessible: usability builds on accessibility. For example, an architect might design the rooms of a building to be maximally usable to people in wheelchairs by making wide doorways and placing light switches lower on the wall. But if the only way to get into the building is by staircase, all of the usability features in the individual rooms are meaningless.

Accessibility supports diverse conditions. Usability supports the conscious and unconscious actions users take when interacting with a web page or website. Examples of conscious actions include users following links or navigation buttons to find material on your site or even resizing a browser window to view other applications (like an email program) while looking at your site. Unconscious actions include tapping or clicking links and scrolling through page content.

Findability and wayfinding are the fundamental usability concerns of basic websites. Findability determines whether users can successfully find relevant information through conscious action, whether from a result for your site in a search engine or through your site's navigation and contextual links. Wayfinding enables users to establish a sense of where they are in your site and how to get to other areas, if necessary.

To determine the degree to which websites are usable requires **usability testing**, where usability specialists observe actual users interacting with a site. For individuals designing websites on their own, a formal, extended usability test may not be feasible. But as Steven Krug (2014) suggests, testing your site with even one user—a friend, a family member—is better than testing it with none. Jakob Nielsen (2000) notes that most serious site usability problems can be discovered by testing with just five users.

Testing has its place. The end of this chapter will suggest ways for you to conduct your own mini usability tests. However, usability and usable design principles can inform how you write and design for the web from the very earliest stages.

## WHAT IS USABILITY?

Usability, in its most general sense, describes an interface's ease of use and methods for improving ease of use (Nielsen 2012). The key questions usability professionals ask is whether a design does something useful or valuable, and if so, whether it is easy for its intended users to use.

But usability can also include emotional dimensions of a website. As usability and emotional design researcher Donald Norman (2004) has observed, "Usable designs are not necessarily enjoyable to use" (8). Designers should aim to build a site that not only supports the easy accomplishment of a meaningful or valuable action—commenting on a blog post, locating an informational page about a site—but that makes the user's experience of actions enjoyable. Norman observed that users perceive designs that are beautiful or fun as being easier and faster to use, even if laboratory experiments reveal that a utilitarian design and an emotional design allow people to accomplish the same task in the same amount of time, or the same amount of effort.

I'll come right out with an embarrassing truth. Web writers and designers (including me) build sites with a wild fantasy in mind. The fantasy goes something like this: Visitors will open their browsers and go straight to my website. Desktop users will maximize their browser windows to fill their entire screens so they can experience the site as the sole focus of their attention. Mobile users will turn off their music and turn off all of their notifications. Nothing will interrupt or otherwise come between them and a pure experience of this incredible website. These imaginary visitors will thoughtfully consider the site's craftsmanship, pausing to reflect on the gorgeous photographs and stunning design choices. They will read the pure poetry of every single word, follow every link with deep interest and fascination, and basically spend as much time reading and thinking about the site as I spent writing and designing it.

That never happens. But designing to that fantasy seems to happen a lot, judging by writers and designers who unselectively post tons of content and design poor navigation. Designers operating under that fantasy incorrectly assume that everything on the site will be found eventually, simply because they also assume their users will look at everything.

To develop a more realistic picture of why users visit a site, and what they do there and how, we can use a framework that's become popular in human-computer interaction, called activity theory (see Kaptelinin and Nardi 2006, for a fuller but approachable introduction). A basic component of activity theory is a flexible, three-tiered hierarchy for thinking about user behaviors:

- At the top of the hierarchy is the user's activity, which is always motivated by some objective: using the web to find a movie to watch, a chili recipe for dinner, or Professor Smith's office hours.
- Activities are carried out through the next level of the hierarchy, individual actions: entering search terms on Google, exploring relevant results, reading pages on promising sites a bit more closely. Actions always have a particular goal: returning search results, clicking a link to explore a result, reading to decide whether the result is relevant.
- And individual actions themselves are often executed in part at the lowest level of the hierarchy, operations (typing, clicking, tapping, swiping, scrolling), which are normally carried out unconsciously.

I have seen many beginning web designers struggle to consider user activity. Most often, beginners are focused only on generating content. They may have a lot of really good ideas for the content they want to present, and some equally interesting ideas for their design and interfaces. But the points they sometimes forget to consider are who their users are, what tasks those users will want to complete, and the broader activity that the users are engaged in that leads them to a particular site.

## ACTIVITY: WHO ARE YOUR USERS? WHY ARE THEY AT YOUR SITE?

Users rarely show up at any website randomly, unless they're using a site or social app that just serves up random links to potentially interesting websites. And even if they do use such a site, they are still engaged in a specific activity (finding new and interesting websites) that might lead them to your site.

Activities are always shaped by the broad objective that people are looking to accomplish when they visit your website. For example, an employer looking to hire qualified candidates in your area of expertise might turn up your résumé in a Google search. A potential member of your club might enter your URL from a flyer or postcard. A new customer might find your site by following a link from an online review of your businesses or from a social media site or app. More randomly, you might have written a blog post about a problem and fix for the smartphone you own, which attracts the attention of someone else looking to fix the same problem.

In each of those cases, someone discovers your website in pursuit of some broader activity: a job search, joining a club, hiring a business professional, or just trying to fix a phone.

It's essential to develop a realistic list of potential visitors to your site in order to determine common user activities that would lead someone there. The more specific the list of people, the better. It'd be great if everyone in the world flocked to your website. But they won't. And it would be impossible to design a site that appeals to everyone while still meeting your own goals for the site. So "everyone" is not a useful category of users.

For individual portfolio sites and blogs, more concrete groups of people might include employers, school admission committees, or even fellow hobbyists or colleagues in your profession/field. For businesses, the list would include customers, shareholders, and even employees.

Clubs and organizations would list current and potential members, donors, and so on.

From that list, you will want to think about the explicit objective that each kind of visitor might have and develop an action list with items like:

- Potential employers finding my résumé
- Like-minded hobbyists contacting me
- School admission committees seeking a list of my recent projects
- Customers viewing how much our business charges for products and services
- New club members printing and mailing membership and payment forms

Just like the "everyone" audience category, it's tempting to say, "Employers looking at every last page of my website." But that rarely, if ever, happens. Keep your list to specific and reasonable objectives.

## ACTIONS: WHAT ARE YOUR USERS DOING?

Activities are always carried out through individual actions. The individual actions a site visitor takes are the primary concern of usability. And the most common actions that occur on a website can be broken down into Morville and Rosenfeld's (2006) four general types of information-seeking behaviors: finding everything, finding a few quality things, finding a specific thing, and refinding something found before.

### Finding Everything

Again, this type of behavior is pretty rare, like the fantasy scenario above. Google and other search engines are left to handle this type of information seeking, and then individual users search on what the search engines have found. Unless you have a very small site (or an obsessive fan or proud grandmother), do not bank on anyone looking at every single thing on every single page.

Some websites include a site index page, which is an alphabetical hyperlinked listing of every single page on the site. A site index might be useful as a last resort for someone trying to find something or to see a list of everything. Other sites duplicate the spirit of a site index by linking to every single page from the navigation area. On small sites, it may be feasible to link to every page from the navigation. But on sites with more than a few pages, trying to cram everything into the navigation often results in hover-driven fly-out or pop-up menus that try (and often fail) to manage information overload. Forget about using them on a mobile screen. Chapters 18 and 21 present methods to simplify the navigation and build a shallow architecture that better serves users.

## Finding a Few Quality Things

Because finding everything is such a rare user goal, it is better to concentrate your design efforts to address more common behaviors. Finding a few quality things is a more typical behavior. Even photography enthusiasts rarely want to see every photograph someone's ever taken— just a few compelling ones. Customers don't have the time or interest to see every single item that an online electronics retailer sells, and instead prefer a few that fit their needs and price range. That type of information-seeking behavior is especially common when users are not exactly sure what they're looking for. And that describes many users.

Designing for that kind of user behavior can help determine what to include in your site navigation. For example, you might have a navigation item that links to an overview of your portfolio, rather than listing in the navigation every item in the portfolio. In that approach, your navigation is meant only to lead users to a specific area of your site. Once there, users might encounter a compelling overview page that uses preview images and engaging summary descriptions that entice users to click. As part of providing wayfinding, which is key to supporting the goals of browsing-like behavior, you might visually highlight the Portfolio item on your site navigation whenever someone is viewing any page related to your portfolio (see the book's companion site for examples).

By providing wayfinding devices such as visual cues in your navigation, you can encourage users to explore other areas of your site simply because they can be confident of where in your site they are. Finding a few quality things is, after all, an exploratory behavior. But a one- or two-word navigation item like *Portfolio* or *My Work* may not be enough to entice otherwise curious users to click. A compelling, hyperlinked image—such as a sample from your design portfolio, if you're a designer—elsewhere on your page might be more appealing, simply because the content of the image may fit better with the vague idea of what a visitor to your site is looking for. It also promises a reward, such as a closer look at something that already looks interesting.

A site with attractive previews and promotional content may even alter a user's actions; visitors to a business's website might discover a product or service that they didn't even realize they wanted or needed previously.

## Finding a Specific Thing

Users are sometimes looking for a specific thing. Creating a usable design for that kind of behavior involves helping users to find what they know (or reasonably expect) appears on a given website. Website statistics, which some web hosts provide (see Chapter 25), sometimes reveal that this behavior begins with a web search; I find that people sometimes search Google for my name plus *vita* or *curriculum vitae*, which are the words for an academic résumé. As an academic, I'm expected to have a vita. Those users are looking for it specifically.

Other examples of known items that users often expect include About and Contact pages. An About page may include a history or biography that offers more information about the person, business, or organization a website represents. Users may also expect some means for contacting the person or organization behind a website. Links to these kinds of specific pages should appear in most sites' navigation areas. A home page may even have a brief About Us or About Me blurb that links to the full About page. And sometimes, the content of an About-style page makes perfect copy for the home page.

Users may be interested enough in site content that they will share it as a link on Twitter, Facebook, or another social media site. That may result in a new user visiting your site on someone else's recommendation. Such a user might want to move back up to your site's overview pages or home page. A site navigation that uses wayfinding devices to indicate the general area of your site that a visitor is in provides a necessary sense of "You are here." A link to your home page on every page, usually in your site's branding (see Chapter 15), may also benefit curious users. The presence of site navigation and home links (and a compelling design) may actually transform visitor behavior from seeking a specific thing, even something recommended by someone else, to finding a few more quality things.

## Finding a Thing Found Before

There is a reason that most web browsers have a bookmarking function: when someone finds something useful on the web, they can bookmark it to return for future reference. That doesn't always happen, though. We've all had the frustrating experience of vaguely remembering a really interesting page or site, but not having any exact record of what or where it was.

This is where whole-page design and especially site branding comes into play. A strong visual design can help to cue users as to whether they have been to your site or a particular page on your site before. Visual cues, such as a memorable image or color scheme, can also help users to remember a page previously visited. That is why I advise against things like randomly displaying one of a set of images on a page. It's a fun thing to design, but it is probably more fun for the designer to create than the user to experience on return visits.

## OPERATIONS: HOW DO YOUR USERS DO WHAT THEY DO?

Clicking or tapping on contextual links, thumbnail images, and navigation items. Entering text in a text box. Using the Tab key to move through the links on a page. Each of these is an example of the unconscious operations that support actions on a page. Add to that list more passive operations, like being able to comfortably read the text of a page (see Chapter 17), or see an image clearly because it's not overly compressed or run at a dinky size (see Chapters 3 and 19).

## HUMAN INTERFACE GUIDELINES

The manufacturer of your favorite operating system or mobile device has probably published a set of human interface guidelines.

Although the example guidelines below are primarily written for developers creating native applications for each manufacturer's platform or operating system, they offer useful guidance even when designing and organizing actionable elements on a web page and determining how large or small to size controls for touchscreens.

- Apple's Human Interface Guidelines: `https://developer.apple.com/design/`
- Google's Android Interface Guidelines: `https://developer.android.com/design/index.html`
- Microsoft's Windows Design and UI Guidelines: `https://developer.microsoft.com/en-us/windows/design`

When an item is difficult to tap or click, or simply not clickable despite appearing otherwise, or when text is difficult to read because it's too small or not run in a high enough contrast with a background color or image, users experience a breakdown. In a breakdown, something that usually happens unconsciously suddenly requires concentration and mental effort. Everyone's had the experience of going to a site whose navigation required very precise mouse positioning and clicking—either to activate a desired link or, because of a densely packed navigation, to avoid clicking the wrong link. Users should be focused on your content, not on activating the right item in a navigation bar.

The easiest way to build a site that's usable on the operational level is to let users be sloppy:

- Prefer large, clickable areas on links, navigation items, and images. Leave generous, neutral space between them. Consult some of the many human interface guidelines available on the web (see the "Human Interface Guidelines" sidebar). A test I often do is to see if I can mouse over page controls by moving my mouse with my elbow, which offers less control than my hand. On my phone, I try to tap things with my thumb, using my nondominant, left hand.

- Provide high-contrast text run in a comfortably large font, with the ability to increase the font size further without breaking the page's layout, perhaps by employing DOM scripting (see Chapter 20).
- Never interfere with the expected behavior of scrolling, tapping, or clicking. Beginning web designers often want to open every single link in a new tab or window. Don't make that decision for site visitors. People know how to open links in new tabs if they wish (and if they don't, they'll never be the wiser). Control over tabs and windows belongs to users, not designers.

If users can be sloppy—that is, if they aren't constantly encountering breakdowns—they can better focus on their goals and actions.


## FIVE QUICK BUT USEFUL MINI USABILITY TESTS

Steven Krug's (2014) book *Don't Make Me Think, Revisited* is a great resource for anyone looking to conduct their own basic usability tests (I especially recommend his chapter "Usability Testing on 10 Cents a Day"). Krug recommends iterative testing: don't just test once, but test, make changes, and test again—even if it's with the same friend or colleague who's agreed to help you out. A version control system will assist you in making small adjustments that you can test and then either improve or reject later (see Chapter 6). It's also important to test your site throughout the design process, if possible. With each round of improvements, additional rounds of testing may reveal other issues that were missed the first time around.

Here are some simple usability tests, which are oriented around the four information-seeking behaviors above:

- **Finding everything that there is.** Most usability tests begin by showing a user the site you want to test. But the usability of a site, particularly for an everything-seeking behavior, begins in a search engine. This test, which is only effective on sites that have been indexed by Google and other search engines, asks users to begin from a web search. Provide a few different scenarios for users: "You're an employer seeking résumés of people in my profession"; "You're a college freshman looking for information about the chess club." Watching what sites they click on, and asking why, can provide insight for how you should structure your pages and the key terms they might contain. If you want to limit your test user's results in a Google search, add `site:example.com` after the search terms to limit results to a specific site (e.g., `vita site:karlstolley .com`).

- **Finding a few quality things.** This test begins on your site itself. You might ask a user to find items from your portfolio, or information about your club, its membership, and how to become a member. You can also conduct a more open-ended test, perhaps with a scenario like, "If you were a potential customer, what would you look at to decide whether to buy from us?"

- **Finding a specific thing.** Have your test users locate your résumé, an About page, or a Contact page. Have your users find something a little more specific, like a particular item in your portfolio. With this type of test, time might be important, so casually keep an eye on the clock of your computer or phone. Do not use a stopwatch, though. Its presence might unnecessarily stress your test users, as though taking a long time is their fault—not your site's.

- **Finding a thing found before.** If you're working with someone who tested your site previously, try repeating the test above. Otherwise, have your test users find a few different, specific things and then—assuming that first test didn't go disastrously—have them refind the first thing you asked.

## Improving the Quality of Your Tests

Be sure to conduct each test on different devices, especially smart-phones. A design decision that works well for a desktop-sized layout of your site might prove to be a serious problem on a phone. When students do usability testing in my classes, I always encourage them to let their usability-test participants use their own devices. It is eye opening to see the real conditions under which people browse the web: the number of panels and tabs they have open on their browser, how large their browser is sized relative to the overall size of their screen, and even how many people have phones with huge cracks in the screens. All of those factor into the experience and usability of a site. Design accordingly.

Here are a few additional ways to get quality results from your tests:

- **Explain that your site is a work in progress** regardless of what state it's in. Sites are always, to some extent, works in progress. Tell your participants that you know you need help to improve it. If your test participants are close friends or colleagues, they may not want to criticize the site for fear of hurting your feelings. But if you make it clear that you know there are issues to be improved, your test users will likely understand that they can help you more by sharing suggestions and criticisms than by telling you how awesome your site is (although that's nice to hear, too).

- **Modify the tests above to match the purpose of your specific site.** If yours is a portfolio site, think about your expectations of why users would come to your site in the first place, and what they would do there.

- **Ask the test participants to describe aloud what they're doing as they do it.** Listen to what they say, but also watch what they're doing. Among usability professionals, it's common knowledge that what users say and what they do can be quite different. But what they say aloud—"I expected a navigation button for that"; "I'm surprised that image isn't clickable"; "This heading really grabbed my attention, but the writing below it doesn't seem to be what I want"—can be especially helpful for improving specific aspects of your site.

- **Try doing quick revisions while the test users are with you,** at least once you get more skilled writing and designing pages, and have them examine or try out your revised designs. Again, version control makes this much easier. Just create a branch (see the book's companion site for details). You might even find that some people will share design suggestions as you work. You shouldn't necessarily follow the suggestions exactly, but you might think about what's behind them. For example, someone might say, "I really think you should have a big photograph of yourself on your résumé." Unless you're a model, a theater major, or a newscaster, that's probably not essential, but what your test user might be implying is that your site needs to be more personal somehow, more uniquely you. A photograph may or may not be the way to achieve that particular goal. Regardless, asking test users the question "Why?" can usually help you determine why they're offering the advice that they are.

## NEXT STEPS

Designing a usable site means accounting for different user activities, actions, and operations, all built on a solid foundation of accessibility. In the next chapter, I will discuss sustainability, which considers accessibility, usability, and other writing and design issues over time and as your site grows.

## REFERENCES

Kaptelinin, Victor, and Bonnie A. Nardi. 2006. *Acting with Technology: Activity Theory and Interaction Design*. Cambridge, MA: MIT Press.

Krug, Steve. 2014. *Don't Make Me Think, Revisited: A Common Sense Approach to Web Usability*. Berkeley, CA: New Riders.

Morville, Peter, and Louis Rosenfeld. 2006. *Information Architecture for the World Wide Web*, 3rd ed. Sebastopol, CA: O'Reilly Media.

Nielsen, Jakob. 2000. "Why You Only Need to Test with Five Users." Nielsen Norman Group. https://www.nngroup.com/articles/why-you-only-need-to-test-with-5-users/

Nielsen, Jakob. 2012. "Usability 101: Introduction to Usability." Nielsen Norman Group. https://www.nngroup.com/articles/usability-101-introduction-to-usability/

Norman, Donald A. 2004. *Emotional Design: Why We Love (Or Hate) Everyday Things*. New York: Basic Books.

# CHAPTER 9

# Sustainability

Accessibility requires designing for conditions. Usability requires designing for behaviors. Sustainability considers designing for conditions and behaviors in two dimensions: time and scale.

Unlike accessibility and usability, which are inherently user focused in that your own ability to access and use your site is only one small part of a broader picture, sustainability determines how well and how easily you are able to develop and refine your site over time. However, a sustainable site also ultimately benefits users: the content, accessibility, and usability of a sustainable site are easier to revise and improve, ensuring the best content and experience for site users.

## WHAT IS SUSTAINABILITY?

Sustainability is associated with development principles in the context of the natural environment. One of the more widely quoted definitions of sustainability comes from the 1987 meeting of the United Nations' World Commission on Environment and Development, also known as the Brutland Commission. Their definition of sustainability reads: "Development that meets the needs of the present without compromising the ability of future generations to meet their own needs."

It is not a major effort to rework this statement with regard to web design: sustainable web design meets present needs of a site's creator and users, without compromising future needs. Going a step further, one might say that sustainable web design meets present needs while also planning for future needs. The web's languages and protocols are always evolving. Much of the advice in this book, despite its title, plans for where the web will be well beyond today.

Unfortunately, people who write and design for the web and other digital media have tended to ignore sustainability at every turn, opting to follow fads and trends or to take the easy path of using a WYSIWYG editor to build the web. It is not enough for a site to be built (a present need). It should also conform to web standards, work across the full range of web-connected devices, and be easy to revise and improve over time and as the site grows (future needs).

## IS A SUSTAINABLE WEBSITE EVEN POSSIBLE?

That all might sound good in theory. And yet everyone has had negative experiences with the relentless pace of change surrounding digital technologies. From file formats to hardware that quickly becomes obsolete, there seems to be little about digital technologies that approaches the kind of stability and permanence that "sustainable web design" requires.

However, sustainable web design is not a guarantee of indefinite stability and permanence. It's more like an attitude toward inevitable change: sustainable design involves making choices that will work now, and likely into the future—while also providing plenty of room for writers and designers to make adjustments to their sites in the future as the conditions on the web continue to evolve.

Designing a sustainable site requires careful planning and organization. Version control, discussed in Chapter 6, is a significant part of any website's ongoing evolution. Thoughtful design choices are essential, even for something as basic as carefully naming files and folders as described in Chapter 5. So are choices that help develop a sound site architecture, as described in Chapter 21. Writing valid, well-formed semantic HTML that describes the structure of your content, and not its visual presentation, contributes significantly to the long-term sustainability of your site: the structure of content is generally more stable than its visual design. A heading is always a heading; whether that heading appears in a serif or sans-serif typeface is inconsequential, in terms of sustainability.

# SUSTAINABLE DESIGN TECHNIQUES

A sustainable website is possible, but its construction is not necessarily intuitive. And a sustainable site certainly cannot be built without planning for the future. The advice in this book is intended to help you to make your site sustainable by employing techniques that will keep it accessible and usable over scale and time. Sustainable web design does not resist change. It prepares your site for change.

The rest of this chapter consists of practical approaches to building a sustainable site: keeping records of your work, naming and organizing all of the elements of your site, favoring directly editable content, and reusing content as much as possible. It concludes by looking at the role of standards and open-source libraries in further pursuit of a more sustainable site.

## Keeping a Record of What You've Done

*What was I thinking?* That's the question that I often ask myself when preparing to redesign a website from a past course or project. Sustainable design is easier to achieve when there is continuity between new work and work done previously. But of all of the things in life that are worth committing to memory, the details about websites that you have created are certainly not among them. Commit them to a Git repository instead (see the "Using a Version Control System (VCS)" sidebar).

If you are hesitant to dive into version control, there are other methods to keep track of what you've done. Early web logs, what are now called *blogs*, were just a record of changes to a website. While that particular use for blogging is not common anymore, any sustainable site will have a record of its development over time, regardless of whether the record appears on the site itself or in a repository or notebook somewhere. In cases where you are collaborating with multiple people on a site, a record also serves the purpose of keeping everyone informed of everyone else's changes.

There are two basic things that you should do to help yourself remember what you've done on your site, especially if you're not using a version control system:

- Keep a wiki, a text or word processor file, or even a notebook where you make notes of your design activity and choices.
- Use the comment syntax in HTML, CSS, and JavaScript to describe what you have written (see Chapter 10).

Retracing your steps and being able to recall the rationale behind a particular design choice will help you keep your site consistent, while preventing you from having to reinvent the wheel when an old challenge surfaces that you already figured out how to solve.

In addition to maintaining a log of your site's changes, it's important to write comments in your HTML, CSS, and JavaScript source. That will help preserve your choices in a human-readable way, and it can even help to teach others who are impressed by your site and want to learn how to do something the way that you have. Chapter 10 describes some basic commenting practices, and the web-available examples that support this book at http://webpg.es/ contain numerous explanatory comments.

## Call It Like It is

Whether you are choosing a domain name, naming files and folders, or writing classes and IDs in your HTML (see Chapter 11), always name

---

### USING A VERSION CONTROL SYSTEM (VCS)

A version control system is a piece of software that can maintain the record of changes to your site over time. There are a number of free and open-source VCSs available, although one of the more popular systems is Git (https://git-scm.com). Essentially, a VCS such as Git establishes a repository of the files for a website or other digital project, and allows you to build a record of the changes you make. A VCS does not do this automatically. It requires you as the writer to periodically commit changes to the repository. If you make a mistake, or wish to return to an earlier version of your project, Git and other VCS software lets you roll back history in a few keystrokes. For an example, you can see the Git repository and history for the Rapid Prototyping Kit at https://github.com/webpges/rpk/.

Chapter 6 looks at version control in depth.

things to reflect what they are, and maintain a consistent naming style across all of your site's elements, including HTML and CSS files, plus images and other media.

As the file-naming advice offered in Chapter 5 suggests, it's never good practice to use words like "new" in file names, as nothing remains new over time. But it's also not good practice to truncate or abbreviate file and folder names; little is gained by calling your résumé page `res .html`; call it `resume.html`. Better yet, create a directory called `re- sume` and put the résumé in an `index.html` file inside the `resume` directory. Be sure, too, that the content of a page matches what its file or directory name suggests. If a URL reads `http://example.com /contact/`, it is reasonable to expect that the page will have information or the means (such as a form) for contacting the site's owner or organization.

In terms of scale, any numbered, or serialized, file names should begin with leading zeros, such as `photo001.jpg`, `photo002.jpg`, `photo003.jpg`. This helps keep the listings of serialized files more readable when you are managing your site's files. Otherwise, `photo10 .jpg` will be listed next to `photo1.jpg`, `photo20.jpg` near `photo2 .jpg`, and so on.

The "call it like it is" rule also applies to the structure of HTML pages. Even on a basic tag level, mark headings with heading tags, lists with list tags, and so on. Take extra care in naming classes and IDs, too. What in your current design is a big purple box may not be in a redesign. So rather than naming a class or ID something like `big-purple -box`, name it `promotional-content` or some other name that describes the content's structure and purpose, not its design (see Chapter 11).

## A Place for Everything, and Everything in Its Place

Being able to quickly find a file that you need to edit helps you simplify your work toward a sustainable website. Take the time to develop a good site architecture (see Chapter 21), and discipline yourself in its maintenance by saving files in their designated places.

It is important that your URLs remain constant and functional over time; in basic websites, URLs are created based on directory structure and file names. You want your site to be found, and you want people to link to your site—but if pages move or disappear without warning when you move or rename files, it reflects poorly on the person doing the linking, not to mention it reflecting poorly on your own site.

For example, if you choose to post a vague directory or file name, like `stuff/` or `res.htm` and later opt to rename it to something more meaningful, you risk making links to the older name obsolete, so be sure to both name things and place things in a thoughtful, sensible site architecture the first time around.

There are some advanced techniques, such as using the Apache web server's URL rewrite module, to redirect old URLs to new and active ones. While those techniques are outside the scope of this book, they do add a degree of flexibility for handling links to old URLs, should you need to construct a new architecture for your site. See this book's companion site for additional information, `http://webpg.es/`.

### Favor Content That You Can Edit Directly

There are certain types of files, such as PDFs, that you cannot edit directly (at least not to a great extent). Instead, you must do your editing in one software program or file, republish it as the PDF, and post that published file to the web. Again, this is a matter of scale: one or two PDFs may not be too much to manage, but dozens or hundreds pose a serious sustainability problem.

With HTML, CSS, JavaScript, and all other plain-text-based files, you only need access to a text editor to do your edits before moving them to your web server. If you use a content management system (CMS) such as WordPress to maintain a dynamic site, you can edit your content using any good web browser. However, if you rely on file uploads of PDFs or word processor documents, using a CMS will not make maintaining the content in those files much easier. The files will have to be changed on your computer and then uploaded through the CMS.

### Don't Repeat Yourself

The idea behind CSS is that you can keep all of the design instructions for all of the pages on your site in one file (see Chapter 12). To maintain a consistent design across your site, you just connect all of your site's HTML pages to one shared CSS file. Making a site-wide change to the design is then only a matter of editing that one CSS file. Publishing an entirely new design is accomplished by replacing your old CSS file with a new, redesigned one.

Like your design, any content that you repeat over pages—your heading, navigation, even brief "About Me" text—can also be kept in a single file, and then repeated over multiple pages using a server-side language or static site generator (see Chapter 23).

But even the page-specific content you mark up in HTML should also appear only in one place. Using CSS and the `media` attribute on the `<link>` tag, you can style one HTML page to display in print differently from how it displays on screen. There's no need, in other words, to have one HTML file for print, one HTML file for screen, and so on. As soon as you introduce multiple copies of the same content, you increase the labor involved in even the smallest changes. If you find a typo, you have to fix it in as many different files as you maintain copies.

## Follow Web Standards

The web design advice in this book adheres to standards for HTML5/ HTML: The Living Standard; Cascading Style Sheets 1, 2, and the stable parts of 3; the Document Object Model and other technologies whose specifications are maintained by the World Wide Web Consortium (W3C), in addition to ECMAScript, the specification behind JavaScript.

Following standards is an important practice that advances sustainability. Even when new versions of standardized languages appear, the older versions can continue to be used. You can, for example, still write in HTML 4.01 or XHTML 1.0 Strict, despite the advances in HTML5. The web is unique in its standards' longevity, because all standards and browser implementations maintain backward compatibility. That stands in stark contrast with popular software programs that eventually stop reading previous versions of their own file types. And certain aspects of older/related standards can make you a better writer of newer ones. HTML5 has a very permissive ruleset. By applying the conservative, explicit rules of the older XHTML 1.0 Strict's ruleset to HTML5, you can develop your own cleaner, well-formed style of HTML.

The alternative to following standards (and it's not really an alternative, if a site is to be accessible, let alone sustainable) is to follow the quirks of a particular browser or piece of web-authoring software. Follow standards for the sake of users of other browsers and for the sake of your future self, should you one day want to make a change or should the web-authoring software company go out of business or sunset the software.

## Build on Top of Open-Source Libraries

Another way to keep a site sustainable is to build on top of actively developed open-source frameworks and code. The Rapid Prototyping Kit (RPK) is one example of this (see Chapter 15). And even the RPK builds on other libraries: for DOM scripting, the RPK makes it simple to build on top of the jQuery JavaScript library (see Chapter 20) or other, lighter-weight alternatives to jQuery. Among other things, jQuery keeps DOM scripting uniform across the remaining quirks of modern and legacy browsers. In other words, rather than writing your own JavaScript that does that kind of work, you entrust that work to the developers of jQuery or another, similar framework.

And so long as you keep your copies of any libraries or frameworks up to date, your site itself stands to improve, thanks to people who continually work to improve the library or framework.

## NEXT STEPS

Sustainable web design isn't magic. It requires thinking carefully about a lot of choices, such as naming things, that are easily overlooked and taken for granted. In the next section of the book, "Strategies for Success," I will discuss the issues of accessibility, usability, and sustainability in action as part of the work of building a standards-compliant, mobile-first responsive website.

# REFERENCE

World Commission on Development and Environment. 1987. "Towards Sustainable Development." *Our Common Future: Report of the World Commission on Environment and Development.* http://www.un-documents.net/ocf-02.htm

# PART III

# STRATEGIES FOR SUCCESS

This section of the book covers the construction and design of individual web pages.

So far, I've discussed web writing and design concerns at a fairly high level, in a somewhat abstract way. This section invites you to dive in and work on your own writing and design. And that will involve learning to write with the languages of the web: HTML, CSS, and JavaScript.

But it would be a mistake to think that writing with the web's languages is a separate category, or even a separate activity, from what is more traditionally considered writing. HTML and CSS are actually languages that describe writing. HTML describes the structure of writing and allows writers to specify which pieces of text are headings, paragraphs, or items in a list. HTML also enables writers to load images or other media and to provide supplementary textual content both for search engines and low-vision users. CSS complements the structural descriptions you write in HTML by helping you describe the appearance of writing, and modifying its appearance as screens increase in size from mobile devices on up. JavaScript makes writing interactive by progressively enhancing pages that build on the core functionality provided by HTML and CSS.

Although the form of a book requires ordering chapters, know that web writing and design is never a linear, step-by-step process. Changes in content may inspire you to change your design, and vice versa; changes to one part of your design, such as the width of a column of content, may cause you to change another part, such as the amount and kind of supporting, sidebar content. The key to creating your pages is flexibility: be ready to make changes.

# CHAPTER 10

# Writing with Source

If you're used to writing in a word processor or a WYSIWYG web editor, one of the first things that may strike you about a simple text editor like TextWrangler or Notepad++ is its lack of buttons and other screen clutter (see Figure 10.1). The lack of buttons can be disorienting at first: word processors, email clients, and other software for writing have conditioned people to write with a lot of software assistance, particularly for formatting.

But the text editor's simplicity is a good thing. There's not much of an interface to learn. In a text editor, what matters is only what you write yourself. And that's what you do in an editor: you write.

In the text editor, nothing you write and nothing about your web pages is hidden from view. The WYSIWYG acronym's popular usage aside, in an editor, what you see really *is* what you get: the content and source code that browsers render as web pages. And that means that, by learning to write HTML, CSS, and JavaScript, you can take full control over every aspect of your pages. More important, when something is wrong with one of your pages, you can be certain that it's something you can research and fix. Sometimes the research dead-ends at a known problem with a particular browser's way of rendering pages. The editor's transparency makes those kinds of conclusions possible.

## ONE PAGE, MANY VIEWS

There are many different views of any given web page. To understand why someone would want to roll back to a piece of software as

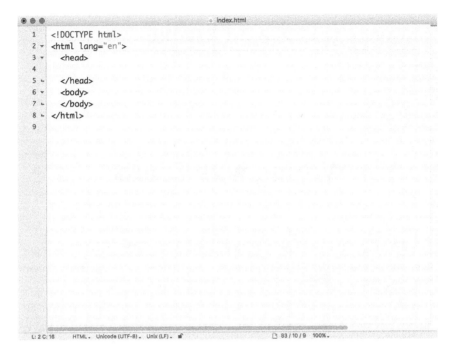

```
1    <!DOCTYPE html>
2 ▾  <html lang="en">
3 ▾    <head>
4
5 ↳    </head>
6 ▾    <body>
7 ↳    </body>
8 ↳  </html>
9
```

**Figure 10.1.**    There is little screen clutter or user interface in a text editor.

primitive as a text editor, it's important first to understand that the text editor is very good at managing its particular view of the page's source. But the editor's view is just one of several views to monitor as you write your pages and build your site:

- **Graphical File View:** The listing of files and folders provided by your computer's operating system is the file view; that is, the list of files that make up your web page or website (see Figure 10.2). It is usually best practice to separate the languages that make up your pages into individual files: HTML in .html files, CSS in .css files, JavaScript in .js files, and so on (be sure that you have configured your operating system to show all file extensions; see Chapter 5).
- **Command-line File View.** This view lists the same files as does the graphical file view, and by default with the files' full extensions. On Unix-like systems, the file view is based around

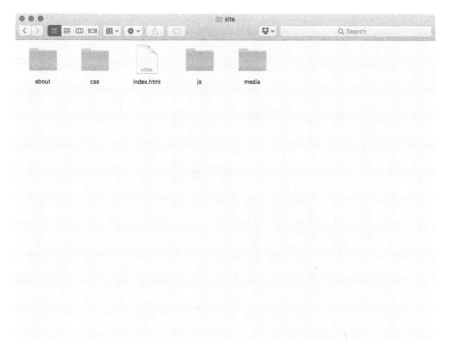

**Figure 10.2.**  A graphical view of the files and directories that make up a website.

the list command, `ls` (see Figure 10.3). Windows uses the `dir` command. The command-line view of files is especially important if you've chosen to work with Git. The command-line file view is also instructive for writing URLs and paths so that when you write a reference from one file, like an HTML page, to another file, like an image, the link between the two actually works (see the discussion of paths in Chapter 21). The structure of URLs and paths written in HTML are identical to Unix-style paths on the command line. `/resume/index` `.html` is both a piece of a URL and a Unix-style path to a file.

- **Source View:** When you use your editor to open an HTML or CSS file, you are looking at the file's source view. You can also access the source view of any page on the web by choosing something like `View > Source` from within a web browser. Looking at the source of other pages on the web is a useful way to learn how other people build pages.

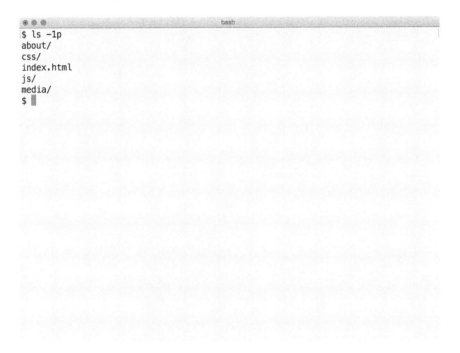

```
bash
$ ls -1p
about/
css/
index.html
js/
media/
$ ▌
```

**Figure 10.3**    A command-line view of the same files and directories as in Figure 10.2.

- **Browser View:** This is how we usually experience web pages. The browser view is how pages display or render in a browser itself. However, each browser or mobile or adaptive device provides a different, unique view of a given web page, as discussed in Chapter 2.

Each view—file, source, and browser—will be slightly different depending on details such as your operating system (macOS, Windows, Linux), your editor (TextWrangler, Notepad++), and your browser (Firefox, Chrome, Safari). Mobile devices and their browsers render additional views of your pages. Available typefaces, screen resolutions, and user preferences also affect views. But what each view represents is the same.

## SOURCE TYPEFACES

Good editors allow all kinds of customizations to how they display source code and other text. The customization that will most affect how comfortable it is to work with an editor is the typeface it uses to render files. Unlike word processors, which store typeface information in the file, text editors store typeface information only as a user preference.

Text editors default almost universally to a fixed-width typeface, usually the old standby Courier. In a fixed-width typeface, every character occupies the same amount of horizontal space. That makes source code easier to read and keeps indentation uniform, because spaces also occupy the same amount of space as any other character.

Although there is nothing wrong with using the default face in your editor, there are probably numerous other fixed-width faces available on your operating system. For example, macOS includes Monaco and Menlo, which are two very good fixed-width faces. Certain editors install their own preferred typefaces. You can also find on the web a variety of openly licensed monospaced typefaces, such as Adobe's Source Code Pro, that you can install on your operating system.

When choosing a typeface for writing source, there are a few characters that should be distinct from one another. There is no room for error in source code, and certain look-alike characters can make life very difficult. A lowercase L, l, should look different from the number one, 1, and the capital I from the pipe character |. Capital O should look different from zero, 0, and 5 should be easily distinguishable from S. It's also important that curly braces, { }, are clearly different from brackets, [ ], and brackets different from parentheses, ( ), because those are all commonly used in web and programming languages. It's also good for side-by-side parentheses not to look too much like an O or zero, (). 

Beyond rendering those lookalike characters distinctly from one another, a good source typeface should feel comfortable to stare at for hours on end. Be sure to size it for comfortable reading, too. On macOS, I almost always have my editor configured to display text in Monaco, which I find is a friendly, readable typeface. As with any other feature in your editor, get to know your available typefaces and look for others that you might legally download from the web. Find what works best for you.

## SYNTAX HIGHLIGHTING

Good text editors also provide more than views of source in simple black and white text in your typeface of choice. Colorized text, known as **syntax highlighting**, makes reading and writing HTML, CSS, Java-Script, and your content more comfortable and efficient.

Any good text editor will provide syntax highlighting. Syntax highlighting offers a set of visual cues about the language features in your files. For example, good editors will display HTML files with tag elements colored differently from the text content that the tags structure. Attributes and their values may be colored differently from the tag element, and so on.

The colors for syntax highlighting vary from editor to editor. Depending on the editor, tags might be colored blue, green, or purple. Some editors allow you to choose different colorized themes to suit your preference. The individual colors do not matter. What does matter is the differences in color between one feature of your source and another. When tags are colored or styled differently from surrounding content, you can tell immediately if you've forgotten to put a closing angle bracket on a tag or a closing quotation mark on an attribute

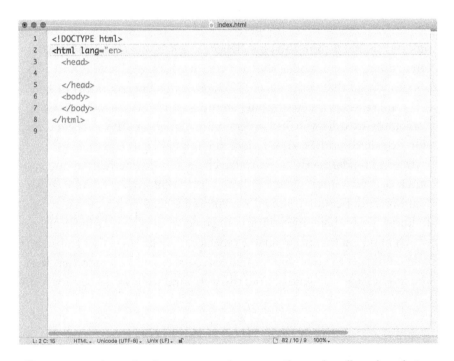

**Figure 10.4.** An unclosed quotation mark on an attribute value affects the coloring of the source that follows.

value. The colors for tags or attribute values will continue to colorize everything that follows as a tag or attribute value (see Figure 10.4).

That is the simplest way to track down common errors that creep into handwritten web pages. If the syntax highlighting of an HTML or CSS file suddenly stops changing over a large stretch—or otherwise looks different from other, similar areas of the file—look for the spot at which the change begins. It's more than likely that you will find the source of the problem nearby. If you still cannot find the error, try running your source through a lint tool and the HTML and CSS validators hosted by the W3C. If the validator and linter come back error-free, you might restart your text editor. Even though they are simple pieces of software, editors can still be buggy and incorrectly highlight your source from time to time.

## SOURCE FORMATTING

Unlike word processors, which format text to a particular printed page size, text editors have no associated page or screen size. If you begin typing a paragraph or long sentence in an editor, it might continue on the same line for as long as you keep typing, without breaking the text onto the next line.

**Source formatting** is the style of line breaks and indentation used to keep source readable. Appreciating and executing good source formatting are necessary skills that you will develop over time as you work with your editor. A lint tool can help you to enforce particular formatting styles in your source code. See the book's companion site for details.

### Line Breaks

There are a couple of different options for handling line breaks. Some editors will display soft breaks, sometimes called soft wrapping, which visually wrap text onto new lines in your text editor's view of the file. But soft breaks are not saved with the file itself. If you view the file's source in a browser, it will appear as one 10-mile-long line.

The better option is to create new lines by hitting the Return key, which some keyboards label Enter or mark with a glyph like ↵. Hard breaks are special, invisible characters that are stored in a file (see the sidebar, "LF, CR, and CR+LF: The Most Boring Sidebar in the Book"). Hard breaks break the lines of your source for anyone viewing it, including people who choose the `View > Source` option in their web browser. Git users will also see that commits and output from certain commands, like `git diff`, reference specific lines in a file. That means that shorter lines are generally easier to work with.

It is tradition to put hard breaks in source files after 80 characters, but running out to 100 characters is fine, too. Line length is mostly a matter of reading comfort. Your editor might offer a visual onscreen

## LF, CR, AND CR+LF:
## THE MOST BORING SIDEBAR IN THE BOOK

The one thing that you cannot see in a text editor, or that you usually don't see unless something has gone very wrong, is the special character that different operating systems put in text files when you hit the Return key for a line break.

This is primarily a Windows issue; the details are below, but suffice it to say that the preferred break for files destined for the web is the Unix-style line feed character, LF. It is preferable because it works well across all operating systems, including and especially the Linux or Unix-like operating system that will probably be run by your web host, as Chapter 5 suggested.

Most Windows editors, including Notepad++, allow you to specify what character should be used for breaks at the end of lines in new files. In Notepad++, go to `Settings > Preferences` and then find the New Document/Default Directory tab. Make sure you choose Unix as the default format. If you open up older files, you can always choose `Edit > EOL Conversion`, and change the current file to Unix. (EOL means "end of line.")

If you're struggling to stay awake, you can skip back to the main text. But if you're interested in a little history/trivia, here goes: Carriage Return and Line Feed, or CR+LF, is the double character inserted by Windows editors to end a line. What it results in is text files appearing double-spaced on LF systems, such as macOS and Linux. (CR by itself is basically ancient, although if you want to fire up your old Apple II or even a Mac OS 9 machine, you'll find a piece of computing history when you press the Return key.)

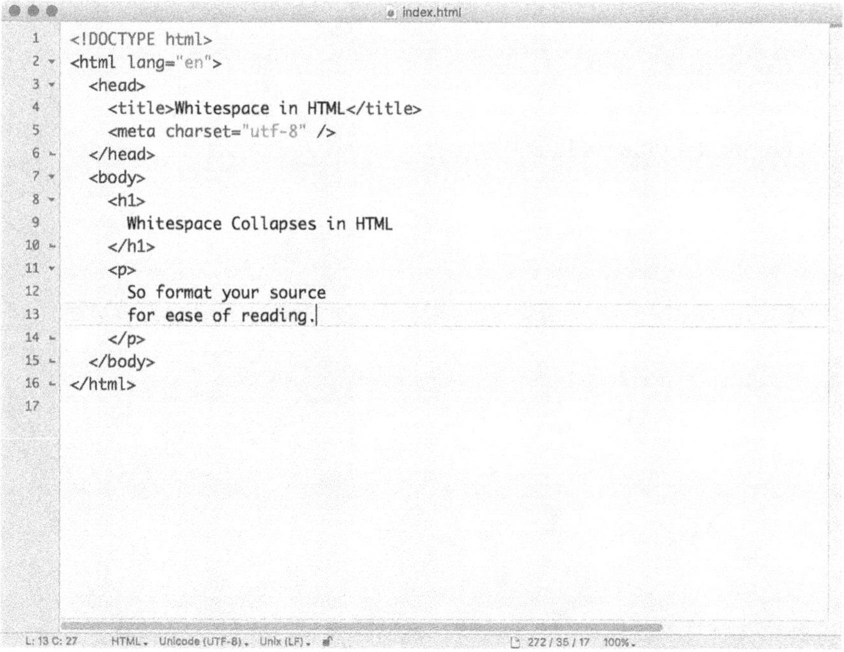

```
 1    <!DOCTYPE html>
 2  ▾ <html lang="en">
 3  ▾   <head>
 4        <title>Whitespace in HTML</title>
 5        <meta charset="utf-8" />
 6  ▴   </head>
 7  ▾   <body>
 8  ▾     <h1>
 9          Whitespace Collapses in HTML
10  ▴     </h1>
11  ▾     <p>
12          So format your source
13          for ease of reading.|
14  ▴     </p>
15  ▴   </body>
16  ▴ </html>
17
```

L: 13 C: 27     HTML ▾   Unicode (UTF-8) ▾   Unix (LF) ▾   ⚓           🗋 272 / 35 / 17   100% ▾

**Figure 10.5.**  Whitespace makes the HTML in this file more readable.

guide to show you where the 80- or 100-character mark is, so you know when to hit Return. Some editors will also allow you to select large, soft-wrapped chunks of text, and automatically insert hard breaks at the end of each line.

You should also insert line breaks whenever it helps make your source more readable (Figure 10.5). Whitespace, which includes spaces, tabs, and hard breaks, is ignored by the browser's rendering of your HTML (Figure 10.6). That is the default behavior of all browsers, except in instance of the <pre> tag coupled with certain settings on the CSS white-space property. Format your source in the editor with as many line breaks and indentations as you like. It will render without any additional whitespace in a browser view.

Because of that, you cannot indent the first line of a paragraph by inserting a tab or five spaces inside the paragraph tag in your source. Use the CSS text-indent property when you need to indent the first line of a paragraph or any other block of text.

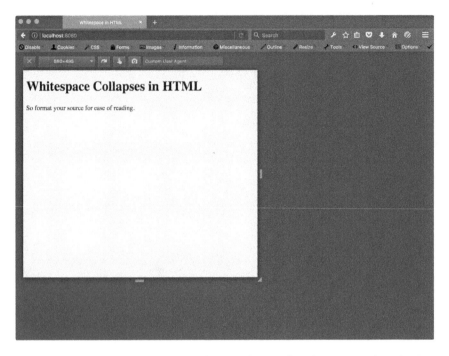

**Figure 10.6.** By default, whitespace has no effect on how browsers render HTML. This is the unstyled HTML from Figure 10.5.

## Indentation

Consistent indentation of source code is important for readability. Some text editors will insert multiple spaces for each strike to the Tab key, while others will insert actual tab characters. Look through your editor's preferences, as you can change this to whatever you wish. Tab characters are easier to delete and reformat than a whole bunch of spaces, but smarter editors recognize when you're deleting spaces for indentation, so there's really no difference. Spaces ensure that your source's indentation looks uniform across any view. You can find passionate, almost religious discussions across the web where people debate indents-as-spaces versus indents-as-tabs.

This book recommends two spaces per tab, and to entab source code with spaces, not tab characters.

Indentation makes HTML, CSS, JavaScript, and any other source code you write more readable by indicating relationships between lines

```
CHARACTER ENCODING: UTF-8 WITHOUT
THE BYTE ORDER MARK (BOM)
```

Another invisible matter your text editor will handle is your text file's encoding; while you should specify UTF-8 as the encoding in the metadata for your HTML pages (see Chapter 11), you must make sure that your text editor is actually encoding UTF-8 (not ANSI or ASCII, which are common default encodings), and without a pesky little creature called the Byte Order Mark (BOM). Most editors, such as Notepad++, have an Encoding menu. Watch carefully, though: Notepad++ has an option for "Encode in UTF-8," which sounds right, except you should choose "Encode in UTF-8 without BOM." Check also for setting up the default encoding of your files in some kind of Preferences menu in your editor; if you accidentally save a file with the wrong encoding, most editors provide some way to convert encoding to UTF-8 without the BOM.

of code. In HTML, indentation makes nested tags more obvious. Here is a heading and paragraph tag nested inside of an <aside> tag:

```
<aside class="tip">
  <h2>Indentation Makes Source Readable</h2>
  <p>
    However, some text editors require you to
    do your indentation manually.
  </p>
</aside>
```

That example indents and breaks onto multiple lines the content inside of the <p> tag, which keeps content itself easier to read and maintain.

Indentations and line breaks can also help make CSS source more readable:

```
body {
  font-family: Helvetica, Arial, sans-serif;
  font-size: 1.185em;
}
```

Indentations are especially important inside of media queries:

```
@media screen and (min-width: 37.5em) {
  #page {
    width: 90%;
  }
}
```

How you format the source for your HTML, CSS, and JavaScript has no impact on how your pages display. But it will have an impact on your ability to collaborate with others, and even how easily you are able to read and understand your own source later. This book's companion site has an up-to-date list of lint tools for HTML, CSS, and JavaScript that will help you adhere to a consistent style when formatting your source.

## COMMENTING ON SOURCE CODE

Every computer language has some sort of syntax for writing comments that are meant for humans, not computers. Just like whitespace, comments have no effect on the display or behavior of your HTML, CSS, or JavaScript files. It's wise to get into the habit of commenting on your source to keep your pages more sustainable. Not only will comments make it easier for you to edit your pages in the future, but they will also help you to think through what you are doing as you write. If you describe, in the comments, what your source means and what you intend it to do, you will deepen your understanding of how web languages work.

So in addition to formatting your source for readability using line breaks and indentation, you can also write comments to your source. In HTML, comments begin with < ! - - and end with - - >. For example:

```
<!--Here is a comment in HTML-->
```

Again, HTML comments are not rendered on your page in the browser's viewport, nor is the browser affected by their contents. However, it is the two hyphens, - -, that close the comment, so do not use a double-hyphen in your comment text itself. This is a hard habit to break for those of us who use two hyphens in email to mimic an em dash. People will also sometimes use a comment to call attention to a specific section of HTML. It's tempting to use a long line of hyphens, but those will break the comment. Use equals signs instead:

```
<!--===== BEGIN PAGE CONTENT HERE: ======-->
```

CSS and JavaScript both use a slash-star (/*), star-slash (*/) pattern to start and end, respectively, comments:

```
/* Here is a comment in CSS */

/*
  Here is a comment in JavaScript, broken
  over multiple lines. This same style of
  comment is allowed in CSS, too.
*/
```

JavaScript also has a syntax for single-line comments, provided that each line starts with two slashes:

```
// This is also a JavaScript comment, but
// each line must start with slashes, because
// each comment ends with a line break
```

Douglas Crockford (n.d.), a leading authority on JavaScript, cautions that it is possible that the */ pattern can appear as a normal part of certain pieces of JavaScript code. He therefore recommends that writers of JavaScript only use the two-slash style of comments. The examples in this book and the RPK follow his advice and use only the two-slash comment style for JavaScript.

## Writing Useful Comments

Writing useful comments is an art of writing all its own. When written well, comments can explain aspects of your source. You can also add line breaks and indentations on your comments, too, to keep them readable:

```
/*
 Hide links that are used only
 by nonvisual browsers to skip
 to different sections:
*/
a.skip {
 position: absolute;
```

```
left: -10000px;
}
```

Here are some good practices for writing useful comments:

- **Write comments as though you were trying to teach someone else what you're doing.** Many teachers will tell you that they never really learn a subject well until they've had to teach it to others. Writing comments that attempt to teach and explain will help anyone who might look at the source of your pages. Instructive comments will help you in the future, after you have forgotten why you wrote some feature in your source code originally.

- **Provide human-friendly descriptions of information meant for the computer.** In CSS, for example, you usually specify colors by numbers—either hexadecimal or RGB (see Chapter 12). It's not easy to remember that #FF3399 is hot pink, nor could someone tell that just by looking at the number. Some designers write color references at the top of their CSS so they know which numbers to write:

```
/*
Colors in this design:
#339900: Deep Green
#FFCC33: Sandy Orange
#993300: Deep Red
*/
```

- **Be careful about referring to line numbers in your comments.** Consider a comment like this:

```
<!--
This closes the <article> tag from line 15:
-->
</article>
```

That comment will only contain accurate information until lines are added or removed before line 15. A better approach is to refer to other structural features in your source code that can be found using a text editor's search function:

```
<!--
 This closes the <article id="feature">
 tag above:
-->
</article>
```

- **Ask questions or set to-do lists for yourself or others you are working with.** Having a question or to-do item within your source is often more convenient than having it stashed away in a notebook or an email.

```
<!--
 Can someone please check the HTML
 below? It's not validating, but
 I don't understand the error
 messages from the validator.
-->
```

- **When you update the source, update the comments.** Comments that refer to changed or removed source code are even worse than no comments at all. Always keep your comments up to date, so that you don't accidentally introduce confusion or misinformation.

## Commenting Out Problem Code

Comments can also be used to isolate a source-code problem. Comments can contain source code, not just human-readable messages. Their effect is the same: to hide the source from the browser, the validator, or any other machine reading the source:

```
p {
  width: 100px;
/*padding: 50px;*/
/*
  The padding is changing the width,
  so I've commented it out for
  testing purposes.
*/
}
```

Yes, you could just delete the problem source. But by commenting it out, you prepare for testing and possibly further revision, while keeping the web browser from reading the problem source as you test. If you determine that the source you've commented out will never be revised, be sure to delete it.

If you're using Git, you can also use branches to try to fix more complex problems. That will prevent you from littering your code with comments and, in the process, losing track of what you were trying to fix in the first place. See the book's companion site for some examples of correcting source-code problems with Git and branches.

## NEXT STEPS

Working with a text editor is an ongoing process of learning and experimentation, as is every aspect of web design. As you work on your pages and read through the remainder of this book, keep in mind the practices suggested in this chapter—particularly indenting and formatting your source, and using comments to explain to yourself what it is that you have written.

The next chapter will look more closely at the HTML language, and how best to write it in your editor of choice.

## REFERENCE

Crockford, Douglas. n.d. "Code Conventions for the JavaScript Programming Language." http://javascript.crockford.com/code.html

# CHAPTER 11

# Structured Content: HTML Overview

Content structured in HTML is the most critical component of any web page. The accessibility, design, and interactivity of a page depend on valid, well-formed semantic HTML. If you think of a web page as a house, then HTML is its foundation and structural walls. CSS is the design and decorations. And JavaScript is something like the household appliances. You might have a nice picture to hang on the wall where you live, but if the walls are so weak that they crumble when you try to hammer in a nail, hanging the picture will be impossible, regardless of its beauty. Poorly written HTML is a crumbling wall.

This chapter introduces the fundamental concepts behind HTML. It also describes the global structure of the `<html>`, `<head>`, and `<body>` tags that all HTML pages require and previews some of the common semantic tags from HTML5. All HTML tags can be enhanced by two attributes—`class` and `id`—that provide additional structure to describe content that's unique to your pages. Chapter 16 looks in greater detail at HTML's block and sectioning elements, which provide additional global structure and play a key role in page layout in CSS.

## HTML DESCRIBES THE STRUCTURE OF WRITING

HTML is an abbreviation for Hypertext Markup Language. HTML is a language that does nothing but describe the structure of writing and the location of media content. You can't use HTML to calculate the answers to math problems or to program robots to attack your enemies. HTML can only describe the structure of a web page's content.

The guiding principle behind HTML is that content should be described structurally, using a language that is separate from visual presentation and design. Adherence to that principle prepares structured content to be interpreted and reused by web browsers and other devices. Multiple media-specific style sheets, coupled with media queries that are described in Chapter 14, enable content to be presented in ideal ways across many different devices. An HTML page can, for example, load multiple CSS files to render on screen one way, and in print in another way. Screen readers and other adaptive technologies rely on well-written HTML to provide a meaningful experience for low-vision users, without the interference that visual design might introduce if design were blended in with the HTML.

HTML is challenging to write largely because the structure of writing is usually communicated in visual ways. Readers flipping through a magazine recognize headings, paragraphs, bulleted lists, and other page features by their visual design. Headings are often large, bold, and offset by multiple lines of space from the running paragraph text. Lists feature bullets, numbers, or even images next to short chunks of text, which might be indented differently from paragraphs.

Writers, too, commonly think in visual ways when they sit down to write. Word processors have conditioned people to highlight a piece of text and change its appearance: making it bold, changing its font and size, or adding color. The idea that a combination of design choices adds structure to the document might never enter a writer's mind.

But on the web, structure is essential to making a web page maximally accessible, even to nonvisual devices such as search engines and screen readers. For that reason, structure on the web is not indicated visually. It's described in HTML, which has a growing set of semantic elements to richly structure the content of a page. **Semantic HTML** is the product of writing the most descriptive tag available in HTML to describe the meaning of every piece of page content. An electronic or postal address might be marked up with the `<address>` tag, while a page footer would be marked up with the `<footer>` tag that first appeared in HTML5. Markup choices are a product of the meaning of page content, not visual design or interactivity. And yet well-structured semantic HTML will simplify the task of enhancing your pages later with CSS and JavaScript.

HTML provides a set of tags to describe the structure of writing and the location of other pages and media content. While there are certain highly specific HTML tags like `<address>` and `<footer>`, there are also general tags that you will write far more frequently: headings, paragraphs, and lists. Headings are marked with heading tags (`<h1>` through `<h6>`); paragraphs are marked with paragraph tags (`<p>`); items in a list are marked with list item tags (`<li>`) and list items are grouped as either unordered (usually bulleted) lists (`<ul>`) or ordered (usually numbered) lists (`<ol>`). Chapter 16 covers those structural blocks in more detail.

Rather than catalog more and more tags here, let's first consider the function of all HTML tags and the basic rules for how they should be written.

## TAGS ARE LIKE QUOTATION MARKS

One way to understand how HTML tags structure writing is to compare tags to quotation marks.

Quotation marks do not make text especially beautiful. They function only to indicate structure. A quotation mark sets off text to indicate structural differences in writing: the speech or writing of another person, the title of a magazine article, or maybe an unfamiliar word or phrase.

Quotation marks also appear in predictable ways, adjacent to the words that they mark and without any spaces:

```
I said, "HTML tags are a lot like quotation marks."
```

Not

```
I said, " HTML tags are a lot like quotation marks. "
```

Once a quotation mark opens, it also must close, or the text becomes confusing:

```
"The Road Not Taken by Robert Frost is a beloved
 American poem.
```

And if single quotation marks appear within double quotation marks, the single quotation marks must close before the doubles:

```
"Tonight I will read you a poem by Robert Frost,
 'The Road Not Taken.'"
```

Quotation marks also appear the same regardless of the content they mark:

```
"The Road Not Taken"
"Ask not what your country can do for you; ask
 what you can do for your country."
```

Despite quotation marks' identical appearance regardless of their purpose, literate humans usually can distinguish whether quotation marks are structuring a title ("The Road Not Taken") or a line from a famous speech ("Ask not. . ."). Humans rely on context and prior knowledge, and sometimes capitalization, to make those kinds of distinctions.

Computers and web browsers are not that smart. They must be told exactly what something is: the purpose of HTML tags is to describe the structure of writing.

HTML tags obey the same rules as quotation marks. HTML, at least on its surface, can be thought of as a set of fancy quotation marks that lets writers semantically describe the structure of writing. If I write an article as a web page and its title is "Simple Rules for Using HTML," I might structure the title as a first-level heading (<h1>):

```
<h1>Simple Rules for Using HTML</h1>
```

Structurally, that text is a first-level heading regardless of whether the CSS styles it to appear big and purple or little and green, in Times New Roman or Helvetica, or whether it even appears visibly on the page at all. The structural meaning, the semantics, of the heading in

HTML will always be the same, no matter how it might be styled later in CSS. That is why HTML that semantically structures writing is the cornerstone of accessibility and sustainability in web design.

## THE SIX RULES OF HTML

There are six rules that you must follow when writing HTML. Some of these rules are taken from the XML-derived XHTML 1.0 Strict (see Chapter 4), whose name implied a very strict ruleset for HTML writers to follow. A strict, unambiguous ruleset may not be fun in many areas of life, but it is necessary for writing any kind of computer language. A **well-formed** HTML document is one that follows the rules of XML. All of these rules will become clearer over the course of this chapter and the rest of the book. It's also good practice to keep an HTML reference handy, such as the one at Mozilla Developer Network.

Here are the six rules of HTML:

**Rule 1.** Every valid HTML document's very first line must be a DOC-TYPE declaration. Not even an HTML comment should appear before the DOCTYPE declaration. Markup validators check your markup according to the type of HTML specified by the DOCTYPE. The DOC-TYPE declaration also prevents web browsers from rendering a page in **quirks mode**, which is reserved for older, nonstandard web pages. Prior to HTML5, the DOCTYPE declarations for HTML and XHTML were long and complex. But in HTML5 and all future versions of HTML, the DOCTYPE declaration is simply this:

```
<!DOCTYPE html>
```

That's short enough that you can probably learn to write it from memory.

**Rule 2.** Every tag that opens around text content must close. If `<p>` opens, a closing tag, `</p>` must follow. (Just like quotation marks.) Some tags, such as line break (`<br />`) and image (`<img />`), do not surround text. Such tags are known as **void elements** (W3C 2013, under "4.3. Elements"). Rather than having an opening and closing tag, void elements self-close with a space and a slash: `/>`. One tag that may not surround any text, but that must appear always with its separate closing tag, is `<script>` when used with the `src` attribute for loading JavaScript. To load a JavaScript file called `site.js`, the script tag would look like this: `<script src="site.js"></script>`. That cannot be shortened to a self-closing `<script />` tag.

While HTML allows for certain tags to remain unclosed, a well-formed XML style requires all tags to close and void elements such as `<img />` to self-close.

**Rule 3.** Tags close in the opposite order that they open, just like single quotation marks inside of doubles:

```
<p>
  To structure text that should be emphasized,
  use the <em>emphasis tag</em>.
</p>
```

In that example, `<p>` opens, then `<em>`; `</em>` closes, then `</p>`. The first tag that opens must be the last to close.

**Rule 4.** All tag elements and attributes, and some attribute values, must be lowercase letters. Here's an illustrative, fake bit of HTML (sometimes called **pseudocode**) that illustrates the element, attribute, and value parts of the tag:

```
<element attribute="value">
```

So in this example,

```
<address class="business">
```

the element, or tag name, is `address`; it has one attribute, `class`, and that attribute's value is `business`. `business` can also be called an attribute value. Not all attribute values must be lowercase. For example, all `<img />` (image) tags require an `alt` attribute for alternative text that users will see or hear on devices that cannot display images. (Chapter 19 will detail methods beyond `alt` attributes for presenting images accessibly.) The attribute value for the `alt` attribute should be a short descriptive phrase or sentence and follow typical capitalization and punctuation rules for a sentence:

```
<img src="apple-pie.jpg" alt="Photograph of
  apple pie." />
```

As that example also shows, tags can have multiple attributes (in that case, `src` and `alt`), which are separated from one another by a space.

**Rule 5.** All attribute values must appear in quotation marks, immediately following the equals sign. To adhere to a well-formed style, there should also never be a space between the equals sign and the opening quotation mark. Use spaces only to separate elements from attributes, and attributes from other attributes:

```
<header id="header" class="masthead">
```

**Rule 6.** All `class` and `id` values should begin with a letter, and must not contain spaces. Never begin a `class` or `id` value with a number or punctuation. Except for special values, such as microformats, you must invent `class` and `id` values yourself, in ways that describe the content of your pages, not their visual design. When reading or writing HTML, you should be able to tell what a thing is, but never what it looks like or how it behaves:

```
<nav id="navigation" class="active">
```

To maintain a consistent style, limit classes and IDs to lowercase letters and the hyphen. Other characters are allowed, including capital letters. But keeping everything lowercase saves you the trouble of remembering whether or not something is capitalized. By consistently using only lowercase letters, you'll be certain that your class is `navigation`, not `Navigation`. Capitalization matters. In CSS, `.navigation` and `.Navigation` refer to two different classes because, like HTML and JavaScript, CSS is **case sensitive**.

Also, some attributes allow multiple values, each of which is separated by a space. For example, a paragraph tag could have the classes of "first" and "summary":

```
<p class="first summary">
  <!--content here -->
</p>
```

For that reason, you cannot use spaces when creating class names. `class="first summary"` does not create a class called *first summary*, but rather two classes: *first* and *summary*. IDs must never contain spaces, as only one ID is permitted per element (W3C 2014, under "3.2.5. Global Attributes"). Additional class and ID features are discussed at the end of this chapter.

Apply all six of those rules consistently to every HTML document that you write.

## THE GLOBAL STRUCTURE OF WEB PAGES

The coming chapters in this book look more closely at the function of different HTML page structures. But stripping away everything else, HTML source is organized like this:

```
<!DOCTYPE html>
<html>
  <head></head>
  <body></body>
</html>
```

The DOCTYPE declaration and each of those tags can appear only once per page. Let's walk through each of them so that you can begin to build a mental model of the structural blocks common to all HTML pages.

### The Root Element: `<html>`

Except for the DOCTYPE declaration, described in the first HTML rule above, HTML pages are entirely contained within an `<html>` tag. While there are some important attributes that should appear on the `<html>` tag, its primary structural function is to serve as the tag that contains both the `<head>` and `<body>` tags. Because of this, the `<html>` tag can be referred to as the **root element** of all web pages. It is the tag that contains all others.

The `<html>` tag should have at least one attribute, `lang`, which specifies the language for the document. On an English-language web page, the `<html>` element would read:

```
<html lang="en">
```

The en abbreviation for English is taken from an ISO standard for representing natural languages as multiletter codes, ISO 639. The United States Library of Congress (2014) maintains a list of ISO two-letter 639-1 codes. For example, if you're writing a page in Spanish, your lang attribute will be es, for *español*. If you have longer passages of text in a language other than what you specified on your <html> tag, you can add additional lang attributes on any HTML elements containing content in the language you specify.

Regardless of the language it's written in, page content does not appear immediately inside the <html> tag. Instead, <html> is divided into two parts: <head> and <body>.

## Metadata in the <head> Tag

Appearing before the <body> tag of every HTML web page is a <head> tag. At minimum, the <head> must contain two important tags, both of which appear in the RPK's HTML files (see Chapter 15).

The first tag is <title>, which should contain a title for the web page. Whatever you write there appears in the title bar or tabs of most web browsers and as the label for pages that people bookmark, either in their browser or through a cloud-based bookmarking service. The contents of the <title> tag will also be the hyperlinked text for your page when it appears in a list of search results or as a social-media share. Because of shoddy web-authoring software, it's not uncommon to see hastily constructed web pages whose title reads *Untitled Document*. Be sure always to include a meaningful title (see Chapter 16).

The second tag that must appear in the <head> is a <meta> tag with a charset attribute:

```
<meta charset="utf-8" />
```

The charset attribute tells browsers and search-engine spiders that the page encodes characters according to utf-8, the abbreviation for Unicode Transformation Format – 8-bit. Remember that it is essential that your editor also encode the text of your HTML file in utf-8, as was discussed in Chapter 10. Later chapters describe additional <meta>

tags for responsive web design (Chapter 14) and sharing on the social web (Chapter 25).

### Page Content in the `<body>` Tag

All of the content of a page that you expect to be visible in a browser's **viewport** must be written inside the `<body>` tag. Most of the work of writing and building the content of your pages happens inside the `<body>` tag. Subsequent chapters break down the typical contents of web pages to help you better structure and organize your page content inside of `<body>`.

## ADDITIONAL STRUCTURE WITH ID AND CLASS

The set of tags that make up HTML, known as its *vocabulary*, goes a long way toward establishing meaningful structure for your page content. But sometimes a page has structures that must be described more specifically than just as headings, paragraphs, and lists (see Chapter 16). HTML includes two attributes for adding more specific structural descriptions: id and class. class and id both provide additional structural information, but they are used for different purposes and follow different rules.

### Uniquely Identifying Pieces of Structure with `id`

Any id value, or unique ID, can only be used once per page. And any given HTML tag can only have a single id value per page. IDs are often used for describing a page's major structural features, such as navigation, header, footer, or content. The id value has traditionally been used with the division tag, `<div>`. However, when a more suitable structural tag is available, be sure to use it rather than `<div>` (see Chapter 16). Consider this HTML fragment:

```
<body>
  <h1>John Smith's Home Page</h1>
  <h2>Portfolio Overview</h2>
  <p>
```

```
    See sample work in
    <a href="portfolio.html">my
    portfolio</a>...
  </p>
  <h2>Latest Projects</h2>
  <p>
    Read all about my
    <a href="projects.html">latest
    projects</a>...
  </p>
  <ul>
    <li><a href="index.html">Home</a></li>
    <li><a href="resume.html">Resume</a></li>
    <li><a href="contact.html">Contact</a></li>
  </ul>
  <p>
    All site content is licensed for use under a
    <a rel="license" href=
    "https://creativecommons.org/licenses/by/4.0/">
    Creative Commons 4.0 International License</a>.
  </p>
</body>
```

In that basic structural form, there is nothing indicating the different content areas of the page, such as a page header, a main content area, a site navigation (the unordered list), or a footer (the Creative Commons license; see Chapter 25). With the addition of some structural HTML tags, whose purpose is to group page content into different common areas, and structurally named id attributes to distinguish the different sections, the page's source might look like:

```
<body>
  <header id="header">
    <h1>John Smith's Home Page</h1>
  </header>
  <main id="content">
    <section id="primary">
```

```
      <h2>Portfolio Overview</h2>
      <p>
        See sample work in
        <a href="portfolio.html">my
        portfolio</a>...
      </p>
      <h2>Latest Projects</h2>
      <p>
        Read all about my
        <a href="projects.html">latest
        projects</a>...
      </p>
    </section>
  </main>
  <nav id="navigation">
    <ul>
      <li><a href="index.html">Home</a></li>
      <li><a href="resume.html">Resume</a></li>
      <li><a href="contact.html">Contact</a></li>
    </ul>
  </nav>
  <footer id="footer">
    <p>
      All site content is licensed for use under a
      <a rel="license" href=
      "https://creativecommons.org/licenses/by/4.0/">
      Creative Commons 4.0 International License</a>.
    </p>
  </footer>
</body>
```

Note that in most cases, I have used an id attribute with a value that matches the name of the tag. HTML5 permits **sectioning elements** like <header> and <footer> to be used in multiple places in different contexts on the page, for example, but a unique ID marks the primary header and footer for the entire page. The <main> tag should only be used once per page, however, and I've decided to give it an id of content. <main> itself is used only for the unique content of a page, so it should not contain the header, footer, navigation, or any other content repeated on other pages of your site. The <ul> tag on the site navigation already groups the list item tags, but I put the id attribute directly on the <nav> tag that I added.

The parts of the page are now more clearly structured than in the first example, but there is no unnecessary markup either. Some pages that you'll find on the web are a sea of <div> tags. But your users and your web-hosting bill will both benefit if you make every last byte of source-code count. Writing meaningful, lean semantic structure is a good first step toward realizing those benefits. Chapter 16 looks at sectioning elements like <header> and <footer> in greater detail.

## Associating Similar, Repeated Structures with class

Once an id value has been used on an HTML page, regardless of the tag it has been used with, it cannot be used again on that

### IDs IN URLs

Unique IDs also provide a pointer for use in URLs. By adding to your URL the hash (#) followed by a page structure's unique ID, known as a URL **fragment identifier**, you can point a visitor to a particular part of your page. That's a good way to remember that IDs must only appear once per page. Fragment identifiers will not function reliably if multiple elements have the same ID.

For example, to point someone's browser to the main content in the example above, we could write a URL like http://example.com/#content. Most browsers will scroll to the fragment-referenced area of the page automatically. CSS and JavaScript can also make use of fragment identifiers to build additional page enhancements.

page. Structural elements that might appear more than once should be structured with the `class` attribute. For example, it has become conventional to use the `<cite>` tag to structure titles of materials that you refer to or quote from. Suppose you cite different types of materials in your page and want to structurally identify the types of material, perhaps so that you can style them differently in CSS. You might invent a class called `film` and another called `book`, adding the relevant class to the `<cite>` tag:

```
<p>
   I enjoyed Peter Jackson's <cite class="film">Lord
   of the Rings</cite> films, but they still
   weren't as good as the original
   <cite class="book">Lord of the Rings</cite> books
   by J. R. R. Tolkien.
</p>
```

You can add classes to any tag requiring more specific structure. Note that the class and ID names do not appear in a browser view of your web page, but they are indispensable for applying additional CSS styles and enhancing your pages with DOM scripting, as will become clearer in the next several chapters.

## Naming Classes and IDs

Classes and IDs should always start with a letter, and are best limited to lowercase letters a–z and the hyphen. HTML5 is more flexible than its predecessors in allowing additional characters in `class` and `id` values, but for backward-compatibility reasons, stick with the conservative set of lowercase letters and the hyphen.

When naming classes and IDs, always create names that describe the content you're marking: for example, `supporting-content` instead of `sidebar` or `blue-box`. The content's presentation as a sidebar or blue box will change if your design changes. But its structural function of supporting the page's main content will not change. Use the `<aside>` tag for any supporting content, regardless of what class or ID you assign it (see Chapter 16).

## Class-itis

It's all too easy to get carried away and start adding classes all over a page. Some content management systems and page-design frameworks even encourage the use of an absurd number of <div> elements peppered with multiple classes. Some sites are made up almost entirely of <div> tags—even for marking up headings, paragraphs, and lists—a practice that completely misses the point of semantic HTML. <div> has no semantic value, and the HTML5 specification has branded it as "an element of last resort" (W3C 2014, under "4.4.13 The div Element"). If you catch yourself writing something like <div class="major-heading">, stop, think, and use the <h1> tag instead.

Class-itis also results in meaningless, redundant markup. For example, writers sometimes write markup like this:

```
<ul>
  <li class="favorite-foods">Pizza</li>
  <li class="favorite-foods">
    Cheeseburgers
  </li>
  <li class="favorite-foods">Cake</li>
</ul>
```

In that case, rather than adding a class to every single list item, it would be better to add it on the <ul> tag that groups all of the list items:

```
<ul class="favorite-foods">
  <li>Pizza</li>
  <li>Cheeseburgers</li>
  <li>Cake</li>
</ul>
```

That will keep the page's markup lighter, easier to read, and easier to revise. Write as little HTML as possible, while still fully describing your content.

## NEXT STEPS

This chapter has covered the basic rules of HTML, and the major structural features found on every standards-compliant HTML page.

The next chapter will introduce CSS, which you can begin to write while you develop your skills with HTML. See also the chapters in the "Issues and Challenges" section to review HTML's importance to the accessibility, usability, and sustainability of websites.

# REFERENCES

Library of Congress. 2014. "Codes for the Representation of Names of Languages." *ISO 639.2 Registration Authority.* https://www.loc.gov/standards/iso639-2/php/code_list.php

W3C. 2013. "HTML: The Markup Language (an HTML Language Reference)." http://www.w3.org/TR/html-markup/syntax.html#void-element

W3C. 2014. "HTML5: A Vocabulary and Associated APIs for HTML and XHTML." https://www.w3.org/TR/2014/REC-html5-20141028/

# CHAPTER 12

# Presentation and Design: CSS Overview

Cascading Style Sheets (CSS) describe the visual presentation and design of web pages, including typography, color, and page layout. CSS controls the appearance of all content structured in HTML. While you can look at an HTML file rendered directly in a web browser, which will provide its own default styling (Figure 12.1), the CSS files cannot be rendered directly. All you'll see is the CSS source itself. A browser has to apply CSS to the structure of an HTML file. That means you must have HTML-structured content in place before you can test your design work in CSS.

The previous chapter described the firm rules of HTML organization: the first line must be a DOCTYPE declaration, for example, and the <html> tag must contain a <head> and <body> tag, in that order. By comparison, CSS is a complete free-for-all. Any CSS rule can be declared anywhere in your CSS file. See the comments in the Rapid Prototyping Kit's CSS files for suggestions on how to organize your stylesheet. The only real consequences of where rules appear in your stylesheet are that rules written near the top of the file will be rendered first, and rules near the bottom of the stylesheet can override identical styles written near the top. Consider a very short stylesheet with just two rules:

## HTML with Default CSS Applied

- Home
- About
- Contact

**Lorem Ipsum Dolor Sit Amet, Consectetur Adipiscing Elit.**

Proin vulputate a dolor eget facilisis. Phasellus vehicula metus ullamcorper, pellentesque tellus sit amet, vulputate mi. Praesent fringilla nisl a dui volutpat, nec scelerisque nibh porttitor. Nunc ut rutrum odio. Mauris a ante tincidunt, luctus augue sit amet, scelerisque ante. Etiam in commodo ante, vel lobortis ipsum. Vivamus maximus ac est fringilla condimentum. Vivamus neque neque, mollis sit amet ultrices lacinia, ultrices et eros. Donec vehicula est mi, eget vulputate eros porttitor eget. Ut pellentesque scelerisque sapien, eget viverra leo. Pellentesque tellus neque, auctor eu euismod eget, varius eget diam. Sed sit amet aliquet odio, a dictum ante.

Class aptent taciti sociosqu ad litora torquent per conubia nostra, per inceptos himenaeos. Donec a auctor dolor. Integer enim odio, auctor ac augue non, commodo euismod augue. Quisque consequat quis justo ac molestie. Nunc maximus viverra massa, nec rutrum elit hendrerit in. Aenean at dui ut ex pharetra interdum sed nec neque. Curabitur neque nisl, tincidunt a pharetra eu, rhoncus a dolor. Ut lobortis, risus nec pharetra feugiat, velit augue feugiat lectus, ac scelerisque dui leo non velit. Aliquam elementum interdum nulla a feugiat. Praesent efficitur scelerisque auctor.

- Donec eget porta massa, molestie vulputate risus.
- Etiam odio massa, condimentum et eros varius, sodales accumsan diam.
- Quisque eget lorem non massa tempus tincidunt. Nam posuere urna turpis.

Donec vitae scelerisque velit. Praesent pellentesque dui ac gravida sagittis. Vestibulum dictum odio non nisl euismod, efficitur euismod eros facilisis. Vestibulum sed quam libero. Mauris id mi aliquet, hendrerit nisi non, iaculis purus.

- Sed ante risus, hendrerit sit amet ex quis, maximus fringilla quam. Cras iaculis lacinia lacus, vitae cursus ligula. Mauris egestas nunc id elit aliquam, id euismod magna ultrices. Donec commodo diam at suscipit interdum.

    Nulla facilisi. Curabitur at libero vitae nulla suscipit iaculis eget at lacus. Nullam auctor massa nisi, sit amet ornare nisi

**Figure 12.1.** HTML is displayed with Firefox's default styles applied.

```
a { color: red; }
a { color: green; }
```

Those two rules are doing the same thing: specifying the color of the links on the page, which are marked in HTML with the anchor tag, <a>. The top rule will be the first to render. But it will be instantaneously overridden by the second rule: links on a page styled by that tiny stylesheet will appear green. If there were a few thousand lines of CSS between the two rules in that example, it's possible that links might be red momentarily before turning green.

## BASIC CSS TERMINOLOGY AND CONCEPTS

A CSS file is a list of rules, sometimes called *rulesets*. CSS rules comprise two parts: a **selector**, which specifies which structural parts of the HTML document will be styled, and a **declaration block**, which uses curly braces to group a list of one or more **style properties** and their values. Some CSS properties take a single value, while others can take multiple values.

The basic form of a CSS rule, then, is something similar to this pseudocode (using `selector`, `property`, and `value` to show their positions in the rule):

```
selector {
  property: value;
    /*
      For properties that take a single
      value, e.g.,
      color: blue;
    */

  property: value, value, value;
    /*
      Commas separate values ordered by
      preference, e.g.,
      font-family: Helvetica, Arial,
        sans-serif;
    */

  property: value value value;
    /*
      For shorthand properties that
      require multiple values, e.g.,
      border: 10px solid red;
    */
}
```

Every CSS rule opens with at least one selector. Multiple selectors can be listed, separated by commas. For example, to display both the italic, `<i>`, and emphasis, `<em>`, tags in italic, one could write:

```
i { font-style: italic; }
em { font-style: italic; }
```

But because the declaration blocks for i and em are identical, this is a shorter way to write the rule (more information about this in the "Grouping Selectors" section at the end of this chapter):

```
i, em { font-style: italic; }
```

Properties and values are all grouped between curly braces, { }, and each property-value combination, known as a **style declaration**, ends with a semicolon, ;. The curly braces and the style declarations form the declaration block. Declaration blocks can contain many different property-value combinations.

However, not every rule must contain every style declaration that you expect for a given selector. A primary capability of CSS is **inheritance**, where style properties transfer from parent elements to their descendants. For example, setting a text color on the <html> tag will style the text content of the entire page to have that same color, unless another rule says otherwise. Once set on html, there is no need to set the same color over and over again on rules for headings, paragraphs, lists, and so on. That only creates tedious work if you decide to change the page's text to another color. A good CSS reference will somehow note whether or not a given property is inherited (see Figure 12.2), but the majority of inherited properties are text and font related.

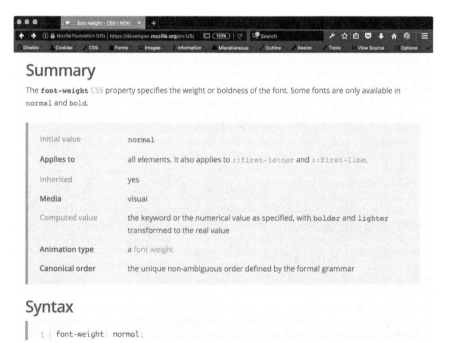

**Figure 12.2.** This portion of the MDN CSS reference indicates whether a property, such as font-weight, is inherited.

For another example, if you want all of your text on a page to run in the Helvetica typeface, you do not need to specify Helvetica for each and every tag you use. Because the CSS `font-family` property is inherited, you can just specify it on the `<html>` tag, which is the ancestor element of all content on an HTML page. A simple CSS file for making text appear in Helvetica would include a style rule like this one:

```
html { font-family: Helvetica, Arial, sans-serif; }
```

The *cascade* in the name Cascading Style Sheets means that style declarations can come from multiple sources (files, selectors, plus the default browser styling—which should be removed using a reset CSS file; see Chapter 15), with the more specific, last-declared rule ultimately being applied to a particular HTML element. Figure 12.3 shows the default browser styling, with the exception of the Helvetica style declaration for the `<html>` tag above, which is inherited by all text on the page.

**Figure 12.3.** Because `font-family` is inherited, all text now displays in Helvetica.

# BASIC SELECTORS

Selectors in CSS describe the HTML structure that will be styled. Using the house metaphor from the HTML chapter, CSS selectors are like instructions to interior decorators for what they should decorate: "the fireplace," "the kitchen cabinets," "the closets in the master bedroom." Except instead of referring to rooms in a house, CSS selectors refer to tags and structural relationships between tags in your HTML.

## Type Selectors

The most basic CSS selectors are HTML tag elements, sometimes called **element** or **type selectors**. While HTML puts the element in angle brackets, like `<body>` or `<p>`, in CSS the element appears by itself: body or p. Any HTML tag can be a CSS selector, and the selector will style the contents of that particular tag the way you specify, wherever it appears on your page.

For example, to set a first-line indent on all paragraphs, you'd write in CSS:

```
p { text-indent: 1.2em; }
```

## ID and Class Selectors

IDs and classes can also be selectors. Class selectors begin with a . (dot) and ID selectors begin with a # (hash). For example, assuming your HTML document has `<footer id="footer">`, to set the background color of your footer to gray, your CSS would be either:

```
#footer { background: gray; }
```

or

```
footer#footer { background: gray; }
```

Either selector works. I prefer to use class and ID selectors without the HTML element. A page will probably have a `#footer`, but the associated element could be a `<div>` or, preferably, the HTML5 `<footer>` tag.

Similarly, if you had a class called warning (e.g., `<p class="warning">`), perhaps on a site with instructions for doing something that might be potentially dangerous like operating a power saw, you could write the selector as either:

```
.warning { color: red; }
```

or

```
p.warning { color: red; }
```

Adding the tag element to the class selector can give you finer-grained control over the look of your page. That is true particularly if you use the same class on different HTML tags, but want to style the class differently, depending on the tag the class appears on. Repeating the paragraph example from above:

```
p { text-indent: 1.2em; }
  /* 1.2em first-line indent */

.warning {
  color: red;
  font-weight: bold;
}
p.warning { text-indent: 0; }
  /* No first-line indent */
```

The .warning selector applies to any HTML element with the warning class, while the p.warning adjusts the text-indent property only on paragraphs, which received a 1.2em indentation earlier in the stylesheet. In short, it is generally better to style the class selector by itself (.warning), and reserve element-prefixed class selectors (p.warning) for additional styles that deviate from the base .warning styles, or that correct or adjust for styles elsewhere in your stylesheet.

## Attribute Selectors

Class and ID selectors are examples of how CSS uses HTML attributes and their values to style pieces of HTML structure. Class and ID values are so common that they have their own syntax: the dot (.) and the hash (#). A slightly more complicated syntax turns any HTML attribute into a CSS selector.

For example, someone writing HTML might add a class like external to links pointing to other sites:

```
<a href="https://www.google.com/"
   class="external">search Google</a>
```

And that external class could work as a selector to style all external links green:

```
a.external { color: green; }
```

But using an attribute selector built around the href attribute can accomplish the same thing:

```
a[href^="http"] { color: green }
```

That selector colors green any <a> element that has an href attribute whose value begins with http, a requirement for all external links to function properly in the browser. Using that selector can also lead to cleaner HTML. There is no longer a need for the redundant external class, because external links can be selected by their href attribute value:

```
<a href="https://www.google.com/">search Google</a>
```

Attribute selectors can be written with several different patterns. Here are some of the more common ones:

- [attr] selects any element with the attr attribute. img[alt] will select all image tags with an alt attribute.
- [attr="value"] selects any element with the attr attribute whose value is exactly value. *[lang="de"] will select any HTML element with de (German/Deutsch) as its lang attribute, using the universal selector, *, which selects all elements.
- [attr^="value"] selects any element with the attr attribute whose value *begins with* value. That was the pattern in the external-link example above. a[href^="http"] will match href values beginning with both http and https protocols, which is why the colon was excluded from the pattern.

- `[attr$="value"]` selects any element with the `attr` attribute whose value *ends with* `value`. For example, `a[href$=".com"]` will select all anchor tags with links pointing to `.com` domains.
- `[attr*="value"]` selects any element with the `attr` attribute whose value *contains* `value` at least once. `img[src*="cat"]` will select any image tag whose `src` attribute refers to an image file with `cat` somewhere in the file name or path, such as `<img src="smelly-cat.jpg" />` or `<img src="photos/cats/photo-023.jpg" />`

Have a look at the MDN reference on attribute selectors (2016a) for additional available patterns.

## Pseudoclass Selectors

CSS provides a number of special pseudoclass selectors, which select an element based on either user behavior or the structure of your HTML document. The more common pseudoclass selectors are used for styling link text appearing inside the `<a>` tag:

- `:link` styles a link in its unvisited state
- `:visited` styles a link that has been visited
- `:hover` styles a link when a mouse pointer is hovering over it, and should usually be combined with
- `:focus`, which styles a link that has been, for example, tabbed to by a keyboard
- `:active` styles a link during the brief moment that it has been activated by a mouse click, finger tap, or the Return key on the keyboard

So to make links green without an underline, hovered/focused links underlined, and visited links red, a style sheet might have a cluster of style rules like:

```
a, a:link {
  color: green;
  text-decoration: none;
```

```
}
a:hover, a:focus {
  text-decoration: underline;
}
a:visited { color: red; }
```

:hover and :focus also work on HTML form elements used for entering information.

There are also pseudoclass selectors for targeting specific elements based on familial relationships, which are described more fully later in the chapter. :first-child and :last-child are the more common of these:

```
li:first-child { /* Styles for the first li in a
  list */ }
li:last-child { /* Styles for the last li in a
  list */ }
```

There are many more pseudoclass selectors available, some of which will be used later in this book, but their support in different browsers varies. Keep the MDN reference handy (2015).

## Universal Selector

One final selector worth mentioning is the universal selector, *, sometimes called the wildcard selector. Used by itself, it will style all elements on the page; for example,

```
* { color: green; }
```

will style all text on the page to make it appear green. However, because color is inherited, it is generally better to set it using the html or body element selector. For both class and ID selectors, the wildcard selector is implied. That is, there is no difference between

```
.warning { color: red; }
```

and

```
*.warning { color: red; }
```

The wildcard selector is at its most useful in relationship selectors. For example, if a page contained the following HTML:

```
<p>
  This is <strong>an example</strong> of
  <a href="example.htm">styling <strong>this
  strong tag</strong></a>
  <em>as well as <strong>this strong
  tag</strong></em>.
</p>
```

only the first `<strong>` tag (marking "an example") is a child of `<p>`. The other two are children of other tags (`<a>` and `<em>`). To style the `<strong>` tags that aren't children of `<p>`, use the wildcard selector:

```
p * strong { /*Style information*/ }
```

That would style all strong tags that are grandchildren of paragraphs: meaning, there must be one or more descendant elements between p and strong for this style rule to be applied.

## RELATIONSHIP SELECTORS

CSS selectors can also be written based on the relationships between elements in HTML pages. CSS, like the Document Object Model (see Chapter 13), understands relationships in HTML using terms you probably already know from your family tree: parents, children, and siblings, as well as ancestors and descendants.

### Descendant Selectors

Descendant selectors are formed by a list of at least two elements or classes/IDs, each separated by a space. The selector styles the last element listed. For example, this descendant selector will style all of the anchor tags (links) in the navigation so that they are not underlined:

```
#navigation a { text-decoration: none; }
```

All anchor tags (`<a>`) inside of `<nav id="navigation">` will appear without the default underlining that browsers apply to links. Other links on the page will still have an underline. To remove underlining from all links, just use the a element selector:

```
a { text-decoration: none; }
```

## Child Selectors

Child selectors are a more specific form of descendant selector. They select an element only if it is a child, or direct descendant, of the parent element. Child selectors are written by putting an angle bracket between two elements. The following selector will style all child `<ul>` tags of `<nav id="navigation">`, but not `<ul>` tags of any more deeply nested lists, which would be descendants, but not children:

```
#navigation > ul {
  margin: 0;
  padding: 0;
}
```

## Sibling Selectors

Sibling selectors target adjacent HTML elements that share a parent. For example, a sibling selector, +, can style paragraphs that immediately follow a heading-two tag (`<h2>`) to run in bold without a first-line indent:

```
h2 + p {
  text-indent: 0;
  font-weight: bold;
}
```

One limitation of sibling selectors is that they only target the sibling appearing after the first. For example, in this HTML:

```
<main id="content">
  <h2>My Heading-Two Tag</h2>
  <p>
    My paragraph text.
  </p>
</main>
```

the sibling selector would allow you to style the paragraph element, but not the heading element. That is, you can say in CSS "style paragraphs appearing immediately after heading-two" but not "style heading-twos appearing before a paragraph." Future versions of CSS might introduce a selector that does the latter, but in the meantime, to style that heading-two, just add a class to it when it appears before paragraphs. Then it can be styled with the class selector.

## SELECTORS AND SPECIFICITY

The *cascade* in Cascading Style Sheets refers to the method by which a browser applies one of a competing set of styles. Multiple selectors can refer to the same elements; for example:

```
a { color: blue; }
a.external { color: red; }
ul#navigation a { color: green; }
```

The first selector styles all link text blue, the second styles links with an external class as red, while the third styles links in the navigation green. But given that all three styles ultimately refer to `<a>` in the HTML, how does a web browser know to style the external links red and all other links blue—given that the selector in the first style is supposed to style all of the links on the page?

Selectors have different levels of specificity in CSS. Andy Clarke has used Star Wars characters to illustrate selector specificity visually (`http://www.stuffandnonsense.co.uk/archives/css_speci ficity_wars.html`). Along with that, Clarke's post refers to a point system for calculating specificity; essentially, elements in a selector get one point, classes in selectors get 10 points, and IDs in a selector get 100 points. When multiple selectors match the same element, the selector with the most points determines how the element is styled. So in the example above, the first selector gets one point, the second gets 11 points (element plus class), and the third gets 102 points (an element plus an ID plus another element).

The more specific style—that is, the style with the most points in this system—is the one that gets applied to the matching HTML structure. That's why the navigation items in the list of styles above will appear green, not blue—even if there were an `<a class="external">` match within `<ul id="navigation">`; to style that would require a selector like `ul#navigation a.external { /*Styles here*/ }` whose point value would be 112 (two elements, one class, and one ID) and therefore more specific.

## Combining Selectors

You can write very descriptive and specific selectors, so long as they match the familial relationships and structural components in your HTML. A match is what triggers a web browser to apply the style. For example, to style a paragraph that is an adjacent sibling of a header-two tag that is a child of `<article  id="main">`, provided that `article#main` is not a child of the body tag, the CSS selector would look like:

```
body * article#main > h2 + p { /*Style
  information*/ }
```

However, you'll probably be relieved to know that it's rare to have to write such complicated selectors. Rare, but possible. (See the "Selectors and Specificity" sidebar above, which will be useful knowledge if you have to write complex selectors.) Complicated selectors like that are also a bad idea, because they rely on such a precise structure. The second the HTML structure changes, the selector is no longer going to match anything. It's often better to apply a simple class to the element that would otherwise appear at the end of a complex selector, and then use CSS to style that class.

## Grouping Selectors

Structural features in HTML are sometimes presented in identical styles. For example, both the `<b>` (bold) and `<strong>` tags might be styled bold in CSS, using two separate style declarations:

```
b { font-weight: bold; }
strong { font-weight: bold; }
```

Using the comma, both selectors can be grouped as a single declaration. A comma-separated list allows many different elements to be styled bold, such as all of the headings:

```
b, strong, h1, h2, h3, h4, h5, h6 {
  font-weight: bold;
}
```

Then, any distinct styles for a given selector could be handled by additional selectors in the same style sheet; for example, h1 has already been styled bold, but to make it purple (as well as bold) requires a style rule that contains only the color property:

```
h1 { color: purple; } /*Already made bold above.*/
```

## COMMON CSS UNITS

Later chapters will cover the specifics of different style properties, like `display` and `position`, which take specific keywords to function properly. This chapter will conclude by looking at units to describe color and length (the generic CSS word for size/dimension), which are set on many different style properties.

### Color

There are three different color models in routine use with CSS. The first is simple color keywords, like red, yellow, blue. A full list of the color keywords can be found at the MDN page on color in CSS (2016c). But color keywords are not useful for more nuanced uses of color. More colors have been added to the list of keywords over time, but they are still limited like a box of crayons. The two primary models for more exacting colors are Red Green Blue (RGB) and Hue Saturation Lightness (HSL). This book will cover only RGB, because HSL is not widely supported in browsers at the time of writing.

RGB colors can be specified by three different methods. The first method uses hexadecimal numbers for red, green, and blue (RGB) color values. This method works very well across operating systems and web browsers. A hexadecimal value is made up of six hexadecimal, or hex, numbers. (Hex numbers run 0–9 and continue A–F; F is the hexadecimal number for decimal 15.) The first two numbers are the red value, the second two the green value, and the third two are the blue value. So to set a color to magenta (red and blue), a hex value of #FF00FF would be required. A Google search for hexadecimal color palette will turn up dozens of pages that show the hex values for colors. You will also see older, 216-color "web-safe" palettes from the days when computer displays were limited to 256 colors. Designers can now use any of the millions of colors that can be specified in hexadecimal.

RGB colors can also be written as decimal numbers, 0–255, using the rgb() **functional notation** method. The hex color #FF00FF can be written in decimal numbers as rgb(255,0,255). As in hex colors, the first number is the red channel, the second is the green channel, and the third is blue.

There is also an RGBa method, which uses rgba() functional notation to introduce an **alpha channel** that sets how transparent the color appears, 0–1. 0 is fully transparent, and 1 is fully opaque, so transparency is always a decimal number. Specifying rgba(255,0,255,0.5) will set a magenta color at 50 percent transparency.

There are many additional color resources and examples available on the book's companion website, http://webpg.es/.

## Length

**Absolute Units**: CSS has support for many absolute units, including print-based units like inches (in), centimeters (cm), and points (pt). The long-time unit of choice for web designers has been the pixel (px). And while print-based units are safely used in print stylesheets, neither they nor the trusty pixel unit are suited to mobile-first, responsive web design. Instead, CSS should be written in relative units.

**Relative Units**: Relative units are based on user preferences and system defaults beyond the control of a web designer. Relative units are essential to accessible, mobile-first responsive design. Later chapters will show how to calculate relative units from absolute units (see especially Chapters 17 and 18).

Here are the four relative units used most often in this book:

- em: The em is the most widely supported relative unit of measure. It is used for all text sizing and vertical units within a typographic grid. The size of the em is based initially on the default font size in a browser, but gains different values as text sizes are increased and decreased on different elements on a page. In traditional typography, the em unit is the width of a capital M in a given typeface. But in most browsers, 1em is initially equal to 16px. Users may configure their browsers with a larger or smaller initial text size. Use of the em unit ensures those users' preferences are respected, and makes it much easier to adjust the typography on a page just by altering the base em on the html selector (see Chapters 16, 17, and 20).

- rem: The rem unit is effectively the same as the em unit, but its value is always relative to the root em unit (font-size specified on the html selector). Support for rem is growing (see Chapter 17), and is generally much simpler to work with than the em unit.

- %: The percentage unit is used for all horizontal grid sizing. Percentages are calculated relative to containing elements. Chapters 18 and 19 will show how pixels can be used as a base unit to calculate percentages to achieve the fluid grids that are part of the foundation of responsive web design.

- vw, vh, vmax: These units are relative to the size of the browser viewport. vw is the viewport width, vh is the viewport height, and vmax is the greater of the viewport height or viewport width. The full viewport width is 100vw, and the full height is 100vh. vmax is the least well supported unit in this series, but the vw unit is the only one used with any regularity (see Chapter 19).

## NEXT STEPS

Now that you've had an introduction to CSS syntax, selectors, and basic units, it will be easier in later chapters to see how both HTML and CSS can be used to build different parts of your pages: content, navigation, headers and footers, and so on. The next chapter covers the basics of one more language, JavaScript. But you might wish to skip ahead to Chapter 14, which includes a discussion of CSS media queries, and return later to work on JavaScript after getting a better handle on HTML and CSS in responsive web design.

## REFERENCES

MDN. 2015. "Pseudo-Classes." https://developer.mozilla.org/en-US/docs/Web/CSS/Pseudo-classes

MDN. 2016a. "Attribute Selectors." https://developer.mozilla.org/en-US/docs/Web/CSS/Attribute_selectors

MDN. 2016b. ":first-child." https://developer.mozilla.org/en-US/docs/Web/CSS/:first-child

MDN. 2016c. "Color." https://developer.mozilla.org/en-US/docs/Web/CSS/color

# CHAPTER 13

# Performance and Interaction: JavaScript Overview

Progressively enhancing the performance and interactivity of your web pages using JavaScript and the Document Object Model (DOM) is known as **DOM scripting** (Keith 2005). DOM scripting is a complex area of web design, but it makes possible the sort of rich web applications and functionality that users have come to expect from sites like Facebook and Gmail. This chapter covers introductory, general approaches to working with JavaScript. Chapter 20 and the book's companion site provide additional guidance in using JavaScript and libraries such as jQuery to further enhance your pages. The "Resources for the Future" section of this book also lists several important books worth reading to enhance your command of JavaScript.

Unlike HTML, which is a markup language, and CSS, which is a declarative style language, JavaScript is a true programming language in that it contains features like variables and control structures as well as complex objects for working with math or dates and times. There is a common misconception that learning to program requires being good at math. That is not really the case for the kinds of programming tasks required on the web, where the most complex math done with any regularity is just counting things.

JavaScript performs data manipulations and minor adjustments to contents of the HTML and its structure, typically by adding or removing classes, via the DOM. JavaScript does not change any of the other relationships outlined in this book: HTML still structures content and CSS handles all design matters.

This chapter focuses on the basic kinds of data that you can manipulate in JavaScript. Chapter 20 will look more at using JavaScript to progressively enhance HTML via the DOM.

## DATA TYPES AND VARIABLES

JavaScript handles many different types of data. These are the most common ones for web development purposes:

- **Strings**: Strings are sequences of characters that appear between quotation marks. They are the bread and butter of interface design, where it is necessary to display different messages to users interacting with a form, or to manipulate the existing text inside of HTML tags. `"Please accept the terms of service"`, `"<h1>"`, and `"$2000"` are all strings.
- **Numbers**: Many programming languages have different types of numbers, things like integers (whole/counting numbers) and floats (numbers with decimals). In JavaScript, a number is just a number, whether or not it has a decimal in it. `0`, `1000`, and `58.4` are all JavaScript numbers. They are not surrounded by quotation marks: to do so would make them strings.
- **Booleans**: There are two Boolean values: `true` and `false`. Booleans are often used in conjunction with control structures, described below.
- **Undefined**: `undefined` is a special value given to variables that have been declared in a JavaScript file but not assigned a value. If I declare two variables, `var x = 5; var y;`, x is assigned the value of `5` but y is assigned the default value `undefined`.

Most of the time when you're writing JavaScript, you're doing something with or according to the value of one of those primitive types of data. And typically, those primitive types are **assigned** to a variable, using the `var` keyword:

```
var greeting = "Hello and welcome.";
var answer = 42;
var human = true;
var isUndefined; // undefined
```

JavaScript variables should always begin with a lowercase letter. There are two different styles for naming variables that contain multiple words. The first is called **camelCase**, so called because of the use of capital letters to distinguish subsequent words. The second is called **snake_ case**, because putting underscores between words apparently makes them look like a snake. It is generally better to aim for shorter variable names, but not at the expense of expressive code. So `username` is preferable to `usrnm`, and `currentUser` or `current_user` to `curusr`. It should not matter whether you choose to write in camelCase or snake_ case, but write in one style, not both. This book uses camelCase.

Also, on the line above `var isUndefined; // undefined`, the `// undefined` portion is the style of comment that is safest to use in JavaScript. Recall that multiline comments must have `//` on each line:

```
// This is a multiline
// comment in JavaScript
```

## Reserved Words

There are certain keywords in JavaScript that are reserved, meaning that you cannot use them to name variables or functions in your code. MDN maintains a list of current and planned keywords that you should consult (MDN 2016a, under "Keywords"). The words that trip people up most often are `default`, `new`, `this`, and `typeof`. They and other keywords should never be used to name features in your code.

If you want to avoid accidentally colliding with a reserved word while also making sure that your own JavaScript doesn't interfere with naming conventions in any JavaScript libraries you use, you can prefix all of your variables with your initials or the initials of your project, followed by an underscore if you prefer that style. For example, I might write variables such as:

```
var ksURL = "karlstolley.com"
var ksShowNavigation = true;
```

## Arrays and Objects

Variables are useful when you have a single string, number, or other basic type of data to store. But often there are related collections of values that a piece of JavaScript needs to track. For example, if there were a script that needed to track a user's favorite colors, a beginning programmer might write something like this:

```
var color1 = "red"
var color2 = "blue"
var color3 = "green"
```

And that's for just three colors. You can probably see the problem: what happens at five colors, or 10? Or one more than whatever a set of variables written like this can contain?

JavaScript, like most contemporary programming languages, includes a data structure called an **array**. Arrays are collections of data. Rewriting the colors from above as an array would look like this:

```
var colors = ["red", "blue", "green"];
```

Arrays are created by placing a set of values in a comma-separated list, between square brackets. The individual values of an array are indexed by numbers, starting with 0. A square-bracket notation is used to access each of the values:

```
var colors = ["red", "blue", "green"];

colors[0]; // red
colors[1]; // blue
colors[2]; // green
```

Values can also be added to an array, using the array object's push() method:

```
var colors = ["red", "blue", "green"];

colors.push("violet");
// colors = ["red", "blue", "green", "violet"];
```

Arrays are useful when a program needs to track a set of similar values, like colors, especially if their order doesn't matter very much. The next section, on "Control Structures," will look at a way to access the entire collection of values stored in an array.

JavaScript provides another type of collection, called **objects**, for modeling more complex structures. For example, a piece of JavaScript might have an object to describe a user:

```
var user = {
      name: "Mary",
       url: "http://example.com/mary/",
  birthday: "February 8",
      pets: 2,
 logged_in: true,
    colors: ["red", "blue", "green"]
};
```

```
user.birthday; // "February 8"
```

Simple objects like `user` make it easier to group properties of a related concept, in that case, a concept like a user and the details about her. Rather than having separate variables like `name` and `url`, which do not have much context associated with them, objects use a dot syntax for accessing an object's properties, like `user.name` and `user.birthday`. Objects are created with curly braces, and just like arrays, their inner values are separated by commas. Objects take a property name, which should begin with a lowercase letter, and end with a colon, `:`. The example above is formatted to make it easier to browse the values on each property.

The `user` object combines different data types. `user.name` and `user.url` are both strings. `user.pets` is a number, likely the number of pets that Mary has, while `user.logged_in` is a Boolean, suggesting that Mary is logged in to whatever system this `user` object is a part of. Notice that the final property, `user.colors`, contains an array. To access the color red from `user.colors`, a line of JavaScript would reference `user.colors[0]`. Objects can contain arrays and other objects; so too can arrays contain other arrays as well as objects. But ultimately, at the lowest levels, arrays and objects are ultimately just collections of basic data types: strings, numbers, and Booleans.

Additional assignment is all that is needed to modify an object's existing properties, or to add and assign new properties:

```
user.name; // Mary, from the example above

user.logged_in = false;
// Now user Mary is no longer logged in
user.email = "mary@example.com";
// Now user Mary has an email property
```

## CONTROL STRUCTURES

One of the defining characteristics of programming languages is their ability to execute code based on the truth of a condition. For example:

```
var age = 18;
if (age >= 18) {
  // Do something for people aged 18 or older
} else {
  // Do something for people under age 18
}
```

That little script uses an `if...else` statement. The `if` statement checks a truth condition. In this case, whether the variable `age` is greater than or equal to 18 (`age >= 18`). If that is true about `age`, any code inside of the first set of curly braces will run. If that is false, for example if the variable declaration were `var age = 13`, any code in the second set of braces will run.

The `if...else` statement checks a condition for truth once. Other statements, such as `while`, repeatedly check a statement for its truth condition:

```
var x = 0;
while (x < 10) {
 // do something with x ...
 x++; // increment x by 1
}
```

That script assigns x to 0, and then runs a `while` loop that will execute for as long as x is less than 10 (so, up until x is equal to 9). Importantly, the loop itself changes the value of x: x++, where ++ is shorthand for writing x = x + 1. If that line were missing, the loop would run forever, because x would always be equal to 0. That phenomenon is known as an **infinite loop**, which in modern browsers will eventually trigger a JavaScript timeout error. Always be on the lookout for infinite loops, especially if your code or browser becomes nonresponsive.

for loops are similar to while loops, but they handle all of the loop's conditions outside of the loop itself. for loops are commonly used to programmatically access all of the values in an array, such as this:

```
var colors = ["red", "blue", "green"];
for (var i = 0; i < colors.length; i++) {
  console.log(colors[i]);
}

// The JavaScript console will output:
// red
// blue
// green
```

A for loop opens with three items in parentheses, each separated by a semicolon. The first is a counter variable, which is i by convention. It is set initially to 0 (zero). The second is a truth condition, in this case, checking that the number i is less than the length of the colors array. That condition is checked each time the loop runs. And after each time the loop runs, the final item, i++, increments i by one.

Inside the loop in the example above, each color from the colors array is printed by the JavaScript console (see the book's companion website for instructions on how to access the console in your web browser). colors[i] ensures that each color will be printed, beginning with colors[0], which was what the i variable was assigned in the i = 0 portion of the for loop.

## FUNCTIONS AND FUNCTIONAL PROGRAMMING STYLE

Returning to the for loop above: it would be possible to write a reusable function to make it simpler to loop through each of the values in an array. That function could be called forEach:

```
function forEach(arr,func) {
  for (var i = 0; i < arr.length; i++) {
    func(arr[i]);
  }
}

var colors = ["red", "blue", "green"];
var animals = ["dog", "cat", "bird"];

forEach(colors, console.log);
// The JavaScript console will output:
// red
// blue
// green

forEach(animals, alert);
// Three annoying pop-ups that read
// "dog", "cat", and "bird" will appear
// in the browser
```

Functions can be used to store any pieces of code that are used repeatedly. A function created with this syntax must be given a name, like forEach for the function above. And when the function is declared, using the function keyword, it should specify the variables that the function needs. In this case, arr is an array, and func is any function. So written, the forEach function will work with any array and any function that can act on the array's primitive values.

## OBJECT-ORIENTED PROGRAMMING STYLE

JavaScript also permits an object-oriented programming style. Even built-in objects, like Array, can be modified by adding to their proto-type chains (MDN 2016b). Rather than create a forEach function, as in the functional style above, it's possible to add an each method to the Array prototype:

```
Array.prototype.each = function(func) {
  for (var i = 0; i < this.length; i++) {
    func(this[i]);
  }
  return this; // return the object a
  // method is called on
};
var colors = ["red", "blue", "green"];
colors.each(console.log);
// The JavaScript console will output:
// red
// blue
// green
```

Just like the forEach functional example above, this each method is not complete. Both the function and the method require additional code to handle errors. That's beyond the scope of this chapter. However, it's also important to note that because forEach is such a common way to walk through arrays, JavaScript now contains its own native forEach method on the Array object (MDN 2016c). So without declaring any of your own functions or methods, it's possible to just write:

```
var colors = ["red", "blue", "green"];

colors.forEach(alert);
```

```
// Three pop-up boxes appear: "red", "blue", "green"
```

The lesson here is always to look through the JavaScript documentation to discover whether a function or behavior that you need is already part of the language.

The primary difference between functional and object-oriented styles of JavaScript is that functional styles refer to a function and pass values to it. In pseudocode:

```
someFunction(someValue, someOtherValue);
```

By contrast, object-oriented styles call a method directly on an object, optionally passing the method additional values. In JavaScript, functions themselves can be passed in as values, as when `alert` was passed to `colors.forEach`. In pseudocode:

```
someObject.someMethod(someValue);
```

## NEXT STEPS

This chapter has covered the basics of JavaScript, and Chapter 20 will look at the use of libraries like jQuery to interact with the Document Object Model (DOM). But DOM-based progressive enhancement is better left until the HTML and CSS of a site are established. The next chapter returns to a focus on HTML and CSS and the foundations of mobile-first responsive web design.

## REFERENCES

Keith, Jeremy. 2005. *DOM Scripting: Web Design with JavaScript and the Document Object Model.* Berkeley, CA: Friends of Ed/Apress.

MDN. 2016a. "Lexical Grammar." https://developer.mozilla.org/en-US/docs/Web/JavaScript/Reference/Lexical_grammar#Keywords

MDN. 2016b. "Inheritance and the Prototype Chain." https://developer.mozilla.org/en-US/docs/Web/JavaScript/Inheritance_and_the_prototype_chain

MDN. 2016c. "Array.prototype.forEach()." https://developer.mozilla.org/en-US/docs/Web/JavaScript/Reference/Global_Objects/Array/forEach

# CHAPTER 14

# Mobile-First Responsive Design Foundations

HTML, CSS, and JavaScript form the technical foundation for web design. This chapter looks at a corresponding conceptual foundation. Now that phone and tablet access is swiftly overtaking traditional desktop and laptop computers as people's primary means of web access (Pew Research Center 2016), the web must be designed for mobile devices and a wider range of access conditions.

A site built with mobile-first responsive web design (MFRWD) delivers the same baseline HTML, CSS, and JavaScript to all devices accessing the site. That means no special mobile site, which would require doubling up on the number of pages and other assets that need to be written and updated to keep in sync multiple versions of the same site. That's not sustainable.

MFRWD also requires a major change in how people design for the web. When you're writing in a word processor or working in an image editor, you probably open the window containing your project to be as large as possible. For MFRWD, you want to make sure that the browser you use to preview your work is actually quite narrow, to simulate the experience of viewing your site on smaller screens. Firefox Developer Edition provides a special Responsive Design Mode for this purpose. Of course, as you work, you'd be wise to check your site on actual mobile devices. But the number one rule of MFRWD is to start by previewing your work in a very small viewport (Figure 14.1).

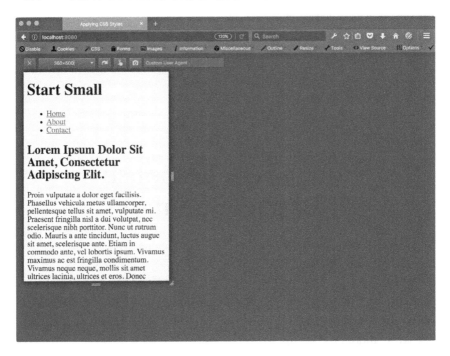

**Figure 14.1.** Start small: Firefox Developer Edition in Responsive Design Mode.

## HTML FOUNDATIONS: THE VIEWPORT META ELEMENT

Strictly speaking, HTML is a language reserved for providing only structured content. It should not contain any kinds of instructions as to how its content displays. But there is one important piece of metadata that belongs in your HTML for MFRWD: the **viewport meta element**. This piece of metadata instructs the browser as to how the document expects the viewport to behave.

Originally developed by Apple for the Safari browser on the iPhone, the viewport meta element is now recognized by browsers across a wide range of mobile platforms, including Android and Windows Phone. The documentation for the viewport meta element can be found at Safari's developer site (Apple Inc. 2016a).

When the first iPhone was released in 2007, there was no mobile web to speak of. Older, so-called feature phones sometimes came equipped with web browsers, but they displayed terribly broken

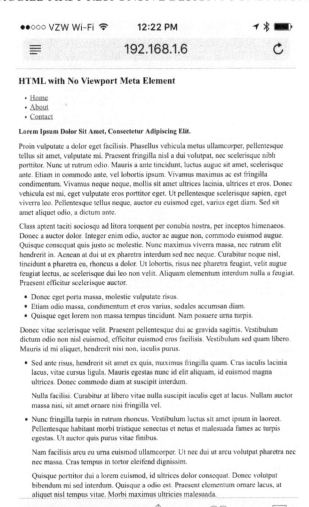

**Figure 14.2.**   Without the viewport meta element, Safari on iOS and other mobile browsers will display even unstyled HTML at unreadably small sizes.

versions of web pages and only after a very long wait over primitive cellular internet connections. To accommodate the web as it was in 2007, engineers at Apple decided to have the iPhone's Safari web browser pretend to be a desktop-sized screen.

By default, without a viewport meta element instructing it otherwise, Safari on iPhone behaves like it is 980 pixels wide. The web of

2007 was designed around screens that ranged between 1024 pixels wide to around 1300 pixels wide. Web designers also routinely designed pages that were 960 pixels wide. Why? Well, 960-pixel-wide designs fit comfortably, if snugly, on a 1024-pixel wide monitor when the browser window is fully maximized to use every last pixel of space. 960 is also a beautiful number for grid-based design (see Chapter 18). 960 divides evenly by 2, 3, 4, 5, 6, 8, 10, and 12. Being equally divisible by so many different divisors means that a 960-pixel-wide design can be divided evenly into many different possible column grids. A relic of that era lives on at the 960 Grid System (http://960.gs/).

Back to the iPhone: given that much of the web in 2007 was designed for 960-pixel-wide pages, by setting Safari to display pages in an apparent viewport width of 980 pixels, most web pages would be displayed in full on the iPhone.

Of course, there is a major catch: to pretend to be 980 pixels wide (far larger than the true pixel-width of the original iPhone itself, which was a mere 320 pixels wide), Safari had to shrink and effectively zoom out from the page. Reading the web on an iPhone in 2007 required tapping different page elements to zoom in close enough to read them.

The viewport meta element can be used to change the default, zoomed-out behavior by passing it certain values as described in Safari's developer documentation (Apple Inc. 2014, under "Viewport").

## Correctly Setting the Viewport

The viewport meta element must be used carefully, though. Disabling user scalability via the user-scalable property, for example, reduces the accessibility of a page and makes it user hostile. So here are the basic, user-friendly values that should be in your HTML's viewport meta element:

```
<meta name="viewport"
  content="width=device-width,initial-scale=1.0" />
```

The meta element takes a name attribute whose value is viewport, and requires the content attribute to list all of the viewport settings

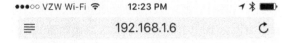

# HTML with A Correct Viewport Meta Element

- Home
- About
- Contact

## Lorem Ipsum Dolor Sit Amet, Consectetur Adipiscing Elit.

Proin vulputate a dolor eget facilisis. Phasellus vehicula metus ullamcorper, pellentesque tellus sit amet, vulputate mi. Praesent fringilla nisl a dui volutpat, nec scelerisque nibh porttitor. Nunc ut rutrum odio. Mauris a ante tincidunt, luctus augue sit amet, scelerisque ante. Etiam in commodo ante, vel lobortis ipsum. Vivamus maximus ac est fringilla condimentum. Vivamus neque neque, mollis sit amet ultrices lacinia, ultrices et eros. Donec vehicula est mi, eget vulputate eros porttitor eget. Ut pellentesque scelerisque sapien, eget viverra leo. Pellentesque tellus neque, auctor eu euismod eget, varius eget diam. Sed sit amet aliquet odio, a dictum ante.

**Figure 14.3.**    With the viewport meta element set correctly, the HTML foundation for mobile-first responsive design is in place.

for displaying the page. The value of `content` may look a little strange, because there are no quotation marks after the equals signs. But remember that `content=""` is the only HTML part. Everything inside is just a value that browsers understand.

A mobile-first design that conforms to the dimensions of all browsers requires the value `width=device-width`. By default,

Safari behaves as though it were 980 pixels wide, so that would be the same as writing width=980 here. But rather than giving width a specific value, this method uses the special keyword device-width, which instructs mobile browsers to display the page at exactly the width the device itself actually is, whatever that width might be. And that is why it's useful to declare the viewport's settings in HTML: absent custom CSS, mobile devices will render their own default styles, but in a way that conforms to the device's native resolution and size.

Next, still within the content attribute value, comes the initial-scale=1.0 setting, which instructs the browser to zoom in at 100 percent, which is actually no zoom at all. A value less than 1.0/100 percent would be zoomed out (much like 980 pixels forces a phone to do), while a value greater than 1.0/100 percent would be zoomed in. initial-scale=1.0 leaves the user's device alone, neither zooming in nor zooming out.

For several years, that was all that was needed to make a maximally accessible, user-friendly viewport meta element.

Unfortunately, some designers apparently believed that dropping that <meta> element into their HTML was all that was required to make a mobile site. If they were doing so on a page designed to be 960 pixels wide (and specified as such in the CSS, with a property like width: 960px), the viewport meta element would actually show only a tiny slice of their page on the screen.

Additionally, advertising networks continued to push down ads with large pixel dimensions, which were sometimes at odds with even a true mobile-first responsive design. So Apple made the decision to create an additional default behavior for Safari, namely, that it would shrink a page down until the very largest element fit, effectively zooming the page back out again. And as I discovered when preparing a page for a workshop that included long URLs displayed on the page, even something like a long URL or a piece of example source code can trigger Safari to shrink the rest of the page.

So beginning with iOS 9, one more value must be added to the viewport meta element: shrink-to-fit, set to no (Apple Inc. 2016b, under "Viewport Changes"). So the complete viewport meta element looks like this:

```
<meta name="viewport"
  content="width=device-width,
    initial-scale=1.0,shrink-to-fit=no">
```

`shrink-to-fit=no` instructs Safari, and other mobile browsers that recognize the viewport meta element, to maintain the width and scale values as set earlier in the viewport meta element.

## Incorrectly Setting the Viewport

There are other values that can be set on the viewport meta element. For completeness, let me briefly list them and explain why they should be avoided:

- `height`: People are accustomed to having to scroll vertically down a page once content is no longer visible. There is no need to set a height on the page's viewport meta element, and weird things can happen if you do. Omit this value.
- `minimum-scale` and `maximum-scale`: These are used to limit how far in and out a user can zoom. Web designers have no business making those decisions for users, who should be able to zoom in or out of a page as far as their device will let them. Do not set these values, ever.
- `user-scalable`: This value is even more user-hostile than the `minimum-` and `maximum-scale` properties, as it will fully disable a user's device from zooming in or out of a page. At one time, Safari on iOS had a bug that inflated the text size of a page on the shift from portrait to landscape orientation unless the `user-scalable` property was set. That is no longer acceptable practice, however, and the text-inflation behavior can be more accessibly overridden by setting `-webkit-text-size-adjust: 100%` in your CSS on the `html` selector (see Chapter 17).

Stick only to the viewport meta element as described above and listed in the Rapid Prototyping Kit's HTML files. Any updates to the viewport meta element will be reflected at this book's companion website.

## CSS FOUNDATIONS: MOBILE-FIRST CSS AND MIN-WIDTH MEDIA QUERIES

A stylesheet organized for mobile-first design puts all mobile/small-screen styles at the top of the stylesheet, immediately following any CSS reset styles. For larger screens, media queries expressed with the min-width condition build your site design up in ever-larger increments. Here's an example that changes the base font-size for a page on a larger view, at a breakpoint (min-width) of 990 pixels:

```
/* Mobile-first styles, outside any media query */
html { font-size: 1.6em; }


@media screen and (min-width: 990px) {
  html { font-size: 1.8em; }
}
```

On viewports smaller than 990 pixels, the text will be sized at 1.6em. That would be the mobile-first style, outside of any media query. On viewports 990 pixels and up, the font-size is 1.8em. Because larger screens are often farther away from the reader's eyes, it's often necessary to increase the size of the text to keep it comfortably readable.

A media query is structured with the @media keyword, followed by a recognized CSS media type. For screen-based designs, that media is screen; for print, it's print. The and allows you to query the media, with a condition written in parentheses. With a min-width: 990px query, the browser will only apply the selectors nested inside the media query when the query is true ("Yes, this view is currently at least 990 pixels wide.") To improve the media query, it is better to express the min-width conditions in ems. 990 pixels at a default 16-pixel em would be min-width: 61.875em ($990 \div 16 = 61.875$). Note that even when the base font-size is changed, browsers activate em-based media queries on their default em size, which is typically 16 pixels.

Web tutorials and other books are full of advice for using max-width media queries, including in the first edition of Ethan Marcotte's (2011) famous book *Responsive Web Design*, which was instrumental in making RWD a widespread practice. However, max-width is better suited to an existing design that must be scaled back down for mobile access. New sites should always be written with `min-width` media queries, with base styles written for mobile devices first, outside of any media query.

Stylesheets that list all base styles outside of a media query achieve two things. First, the few legacy browsers still in use that do not understand media queries will still receive the mobile layout of a site. For mobile browsers, that's perfect. For desktop browsers, a more accessible experience of a page is possible if users just resize their browser windows a little narrower. Second, you will repeat far fewer styles, resulting in a much shorter and smaller stylesheet. Colors as well as typefaces tend to remain constant across all sizes of a design. So too does the baseline grid of text, if it's expressed in ems (see Chapter 17). Setting colors and other baseline styles in the mobile-first area of the stylesheet, outside of a media query, frees you to add only those styles that need adjusting as the screen viewing your site gets larger. Usually that means adjusting only a few things, like your base `font-size` or the widths and dimensions of content areas on the design. `min-width` media queries help you adhere to **the DRY principle**: Don't Repeat Yourself.

## JAVASCRIPT FOUNDATIONS: MEDIA-QUERY-AWARE PROGRESSIVE ENHANCEMENT

Mobile-first responsive web design requires only thoughtfully written HTML and CSS. But there are roles for JavaScript to play in certain situations, such as Scott Jehl's Repond.js (`https://github.com/scottjehl/Respond`) **polyfill** that helps older browsers that do not natively support media queries still render responsive designs (see the discussion of polyfills in Chapter 20). Of course, there is never any guarantee that a user will have JavaScript available, especially in an older browser, so the inclusion of a polyfill is a progressive enhancement that renders only in ideal situations. That means that a mobile-first stylesheet is necessary to make your page accessible on mobile devices and older browsers that do not have JavaScript.

Executing JavaScript that is sensitive to responsive design is a particularly interesting challenge. Although it would be possible to replicate media-query breakpoints in JavaScript itself, Jeremy Keith (2012) developed a simple technique for using JavaScript to read an "otherwise useless" style in CSS. Keith's technique uses the :after pseudoelement on the body selector coupled with the CSS content property, which takes the name of the particular media query that is active. Repeating the font-size switching CSS from above to include properties that can be read in JavaScript:

```
html { font-size: 1.6em; }
  body:after {
    content: "mobile";
    display: none;
  }
  @media screen and (min-width: 990px) {
    html { font-size: 1.8em; }
    body:after {
      content: "medium";
    }
  }
}
```

JavaScript can then access the content value computed for the body:after selector at any given time. A custom JavaScript function that I've called responsiveSize(), which builds off of Keith's technique and sample code, can handle the job:

```
function responsiveSize(target) {
  // size will read the content property on
  // body:after
  var size = window
    .getComputedStyle(document.body,':after')
    .getPropertyValue('content');
  if (size.indexOf(target) == -1) {
    // indexOf string method is -1 if
    // the target isn't in size object
    return false;
    // return false (not the target)
  }
  else {
    return true; // otherwise, return true
```

```
    }
}

if (responsiveSize('medium')) {
    // JavaScript to run at medium size
}
```

Adding the content values (`medium`, `large`, etc.) should wait until all of your breakpoints are set, so you don't end up with something weird like `extra-medium`. Note, too, that `display: none` on the mobile-first view ensures that the CSS-generated content does not appear on the page, nor is it read aloud by screen readers. And because that example stylesheet uses `min-width` media queries, it is not necessary to repeat the `display: none` style again. It's DRY, having already been set in the mobile-first area of the stylesheet. A complete version of this script with examples is available on this book's companion website.

## NEXT STEPS

Mobile-first responsive web design invites designing first for small screen display, and carefully using CSS media queries and perhaps media-query-aware JavaScript to build up for larger screens. Specific techniques for that are the subject of the book's remaining chapters.

The next chapter describes the files in the Rapid Prototyping Kit, which provide a basic foundation for building your own responsively designed site.

## REFERENCES

Apple Inc. 2014. "Supported Meta Tags." *Safari HTML Reference*. https://dev eloper.apple.com/library/safari/documentation/AppleApplications/Refere nce/SafariHTMLRef/Articles/MetaTags.html

Apple Inc. 2016a. "Configuring the Viewport." *Safari Web Content Guide*. https://developer.apple.com/library/ios/documentation/AppleApplications /Reference/SafariWebContent/UsingtheViewport/UsingtheViewport.html

Apple Inc. 2016b. "Safari 9.0." *What's New in Safari*. https://developer.apple .com/library/content/releasenotes/General/WhatsNewInSafari/Articles /Safari_9_0.html

Keith, Jeremy. 2012. "Conditional CSS." *Adactio: Journal* (January 12). https:// adactio.com/journal/5429/

Marcotte, Ethan. 2011. *Responsive Web Design*. New York: A Book Apart.

Pew Research Center. 2016. "Smartphone Ownership and Internet Usage Continues to Climb in Emerging Economies." (February 22). http://www.pewglobal.org/2016/02/22/smartphone-ownership-and-internet-usage-continues-to-climb-in-emerging-economies/

# CHAPTER 15

# Rapid Prototyping and Local Development

Making visible progress on your website will help you stay motivated to complete it. The Rapid Prototyping Kit (RPK) provides a foundational set of files for building a mobile-first, responsive website in compliance with web standards for HTML, CSS, and JavaScript. You can download the RPK from the book's companion website, `http://webpg.es/` or fork it on GitHub at `https://github.com/webpges/rpk/`, if you're interested in using Git with your work (see the instructions on the book's companion website). Once you have a copy, you can open, manipulate, and customize the RPK on any operating system (Windows, macOS, Linux) and edit its files using any good text editor.

This chapter looks at the benefits of rapid prototyping and the process of building a site with the RPK: sketching out a rough layout, structuring content in HTML, and designing site styles in CSS. Setting up a small web server suited to local development, on your own computer, makes it possible to test your site thoroughly before it ever reaches the public-facing web. Specific design and development techniques are explored further in subsequent chapters. But consider this chapter part road map, part crash course.

## BENEFITS OF RAPID PROTOTYPING

Rapid prototyping means getting straight to work on a site. Some books suggest starting the process of web design by developing wireframes, sketches, mockups, and other kinds of throwaway prototypes that aren't part of the final project. There are a few of those books listed in the "Resources for the Future" section near the end of this book, if that kind of prototyping suits you. While those types of development techniques have their place and their benefits, my preference is to get to the work of actually building a site as quickly as possible and looking at it in the browser. Time is precious, so it's better not to spend too much time on work that's going to be thrown away, and better still to be doing things that directly reveal the affordances and constraints of web design with HTML, CSS, and JavaScript.

Keep in mind that a website is never really finished. There are just periods of time when it might not change much. Instead of trying to build the perfect site before going live with it, it's better to get something together that works basically the way you want it to. Then you can devote yourself to the site's ongoing improvement and expansion over time, which is even easier to do if your work is supported by a version control system (see Chapter 6).

As Chapter 3 urged, have some content on hand as you begin to prototype your website. A few rough sketches in a notebook can help guide your design. But the best first step in building a website is to gather and create a representative portion of the site's content. The site's actual content, not placeholder text or stock images, should drive the design of your site. Keep in mind that content may change over time and in response to your design. So stay flexible.

## THE COMPONENTS OF RAPID PROTOTYPING

Rapid prototyping requires only a text editor, a browser, and a local development server, such as the Node.js `http-server`. Those technologies were described in Chapter 5. The RPK provides a few starter files to get you writing more quickly.

One of the reasons that WYSIWYG web editors remain popular is that they enable people to build pages quickly and serve as all-in-one development environments. The pages that WYSIWYGs spit out may not be standards compliant, mobile friendly, lightweight, or easily revised, but they are pages.

## EATING MY OWN DOG FOOD

Many open-source projects try to live by a phrase that I have come to love: "Eat your own dog food." The idea behind this phrase is that people who create digital materials (software, templates, plugins, etc.) for others should use the materials themselves.

That is how the RPK came to be: instead of reinventing the wheel for each of my web projects, I started building a collection of files and directories that would put a lot of things in place that I would otherwise be writing from scratch. I've refined those files over the years based on what I'm teaching in my web design courses.

So in many of my HTML sites, including the site that supports this book, I have eaten my own dog food: they are all based on the RPK, with modifications as necessary. And that is exactly the point of the RPK. It's just a start, and you are supposed to modify it to suit your own needs.

Handwritten, standards-compliant pages can be written quickly, too, and edited and revised even more quickly. The RPK's files and directories are a solid start meant to help you transition from the sketching and planning aspects of your site development to full-on site creation. I call it *prototyping*, but this activity builds more than the throwaway prototypes from wireframing or mockups. This is the real work of building your site. What makes it prototype-like is your attitude: if something doesn't work, modify and improve it. Otherwise, throw the problem piece away and start anew. Commit your good work to Git.

When I am building a new site, I often keep in mind the words of Eric Raymond (2001): "You often don't really understand the problem until after the first time you implement a solution." For this reason, "be ready to start over at least once" (25).

## THE RAPID PROTOTYPING KIT (RPK)

The Rapid Prototyping Kit is a set of foundational files and directories for quickly building a website. Because I use the RPK in my own web design work, I continue to make subtle improvements to it. The book's companion site and the RPK's Git repository will list any changes to the RPK as described here, but the version of the RPK referred to in this book will also always be available. Below is a rough outline of the RPK.

## The Rapid Prototyping Kit Directories

Be sure to clone or download and unzip the RPK's `.zip` file into a directory of your choosing. Make sure it's somewhere on your file system that you can remember. I always create a `Projects/` directory off of my home directory, and keep each of my current major projects in its own directory inside of `Projects/`.

Once you clone or extract the RPK, you will find a few files, described on the book's companion site, plus a directory called `site/` that contains all of the RPK's other files and directories. There is also a `demo/` directory, which is structured the same as the `site/` directory and shows off examples and ideas for how the RPK can be used.

The RPK's `site/` directory is structured as a root web directory, which contains all of the files and directories that make up a website. Eventually you will need to transfer the contents of the `site/` directory (but not the directory itself) to the root directory provided by your web host, once you get to the point of uploading your site (see Chapter 24). But for development purposes, you can build and test your site using the `http-server` app from Node.js. Just change directories into `site/` and run `http-server` (you can also change directories into `demo/` and run `http-server` to try it out). This example command-line interaction assumes you have a `Projects` directory containing the `rpk` directory; adjust your paths accordingly:

```
$ cd Projects/rpk/site
$ http-server
Starting up http-server, serving ./
Available on:
  http://127.0.0.1:8080
  http://192.168.1.6:8080
Hit CTRL-C to stop the server
```

In addition to some HTML files, which are described below, `site/` contains several directories:

- `css/`: A directory for all CSS files; the RPK includes `screen` `.css` and `print.css` for screen and print design, respectively.
  - `gfx/`: A subdirectory inside of `css/` for any graphics loaded by CSS, such as with the `background-image` property.
- `js/`: A directory for all JavaScript files. `site.js` contains all of the JavaScript included with the RPK.
- `media/`: A directory to contain all of the media content for a site, organized into these subdirectories:
  - `audio/`: A subdirectory for all audio files, probably as MP3s.
  - `img/`: A subdirectory for all image files such as JPEGs, GIFs, or PNGs.
  - `video/`: A subdirectory for all video files (see Chapter 19).

The Rapid Prototyping Kit includes directories for each kind of web-native site content that you might wish to post. Chapter 21 provides guidance for adding your own directories to structure and organize your site architecture. The RPK's directory structure can be changed as needed, but if you are new to web design, the default directory structure should help keep the contents of your site organized.

## The Rapid Prototyping HTML Files

In addition to a directory structure intended to help you organize your site's content, the RPK includes an HTML file containing a global structure for all site pages. This file is named `prototype.html`. True to its name, `prototype-with-comments.html` contains the same HTML as `prototype.html` but that explains in detail all of the prototyping features.

The `index.html` file, which has the exact same starter HTML as `prototype.html`, is where you can start building your site. Make copies of `prototype.html` as you need additional pages, once you have added custom metadata and structures as described below. For example, to start an About page in `about/`, on the command line you would do the following inside of `site/`:

```
$ mkdir about
$ cp prototype.html about/index.html
```

That will create a directory-based URL similar to `http://example`
`.com/about/`. So will creating the directory and copying the file with
the GUI on your operating system. The `index.html` portion of the
URL can be omitted, as almost all web servers will serve that automatically when `/about/` is requested. You will need to change paths in
`about/index.html` that point to your CSS and JavaScript files (see
Chapter 21).

The `<head>` area of the RPK includes the `<title>` tag as well as
meta elements for the character encoding and viewport (see Chapter
14). There are also meta tags for use with the Open Graph protocol for
sharing your work on social sites (see Chapter 25), but they are commented out by default. Remove the comments to use the Open Graph
meta tags. If you choose not to use them, it's best to delete those lines.

The RPK's `<body>` is sectioned using structural elements described
in Chapter 16. The RPK's HTML and accessibility features will help
you begin to structure your site's page content immediately, and enable
you to build CSS over the top of that structure for a standards-compliant, responsive page design.

Most web pages, regardless of their purpose, share a few common
areas. The RPK includes them:

- A header with the site name and tagline for branding purposes
- A navigation area, inside the header, to help users find their
  way to other pages on the site
- A content area, `<main id="content">`, that might consist
  of one or more subdivisions of content, using `<article>` or
  `<section>` as the outer sectioning element (see Chapter 16)
- A footer area with copyright and licensing information and
  other information about the page or site

The next several chapters describe the purpose and general design approaches to those structures, which are shared across all pages in your
site.

The RPK's HTML also reflects a sensible source order, meaning its
ordering of content divisions—header, navigation, content, footer—
would make sense and be useful even in the absence of page design, or
if the page were being read aloud to a low-vision user. It also works well

in a small-screen setting, where the page would be displayed as a single column, in the order described in the HTML.

## The Rapid Prototyping CSS Files

One of the reasons that beginners struggle with CSS design is that it's often a toxic mix of designing for a page, but against the browser. When you view a plain HTML file, without any of your own CSS styles, the web browser itself is actually styling the page with its own built-in set of CSS styles. And every browser is a little different in its default styles. That makes cross-browser CSS design unnecessarily frustrating, even for simple things like sizing text.

That is why the RPK's screen and print CSS files open with a modified, minified version of Eric Meyer's (2011) reset CSS, which has the effect of removing any styles that might be added by a web browser. It removes all margin and padding around elements, makes uniform all of the font sizes on the different headings, and ensures that browsers unaware of HTML's newer block elements, like `<article>` and `<aside>`, display them as block elements with `display: block`. The full, readable reset CSS can be found in the RPK in `css/_reset.css`. I make it a habit of naming reference files such as that with underscores, to remind myself they are not to be linked to or used directly on a site.

The basic lesson from reset CSS is that you have to specify every aspect of your design. Everything is completely unstyled: there is no space around any of the headers, paragraphs, or lists, which lack even bullets. The idea behind this is that you are now free to style your page exactly as you want it to appear. If you need bullets on your unordered lists, for example, you have to specify them in your CSS. It's potentially extra work to add bullets, yes, but only if you want those and other design features to appear. If, for example, you want no bullets next to your navigation list, no problem. They're not there anyway, because the reset CSS removed them. But if you do want bullets, you can be more confident that they will appear as you intend across standards-compliant web browsers.

Just be sure to begin writing your styles below all of the reset CSS, or your styles, too, will be reset. There's a comment in the CSS file indicating where you should begin writing your styles. The `screen.css` file opens with a few useful styles for site typography (see Chapter 17) and responsive media (see Chapter 19). The `print.css` file contains those plus a few additional styles for handling black and white printing and outputting the contents of URLs when printing a page with links. Full comments and details are in the `print.css` file.

Remember, too, only to include a single `screen.css` and `print.css` file for your site. All of your pages should link to `screen.css` and `print.css`, so that changes to your site's display on screen or in print can be made by editing just one CSS file. See Chapter 16's technique of adding a class to `<body>` when a particular page needs to deviate from your shared styles.

### The Rapid Prototyping JavaScript File

The RPK JavaScript file includes a few progressively enhanced utility functions, including swapping out the `nojs` class with `hasjs` on the RPK's `<html>` tag (see Chapter 20). It also loads the jQuery library, should you want to build your site with jQuery. Full details of the RPK JavaScript appear in the `site.js` file's comments.

## WRITING AND DESIGNING WITH THE RPK

Chapters 16 through 20 cover the specifics of working with different aspects of your page structure and design, but here is a rough outline of how to proceed with creating your website using the RPK. Note that this is rarely a linear process; for example, your content may force you to rethink your page design, and vice versa. Still, every writer should address each of these tasks as part of web writing and design, with or without the RPK:

- **Generate and gather your text and image content.** You will need to have structured HTML available before you can test your design work in CSS; so drafting your text, and preparing some images and media (see Chapter 19), will allow you to accurately describe the structure of your page content as discussed in Chapter 16.
- **Set up your basic metadata, branding, and rough navigation.** Edit the `prototype.html` file to set up the basic metadata,

branding, and navigation for your site and save it, so that you can create pages based on your own starter page that has most of your shared page features in place. You can replace the RPK's starter `index.html` with the contents of your own modified `prototype.html`, if you like. Chapter 23 introduces general approaches for building reusable sets of shared content features on dynamically generated sites.

- **Develop a representative page from your site.** The urge that most designers have is to start with the home page, but it is often very different from the content pages of a site. I recommend starting with an About page. Not only will that likely be representative of your site's other pages, but its contents might help you to clarify what other pages the site should include.

- **Mark up your text and image content in HTML.** Once you have a rough draft of your content, start tagging it with HTML, particularly its headings, paragraphs, and lists (see Chapter 16).

- **Begin to develop site typography.** Working with a mobile-sized viewport window, start establishing in your CSS a baseline grid and typographic scale as described in Chapter 17. The book's companion site has additional guidance on web typography and typeface selection.

- **Sketch out a rough layout for your site, and start building it in CSS inside media queries.** This is mostly about geography, not the site's complete look: As the screen viewing your site gets larger, where will the header and footer appear? The navigation? Your content and subcontent areas? Your rough sketch will guide your work in Chapter 18 on responsive grid-based page layout. Once you know you are able to position your page elements where you want them, you can use your image editor to create a striking design, or you can experiment further by writing your design directly in CSS.

- **Use an image editor to prepare responsive images.** With your layout in place, you can begin to finalize dimensions, particularly widths, for presenting each image on your page across different viewports and layouts (see Chapter 19).

## Cultivating a Long-Term Attitude toward Site Development

A website is, to some extent, always in draft form. You will want to make changes to your content as your career progresses, or as your business or organization grows. Your design might start to look dated, and you will want to update it, too. Here are some basic habits to help cultivate a long-term attitude toward site development (see also Chapter 9 on sustainability):

- **Write as little source as possible.** Beginners in my web design classes tend to write way more HTML markup and CSS styles than are necessary. I think this happens because they are nervous about working in these new languages, and expect that interesting pages will have lots of markup and CSS styles. That is not true. The guidance in the chapters that follow, along with examples at the book's companion site and in the RPK `demo/` directory, will show you how to write lean source, which makes a site much easier to revise and maintain.

- **Think about relationships between your page elements.** One of the strengths of both CSS and JavaScript is their leverage of relationships between page elements. For example, perhaps there is a paragraph you want to display entirely in bold, so you first write something like this:

```
<p><strong>
  This paragraph's text is all in bold.
</strong></p>
```

But when you see that kind of markup, where two or more tags mark the same content, it's time to rethink your strategy. One alternative to that use of the `<strong>` tag is to add a class to the paragraph, like `<p class="important">` and then in the CSS specify `.important { font-weight: bold; }`. Don't forget to remove from your markup any unnecessary tags, like `<strong>` in that example, when you make those types of revisions.

- **Think about the general, then move to the specific.** The advice above suggests to begin site design by working with a representative content page from your site. That approach should help you think about what most pages will include structurally and how they will be designed. From that, you can design pages, such as the home page, whose structure and design are different from most other pages on the site. Chapters 16 and 18 suggest using a class on the body tag to give you a hook to style different types of pages, while maintaining lean source and a single CSS file.

- **Devote a little time every week or so to improve something on your site.** Like any other skill, your web writing and design skills depend on frequent exercise. Coming back to your site regularly, as your schedule allows, will keep your current skills fresh and help you to learn new ones. See the "Resources for the Future" section of this book for material that will advance your abilities and keep you current on the latest and best approaches to web design.
- **Use Git or another version control system.** If it has been a while since you last worked on your site, the git log command should be all that it takes to help you remember what you were doing. Add and commit comments with to-do lists in them in your source code, too, so you know what to work on next.

## NEXT STEPS

The remaining chapters in this section of the book take a finer-grained approach to the major components of your pages, beginning Chapter 16 with text content structured in HTML. Chapter 17 will look at setting up typographic styles for your site, while Chapter 18 looks more closely at page layout. Chapter 19 will cover the preparation and delivery of responsive media.

## REFERENCES

Meyer, Eric. 2011. "CSS Tools: Reset CSS." http://meyerweb.com/eric/tools/css/reset/

Meyer, Eric. 2011. "CSS Tools: Reset CSS." http://meyerweb.com/eric/tools/css/reset/

Raymond, Eric S. 2001. *The Cathedral and the Bazaar: Musings on Linux and Open Source by an Accidental Revolutionary*. Revised and expanded ed. Sebastopol, CA: O'Reilly Media.

# CHAPTER 16

# Text Content

The purpose of HTML is to structurally describe all of the content that makes up a page. This chapter walks through a systematic approach to marking up text content in HTML. After touching on a single necessary content tag in the `<head>` area, the chapter covers the basic HTML block tags that should mark all page content, including branding and navigation: headings, paragraphs, and lists. Related blocks can then be grouped into larger semantic structures using the new sectioning elements introduced in HTML5.

## CONTENT IN THE HEAD AREA

There is only one content tag of consequence in the `<head>` area of HTML documents (see Chapter 11). That is the `<title>` tag, whose contents appear in browser tabs and as the links in search results.

Ideally, a title tag should include both the name of the site and the specific page.

Putting the site first, either its name or domain, is generally good practice unless there is a reasonable expectation that someone would have multiple tabs opened on the same site:

```
<title>Example.com: About Us</title>
```

If multiple tabs are open, of course, they may be truncated to *Example .com* in that case, making it difficult to keep them organized. While it's usually safe to assume someone will only have one or possibly two tabs open on your site at once, if you're building a site that functions as a reference or guide, it might be better to open with the name of the page title:

```
<title>About Us: Example.com</title>
```

Use only colons to separate portions of the text inside of `<title>`. Other punctuation marks are used on the web, including double colons (`Example.com :: About`) or pipe characters, `|`. Avoid using stand-alone punctuation to create design in `<title>` tags, as they will be read aloud in screen readers: *Example dot com colon colon about* in the double-colon example. And while some sites separate title components with a dash, note that some screen readers speak the contents of the title tag with *dash* followed by the name of the browser (Krantz 2004). That means that users of screen readers may habitually skip to the next section of the page as soon as they hear *dash*.

There is a set of `<meta>` tags that can be used in the `<head>` for social sharing. Those are discussed in Chapter 25.

## CONTENT IN THE BODY AREA

All of a page's content that is rendered in a browser's viewport appears in the `<body>` area of an HTML document. That is where you will spend the majority of your time writing HTML. The rest of this chapter looks at systematically marking up content, starting with blocks, which might contain phrases or inline elements, and then grouping blocks into specialized sectioning elements to add global structure to your page.

For sites with complex designs that vary slightly from page to page, it's useful to add a class on `<body>`. For example, a Résumé page might have `<body class="resume">` and an About page might have `<body class="about">`. Your CSS can then use that class as part of a descendant selector to make adjustments for a particular page or section of your site (see Chapter 12 on descendant selectors).

## STRUCTURAL BLOCKS: HEADINGS, PARAGRAPHS, AND LISTS

You can build a solid web page using only headings, paragraphs, and lists. Why? Well, most writing is made up of headings, paragraphs, and

## CONTENT MODELS IN HTML5

The HTML5 specification defines a more complex taxonomy of content models than *block*, *inline*, and *sectioning*, which are the simpler terms used in this chapter. The terms are different, but whether something is described as *inline* or *phrasing content* (the HTML5 term) should have no impact on how you write structural HTML.

See the book's companion site for additional information about the content models specified in HTML5, if the topic interests you.

lists. On a well-structured HTML page, every piece of content is ultimately part of a heading, paragraph, or list.

Conveniently enough, there are three basic types of structural blocks in HTML for marking up written content: headings, paragraphs, and lists. Blocks are nothing more than text that, in the absence of any fancy formatting (such as a plain text email), would probably be separated by empty lines:

```
Primary Colors


There are three primary colors that occur in nature.
They are:


Red
Yellow
Blue
```

Marked up in HTML, those blocks of text could be described semantically with the heading, paragraph, and list tags:

```
<h1>Primary Colors</h1>
<p>
 There are three primary colors that occur in
 nature. They are:
</p>
<ul>
  <li>Red</li>
```

```
<li>Yellow</li>
<li>Blue</li>
</ul>
```

Let's look at each type of block piece by piece.

## Headings

There are six levels of headings in HTML. `<h1>` is a top-level heading; `<h2>` a subheading; `<h3>` a sub-subheading, and so on. Stylistically, it's usually better to limit your use of `<h1>` to once or twice a page; `<h2>` can be used often, as can `<h3>`, provided that `<h3>` is used for subheadings that separate content introduced by an `<h2>`.

When using headings, though, remember that their purpose is to break up long stretches of text with meaningful labels. `<h1>` might provide the site title (as in the RPK). `<h2>` can mark up the titles of individual pages, whose major sections are subdivided by `<h3>` tags; the sections labeled by `<h3>` tags could then be broken up further by `<h4>` tags.

Consider a concrete example. Imagine the markup for a résumé; taking away all of the content and leaving only the headings, it might look something like:

```
<h2>Résumé</h2>
  <h3>Objective</h3>
  <h3>Work Experience</h3>
    <h4>Industry</h4>
    <h4>Government</h4>
  <h3>Education</h3>
  <h3>Software Skills</h3>
```

The indentations in that example are only to enhance readability of the HTML source code (see Chapter 10). Particularly for the two `<h4>` tags, indents also illustrate that the heading tags are used to further subdivide content under a shared heading, not for enumeration. I once had a web design student who kept adding more and more numbers to his headings each time he used one. When I told him there was no such thing as an `<h27>` tag, he took the news pretty hard. The most minor subheading in HTML is `<h6>`.

## Paragraphs

There is only one paragraph tag in HTML: `<p>`. You should use the paragraph tag only to describe paragraphs of text—and nothing else. If something is structurally a heading, do not use the paragraph tag. I also often see beginners misuse the paragraph tag like this:

```
<p><h2>This is So Wrong</h2></p>
```

I'm not quite sure why beginners tend to do that. I suspect it may have something to do with word processors displaying the paragraph mark (or *pilcrow*), ¶, after every break (including after headings and lists). But reason it out, HTML-style: if something is a heading, it's a heading—not a paragraph. Paragraph tags should appear only when you have a need to describe content whose structure is an actual paragraph, not a heading or a list. Do not use the paragraph tag as an all-purpose tag. Be sure you're marking up at least a complete sentence or a standalone phrase. Otherwise, use a heading or a list tag.

## Lists

Lists are an extremely useful structural element in HTML. In addition to helping readers quickly read through content, lists are also useful for marking up site features such as navigation and menus, and even for postal addresses and contact information.

There are three types of lists in HTML: ordered (`<ol>`), unordered (`<ul>`), and definition (`<dl>`). Individual items in ordered and unordered lists are marked up with list item tags (`<li>`):

```
<li>Red</li>
<li>Yellow</li>
<li>Blue</li>
```

A good approach to marking up lists is to begin with the list items first. Then, determine whether there is any specific order to the items: for example, if they are steps in a process, or an enumerated list of things, they should be grouped using the `<ol>` (ordered list) tag. If the items are more or less in random order or if their order does not matter, as with the primary colors, group the list items with the `<ul>` (unordered list) tag:

## SPECIAL CHARACTERS

The HTML specification defines a set of **character entities**, which a browser will display as a special character. HTML character entities must be used if your text content includes angle brackets, which would be interpreted as part of HTML tags, and the ampersand, because it is used to indicate the start of an entity. The three characters for which you must use entities are:

```
&lt; to display <
&gt; to display >
&amp; to display &
```

The HTML specification includes many other character entities, but do not use them. Other than the three character listed above, which should always be presented as entities, pages encoded as UTF-8 should include special characters directly in the HTML source code.

Word processing programs and certain operating systems will create some special characters automatically, including typographers' quotes and even the copyright symbol, ©, if you type (c). Your text editor may also make certain substitutions for you, such as replacing double hyphens with em dashes. To insert special characters in your source code, including emoji, search the web to find out how to access a list of the nonkeyboard characters for your operating system. Certain operating systems also support special modifier keys for inserting em dashes and accented Latin characters.

```
<ul>
  <li>Red</li>
  <li>Yellow</li>
  <li>Blue</li>
</ul>
```

Navigation areas are structurally just lists of links:

```
<ul>
  <li><a href="/">Home</a></li>
  <li><a href="/about/">About</a></li>
  <li><a href="/contact/">Contact</a></li>
</ul>
```

This chapter will return to the topic of navigation with the <nav> sectioning element. Chapter 21 goes into greater depth about site architecture, including navigational problems and their solutions.

The syntax for definition lists is more complex than ordered and unordered lists. Definition lists are grouped with the <dl> tag, and include one or more definition term tags (<dt>) followed by an associated definition tag, <dd>:

```
<dl>
  <dt>CSS</dt>
  <dd>
    Cascading Style Sheets, the design
    language of the web.
  </dd>
  <dt>HTML</dt>
  <dt>XHTML</dt>
  <dd>
    Hypertext Markup Language, sometimes
    Extensible Hypertext Markup Language,
    the structural language of the web.
  </dd>
</dl>
```

Although semantically very useful, definition lists can be challenging to style because there is no element allowed in HTML for grouping <dt> tags with their associated <dd> tags. For that reason, it's sometimes better to use nested ordered or unordered lists rather than definition lists.

## Nested Lists

Lists can be nested in HTML, meaning that individual list items can contain their own sublists (not unlike an outline for a term paper). But nested lists must be structured in a particular way. Nested lists are, in HTML, considered structurally to be a part of a parent list item. Taking the primary color example, we could nest lists with synonyms for each color:

```
<ul>
  <li>Red
    <ul>
      <li>Crimson</li>
      <li>Scarlet</li>
    </ul>
  </li>
  <li>Yellow
    <ul>
      <li>Lemon</li>
      <li>Gold</li>
    </ul>
  </li>
  <li>Blue
    <ul>
      <li>Navy</li>
      <li>Cobalt</li>
    </ul>
  </li>
</ul>
```

Notice that on Red, the list item opens, the word Red appears and then a nested unordered list opens, with two list items of its own: Crimson and Scarlet. Then, that unordered list closes, and finally the list item tag that opened before Red closes.

## Block Quotes

The `<blockquote>` tag is used to structure paragraphs and long stretches of material originally from another source. For example:

```
<p>
  The Constitution of the United States
  opens with:
</p>

<blockquote>
  <p>
    We the People of the United States,
    in Order to form a more perfect
```

## VALIDATION ERRORS, AND HOW TO FIX THEM

As you are writing your HTML pages, it is important to regularly upload your files and check them against the W3C Markup Validator at `http://validator.w3.org/`. Don't wait until your pages are completely finished; errors are easier to catch if you get into the habit of validating after small sets of changes to your HTML.

And don't be surprised if you get errors. The important thing about validator output, particularly when there is an error on your page, is to worry only about the first error that's listed. Early errors (like forgetting to close a tag near the top of the page) have a snowball effect on the validator, causing it to report dozens, sometimes hundreds, of errors—even if there's only a single one on the page.

The validator is just a machine, after all. So do not assume that the number of errors the validator reports reflects the reality of your page. Look for the first error it reports, try and fix it, and then revalidate. Five times out of seven, you'll find that your page only had an error or two, particularly if you were cautious as you were writing the page to begin with—and checked them often in the validator. For additional checks on your code, be sure to use an HTML lint tool. See the companion site at `http://webpg.es/`.

```
       Union, establish Justice, ensure
       domestic Tranquility, provide for
       the common defence, promote the
       general Welfare, and secure the
       Blessings of Liberty to ourselves
       and our Posterity, do ordain and
       establish this Constitution for
       the United States of America.
    </p>
</blockquote>
```

The `<blockquote>` tag may appear with other block-level tags inside of it (headings, paragraphs, or lists). Using CSS, you can indent blocks of quoted material:

```
blockquote {
  padding-left: 2.4em;
}
```

If you need to style a paragraph within a block quote differently from your other paragraphs, use the descendant selector `blockquote p` in your CSS.

## STRUCTURAL INLINE PHRASES: ANCHOR, STRONG/BOLD, EMPHASIS/ITALIC, AND CITE

Of course, not all writing is structured in blocks: some structure is limited to words and phrases that appear inside of blocks.

### Anchor Tags

The anchor tag, `<a>`, is behind the web's signature feature: the hyperlink. The anchor tag is used to turn phrases of text into links that can be activated to take a user to another page on your website or any other resource on the web.

`href`, or hypertext reference, is the most important attribute on the anchor tag. The value of `href` is the path or full URL to the page you wish to link to (see Chapter 21). External links must always begin with `http://` or `https://`. This markup:

```
<p>
  Read the latest headlines at
  <a href="https://news.google.com">the Google
  News portal</a>.
</p>
```

will create a hyperlink from the text *the Google News portal*, which can be clicked on or otherwise activated by a user.

### Bold and Italic

By default, web browsers use the `<strong>` tag to display text as bold text, and the `<em>` (emphasis) tag to display text as italic. However, their structural names will also instruct screen readers to read text in voices that indicate "strong importance" or "emphatic stress" (W3C 2014). The exact difference between those two remains a matter of some dispute in the web design community.

There are other uses of italic in printed material that have corresponding semantic tags in HTML. For titles of works, use the `<cite>` tag:

```
<p>
  Read the online Web magazine <cite>A List
  Apart</cite> for the latest developments
  in web design.
</p>
```

If you're using an unfamiliar term, or a term from a different language, use the definition tag, `<dfn>` when it is first introduced and defined in your content, optionally with the correct language identifier on the `lang` attribute (see Chapter 11):

```
<p>
   Her remarks perfectly captured the
   <dfn lang="de">Zeitgeist</dfn>, or
   the mood of that period in time.
</p>
```

By default, the `<cite>` tag will appear in italic text; but as with `<strong>`, `<em>`, `<dfn>`, and any other tag, its display is ultimately dictated by CSS, not HTML. The `screen.css` file in the RPK includes those styles for strong, emphasis, and cite, but you can change them to appear however you wish.

In cases where there's no need for a screen reader to change voice and where there is no semantic importance to a phrase, use `<b>` or italic `<i>` tags. The HTML Language Reference (W3C 2013) notes that `<b>`, as well as `<i>`, "represents a span of text offset from its surrounding content without conveying any extra emphasis or importance." For example, long list items might better draw people's eyes if they open with a phrase styled in bold or another color. That's a perfect case for using the `<b>` tag:

```
<ol>
  <li>
    <b>A few words in bold text</b> can
    help guide people's eyes without
```

```
      using the semantic importance of the
      strong tag.
    </li>
</ol>
```

There is no special meaning to A *few words in bold text*, so it is a good candidate for the <b> tag here. If you're unsure whether to use bold or strong, or italic or emphasis, err on the side of caution and use the more semantic strong and emphasis tags.

## SECTIONING ELEMENTS

Content structured as headings, paragraphs, and lists forms the foundation for a semantic HTML page. HTML5 introduced several new sectioning elements to group related blocks into additional semantic structures. Those new elements should be used whenever possible, rather than the old, semantically meaningless <div> tag that was once used for structural grouping purposes.

### Header and Footer

Most pages have repeated content that functions as a header and footer. A well-structured page will usually open with a <header> tag just inside of the <body> tag, and close with a <footer> tag just before the body closes.

According to the HTML5 specification, <header> "typically contains a group of introductory or navigational aids" (W3C 2014). For a <header> that opens the entire page, a top-level heading element <h1> might contain the hyperlinked site name and a paragraph with a tagline, as in the RPK:

```
<header id="header">
  <h1><a rel="home"
    href="http://example.com/">Example.com</a>
  </h1>
  <p class="tagline">Showcasing the very best
    examples on the web</p>
</header>
```

Stylistically, I prefer to mark all major page sectioning elements with an id that matches the name of the major element. The next section looks at enhancing the page <header> with "navigational aids," and Chapter 18 will describe referring to those id attributes in CSS to build the page layout.

Just as a header likely opens a page, a footer typically closes it. The HTML5 specification notes that "a footer typically contains information about its section such as who wrote it, links to related documents, copyright data, and the like" (W3C 2014). A basic whole-page footer might look similar this one, which is taken from a website that I created:

```
<footer id="footer">
  <p class="copyright">
    Site contents and design © Karl
    Stolley. Licensed under <a rel="license" href=
    "https://creativecommons.org/licenses/by/4.0/">
    Creative Commons</a>.
  </p>
</footer>
```

For more information about Creative Commons licensing, see Chapter 25.


## Navigation

HTML5 introduced the <nav> element to mark "a section of a page that links to other pages or to parts within the page" (W3C 2014). The unordered list of navigation items in this chapter can be tucked neatly into the <nav> element, which I've assigned an id of navigation:

```
<nav id="navigation">
  <ul>
    <li><a href="/">Home</a></li>
    <li><a href="/about/">About</a></li>
    <li><a href="/contact/">Contact</a></li>
  </ul>
</nav>
```

And because the <header> element may contain "navigational aids," it is often good semantic practice to nest the <nav> section inside of <header>:

```
<header id="header">
  <h1><a rel="home"
    href="http://example.com/">Example.com</a>
  </h1>
  <p class="tagline">Showcasing the very best
    examples on the web</p>
  <nav id="navigation">
    <ul>
      <li><a href="/">Home</a></li>
      <li><a href="/about/">About</a></li>
      <li><a href="/contact/">Contact</a></li>
    </ul>
  </nav>
</header>
```

Including <nav> as the last element inside of the <header> maintains a sensible source order. Chapter 18 demonstrates techniques to position the navigation bar at the very top of the page layout using CSS, independent from where the navigation appears in the HTML. Again, to keep a page accessible, it's important to structure the HTML as though there were no design. People who require assistive technologies and people with older, less capable browsers will have a better sense of a site's contents if its pages open with a heading and tagline.

## Article, Section, and Aside

Content that is not part of the page header, navigation, or footer usually belongs in one of three sectioning elements: <article>, <section>, or <aside>. Here is the HTML5 specification's description of each one (W3C 2014, under "4.3 Sections"):

- **Article**: "a complete, or self-contained, composition in a document, page, application, or site and that is, in principle, independently distributable or reusable"
- **Section**: "a generic section of a document or application. A section, in this context, is a thematic grouping of content"
- **Aside**: "a section of a page that consists of content that is tangentially related to the content around the aside element, and which could be considered separate from that content"

As Jeremy Keith and Rachel Andrew (2015) note, "self-containment" is the only distinguishing characteristic between `<article>` and `<section>`. What I teach my students is this: if a chunk of content is meant to be read from start to finish, it is self-contained and probably belongs in an `<article>` element. If a page itself is meant to be read from start to finish, all of its content belongs in a single `<article>` element, probably with a unique ID: `<article id="primary">`.

Conversely, if a page includes a list or overview of thematically related content, such as the overview page to a professional portfolio that provides previews of multiple samples of work, the page's content probably belongs in a `<section>` element. Then, within the whole-page `<section>` element, there might be multiple `<article>` elements for each self-contained preview. An old-school newspaper analogy is useful here: a newspaper has a sports section that's folded separately from the entertainment section. And each of those sections has multiple articles. Online news outlets are organized similarly.

That said, it's also possible to structure very long `<article>` elements into multiple `<section>` elements. In that case, the outer `<article>` element is still self-contained and meant to be read straight through.

Note that the HTML validator will throw a warning if an `<article>` or `<section>` element does not include a heading (`<h2>` through `<h6>`), ideally at the top of the element and optionally inside of a `<header>` tag. It is permissible and sometimes very useful to include `<header>` and `<footer>` elements for each article, and sometimes in sections as well.

`<aside>` is the conceptually simpler sectioning element of these three. What matters most is the placement of the `<aside>` element in your HTML. An `<aside>` nested inside of an `<article>` or `<section>` element should be "tangentially related" only to the content inside the article or section. Pull quotes and content like "quick facts" are strong candidates for `<aside>` appearing within another sectioning element.

An `<aside>` appearing outside of an article or section should be tangentially related to the whole page or site. Advertisements can appear in `<aside>`, as can content like lists of favorite or related sites.

## Main

Although not technically a sectioning element according to the HTML5 specification (W3C 2014), the <main> element is useful for marking the central, unique content of a page. It can appear on a page only once. The specification describes <main> this way: "the main content of the body of a document or application. The main content area consists of content that is directly related to or expands upon the central topic of a document or central functionality of an application." I have found it useful to give <main> an id value of content: <main id="content">. That ID can be referred to from accessibility links that use the #content fragment identifier, as in the RPK (see Chapter 11 for more on fragment identifiers).

The body of most HTML pages can be sectioned into a header, followed by a main element, possibly followed by a whole-page aside, and closed by a footer:

```
<body>
  <header id="header">
    <!-- header content -->
  </header>
  <main id="content">
    <!-- main content, grouped in an <article> or
      <section> -->
  </main>
  <aside id="supporting">
    <!-- tangential whole-page supporting
      content -->
  </aside>
  <footer id="footer">
    <!-- footer content -->
  </footer>
</body>
```

The primary limitation to <main> is that it should not contain any content that is repeated over other pages. Main should not include a site's repeating header, footer, and navigation elements, nor should it include any <aside> elements that appear on multiple pages.

For examples of many different possible sectioning element patterns, see the book's companion website.

## NEXT STEPS

Marking up text content is a matter of being honest and consistent: if something is a paragraph, mark it as a paragraph; if it's a list, mark it as a list. Once that work has been done, taking a step back to consider the shared purpose and relationships between your headings, paragraphs, and lists should help you decide how to mark up a page's primary header and footer, and whether to group the page's content as an `<article>` or `<section>`, and which of the page's sectioning elements to nest inside the `<main>` element.

The next chapter looks at building typographically rich styles in CSS to make your page content attractive and readable.

## REFERENCES

Keith, Jeremy, and Rachel Andrew. 2016. *HTML5 for Web Designers*, 2nd ed. New York: A Book Apart.

Krantz, Peter. 2004. "The Sound of Accessible Title Text Separators." http://www.standards-schmandards.com/2004/title-text-separators/

W3C. 2013. "HTML: The Markup Language (An HTML Language Reference)." https://www.w3.org/TR/2013/NOTE-html-markup-20130528/

W3C. 2014. "HTML5: A Vocabulary and Associated APIs for HTML and XHTML." https://www.w3.org/TR/2014/REC-html5-20141028/

# CHAPTER 17

# Web Typography

Typography is arguably the most important aspect of visual design on the web. A site with even a simple, single-column layout can look stunning if its type is sized methodically and set correctly on a consistent baseline grid. Particularly in mobile-first responsive web design, where the smallest possible design can usually only run comfortably in a single column, solid typography is essential.

Historically, typography had been the most limited visual design feature of web and screen-based design in general. Print designers have always had access to unlimited libraries of type, assuming they could afford them. And delivery of high-resolution typefaces from a computer to the printed page has long been standardized.

Two recent developments are improving the quality of typography achievable on the web and screens generally. First, pixel densities are increasing on screens of all sizes, beginning with mobile phones and now on high-end tablets and laptop and desktop displays. The jagged, blotchy, pixelated look of type on screen is becoming a thing of the past: increased pixel density means more pixels available to render typefaces on screen, giving type on high-density displays the crisp look of printed pages.

The availability and legal, web-friendly delivery of quality typefaces have also improved considerably. Web designers were once limited to a small number of **system fonts**, which are typefaces that commonly ship with operating systems. It was not technically or often legally possible to load a typeface with the same ease as an image or media file. Those limitations resulted in largely unsustainable and inaccessible workarounds like providing text as images or Flash-based tricks to deliver limited spans of text in a special font.

On the technical side, the W3C (2013) finally standardized the delivery of web fonts in the CSS3 specification for `@font-face` in October 2013. Even though `@font-face` had been around since CSS2, browser makers never implemented it. Most browsers now support `@font-face` (see `http://caniuse.com/#feat=fontface`), so the technical limitation to typeface selection is largely a nonissue.

There are also numerous typeface-hosting services; a list of them is available on this book's companion site. Some of those services, such as Google Fonts, have licensed typefaces for use free of charge. Reputable typeface hosts serve fonts in multiple formats to better ensure their correct display across all browsers and operating systems. System fonts are still important and must be listed as fallbacks in CSS, should `@font-face`-delivered typefaces fail for whatever reason. See the discussion at the end of this chapter.

The techniques outlined in this chapter will help you establish a consistent setting for the type of your page, independent of the typeface you use to set it. While there are resources related to typefaces and web-font services on the book's companion site, as well as additional readings on type and typography in the "Resources for the Future" section at the end of the book, this chapter will focus on the fundamentals of establishing a typographic scale and setting type on a baseline grid.

## TYPOGRAPHIC PEDANTRY: TYPEFACE vs. FONT

Strictly speaking, typographers refer to *typeface* when they're talking about a particular family, and *font* when talking about a specific size and weight from the family. *Font* is also appropriate for describing a digital file that contains a typeface. So, Caslon is a typeface; 12pt Caslon is a font. The file `adobe-caslon.otf` can also be called a font.

This chapter refers primarily to *typefaces* except when covering specific settings of type and CSS properties, all of which favor *font* over *typeface*. The "Resources for the Future" section of this book includes a number of classic, essential titles on typography.

A bonus chapter available on this book's companion website provides additional guidance on rich web typography. It includes a list of typeface providers and advanced CSS for using OpenType features, such as ligatures and alternate character sets, with typefaces and providers that support OpenType.

## FOUNDATIONAL TYPOGRAPHIC CSS

There are two properties, `text-rendering` and `text-size -adjust`, with **vendor prefixes**, that should appear at the top of your stylesheet on the `html` selector. This chapter and all of the CSS advice in this book assumes you're using a reset stylesheet (see Chapter 15). The following styles are included in the Rapid Prototyping Kit:

```
html {
  text-rendering: optimizeLegibility;
  -webkit-text-size-adjust: 100%;
  -moz-text-size-adjust: 100%;
  -ms-text-size-adjust: 100%;
  text-size-adjust: 100%;
}
```

The `text-rendering` property "emphasizes legibility over rendering speed and geometric precision. This enables kerning and optional ligatures" (MDN 2016). There's a discussion of both kerning and ligatures in the OpenType on the book's companion site, but for now it's enough to say that setting `text-rendering` to `optimizeLegibility` will tell capable browsers to expend additional computing resources to make your text look the very best it can, in the typeface you've chosen. That should not introduce any performance problems to your page, unless it is extremely long (beyond several thousand words).

The `text-size-adjust` property, prefixed above with vendor prefixes for major browsers, ensures that no text-inflating algorithm is applied to your text on a rotation change. Without the `text-size-adjust` property, someone viewing your site on a phone in portrait orientation who switches to landscape orientation might see all of your text magnified. For a carelessly designed page, that's probably a desirable effect. But because the advice in this book advocates thoughtful mobile-first responsive design, it's your responsibility to control the presentation of text at all sizes. text-size-adjust ensures that your carefully designed text treatments display as specified in your stylesheet.

## Base Font Size and Line-Height (Leading)

The two remaining elements you should set on your html selector are font-size and line-height. Font size on html sets the base size of the type on your page. This should be expressed in em units. line-height specifies the amount of space that each line of text occupies. Both font-size and line-height are inherited properties, so setting them on the html selector sets their values for the whole page. Sections later in this chapter discuss how to style deviations from a page's base font size and line height.

By default, most browsers treat 1em as equal to 16px. Depending on the typeface you select and the screen you preview it on, 1em may be too small to read comfortably. I teach students to begin by setting text a little larger, to the em equivalent of 18 pixels, or 1.125em. Why 1.125? This is the simple formula, explicitly described as such in Ethan Marcotte's (2014) book *Responsive Web Design*:

```
target ÷ context = result
```

If the target is 18 pixels, the context is the browser default of 16 pixels. The result is the em unit to set font-size on the html selector:

```
18 ÷ 16 = 1.125em
```

The benefit to em units is that they are relative to the default type size of any given browser. For low-vision users who increase their browser's default type sizes, a design based on ems will harmoniously scale up. The 16-pixel em provides a mathematical basis for the size relationships for the rest of the type styles in your stylesheet.

Type should be set on a **baseline grid**, which is set using the CSS line-height property. To determine the line-height, which is analogous to *leading* (pronounced "ledding") in print contexts, I usually start with a comfortable line height of approximately 120 percent of the font size, rounded up to the nearest even pixel: 120 percent of the base `font-size` for the page, 18 pixels, is 21.6 pixels, which I round up to 22 pixels.

With a pixel value for the line height, it's possible to calculate its value in ems, based on the new 18-pixel context that is established by the `font-size` property on `html`:

```
22 ÷ 18 = 1.222em
```

Although ems will work with any number you'd like, I find it helpful mathematically to think of half line-heights in certain cases, such as after individual list items. 11 pixels is a tidy number, half of 22. I like it better than 10.8, which is half of 21.6, the exact 120 percent value of 18. More on half-heights for spacing blocks later in the chapter.

Putting it all together, the CSS for setting the base `font-size` and `line-height` and a page's typographic foundations looks like this:

```
html {
  font-size: 1.125em; /* 18px / 16px =
    1.125em */
  line-height: 1.222em; /* 22px / 18px =
    1.222em, or ~ 120% of the font size */
  text-rendering: optimizeLegibility;
  -webkit-text-size-adjust: 100%;
  -moz-text-size-adjust: 100%;
  -ms-text-size-adjust: 100%;
  text-size-adjust: 100%;
}
```

My habit is to write the `target / context = result` formula next to any em unit (using a / to separate the context divisor instead of the fancy ÷, which cannot be typed directly on most keyboards). I also list any styles derived from calculations at the top of a CSS declaration block. Be sure to keep any math you do inside of a CSS comment, which opens with /* and closes with */. Quick annotations will help you remember how you arrived at any given relative unit. Do double- and triple-check your calculations from time to time, because it's as easy to make errors there as in any other part of a stylesheet.

For additional baseline type and grid settings at different sizes, see the book's companion website, `http://webpg.es/`.

## EM UNITS, REM UNITS

The em unit is a relative unit of measure, originally derived from the width of an imaginary square around a typeface's uppercase M. The great thing about em units is that, being relative, you can use them to establish the size relationships between all page elements. By modifying just the base `font-size` on the `html` selector in the CSS, all other size relationships will scale up accordingly.

However, there are cases where setting type in em units can get really complex. If you have a sidebar displayed in slightly smaller text than the main content of the page, with a headline that's slightly larger, and a subhead slightly smaller than that, the number and complexity of `target ÷ context = result` calculations can get overwhelming. I personally don't mind that complexity, because it's usually a sign that I need to rethink my design and aim for something simpler.

But if complexity isn't your thing, there is comparative simplicity in the `rem` unit. The em unit is always relative to any parent element, going all the way back to `<html>`, that's if its `font-size` had been explicitly set. By contrast, the `rem` unit is constant, based on the value of `font-size` set on the `html` selector. `rem` therefore stands for *root em unit*: the value set on `font-size` for the root element of a document, which in HTML is always `<html>`.

You still use the `target ÷ context = result` formula to arrive at `rem` units, but the `context` value will always be whatever pixel-value equivalent you've set your `font-size` to on `html`.

`rem` units are supported on all major browsers, with the notable exception of Internet Explorer older than version 9. See `http://caniuse.com/#feat=rem`.

## TYPOGRAPHIC SCALES

A base `font-size` should be chosen and adjusted based on how easily the type can be read in the typeface you've chosen. 18 pixels / 1.125 ems is just a starting point. While it is possible to create a web page with a single `font-size`, it may come across as monotonous and prevent people from quickly scanning the page to find the content most meaningful to them, especially on content-heavy sites.

The question is, once you've established a base size for the majority of text on your page, how do you go about choosing how much larger the headings will be? Or the subheadings? If there are figure captions on the page, how do you go about deciding how much smaller those are than the primary running text?

Computers will of course allow you to choose any font size that you'd like. Sometimes it's tempting to just eyeball it and pick some sizes. But that's a haphazard way to design a page. That is why it is common typographic practice to choose type sizes within a **typographic scale**, which is a fixed set of sizes appearing in some kind of predictable interval. That interval establishes a hierarchy of information, particularly on headings: larger headings often mark more important divisions in page content.

Your word processor and operating system probably have a simple typographic scale already in place. Here is the typographic scale available in macOS's Font Picker system dialog boxes for choosing a font size: 9, 10, 11, 12, 13, 14, 18, 24, 36, 48, 64, 72, 96, 144, 288. Your operating system or word processor probably has a similar scale: rather than making every single whole number available, it suggests certain sizes, usually in **points** (although macOS and other operating systems' dialog boxes may not include a unit, such as points or pixels, at all).

Here's a little history lesson on type sizing. A point is a traditional measure of type, roughly equal to 1/72 of an inch. So printed 72-point type is about an inch tall, measured from the tallest ascender to the baseline, about where the bottom of a lowercase x sits. So measured, 144-point type is about two inches tall. To learn more about ascenders and other type anatomy, see the book's companion site at http://webpg.es/.

Unlike computers, which can render 8-point type or 13.5-point type, the original movable-type printing presses had a fixed number of sizes available. The traditional typographic scale, in other words, is more than just an arbitrary set of numbers. It uses particular ratios *based on* an arbitrary set of numbers, specifically the number 72 and secondarily on the number 12, which is itself 1/6 of 72 (a value called the pica, which is 12 points or 1/6 of an inch). 72 and 12 are both useful numbers for deriving ratios, because both are divisible by 6, 4, 3, and 2, making it possible to neatly calculate half, third, quarter, and sixth values.

Of course, when choosing and setting typefaces for the screen, values expressed in inches, or fractions of an inch, are irrelevant. What matters is the screen resolution, in pixels. The original Macintosh display was manufactured at 72 pixels per inch (ppi), meaning that for every inch of screen space, there were 72 individual pixels. But in the intervening years, pixel densities became 96ppi, at which density a point is approximately equal to 1.33 pixels. Ever larger and smaller screen sizes, in doubled- and tripled-pixel densities, have eliminated any consistent physical size relationship between the pixel and the point.

And yet, the sizes on the traditional typographic scale (9–14, 18, 24, 36, 47, 72, 144, and so on) remain in many font-picking dialog boxes.

## DEVELOPING A SITE STYLE GUIDE

HTML is meant to be flexible enough to allow you to mark up most common structural elements of web content, particularly headings, paragraphs, and lists. You can mark up in HTML as you write, or mark up your existing writing with HTML. But it is useful to create a style guide for your site, especially when you begin to use CSS to design your page content and establish typographic scales and baseline grids. A style guide is even more important when you are collaborating with others on a site, so that pieces of content are marked up consistently and uniformly.

The simplest way to write your style guide is to put together a page that includes all of the structural elements you use to mark up your page content, and provide a sample rendering using the site's actual CSS by linking to the site's CSS file. Then, any changes to your CSS will also change the style guide's appearance. Save your style guide's HTML file as `style-guide.html` for easy reference.

While you can use *Lorem ipsum* text to show off the examples, it's good practice to use the sample text to convey what kind of content should be marked up as paragraphs, lists, or any other structural pages for your site. That will help it serve as a refresher for your memory and as guidance for any collaborators.

See the book's companion website for examples of site style guides.

Predictable, repeated values are pleasing to human beings. We like them visually, and we even like them in sound, particularly music.

## Modular Scales and Music

The intervals of the musical scale have become popular in web design when choosing a typographic scale for setting type at different sizes. There's nothing wrong with using sizes from the traditional typographic scale, but the Modular Scale site at `http://www.modularscale .com/` allows you to experiment with applying different ratios, or intervals, from music, particularly Western music's diatonic scale. The ratio of a perfect fifth, which is what Modular Scale defaults to, is 2:3 or 1.5 in decimal notation ($2 \times 1.5 = 3$). So if `18px` is your base font size on a page, the next larger size you might run is 27 ($18 \times 1.5 = 27$), followed by 40.5 ($27 \times 1.5 = 40.5$). In the opposite direction, the next size smaller from 18, perhaps for setting a caption, is 12 ($18 \div 1.5 = 12$).

The smaller the interval, like a minor second (15:16 or 1.067), the more gradual the change from size to size. A large interval, like a perfect octave (1:2, or 2.0) results in proportionally larger changes from size to size. Smaller intervals are often useful in intricate text settings, like an online dictionary, whereas large intervals can have a loud, energetic feel to them, like a roadside billboard.

So how to choose an interval? One way is to find a piece of music that you enjoy, or a piece of music fitting to the site you're creating. Wagner's "Bridal Chorus," or "Bridal March" as it's sometimes called, is often played at Western weddings. The opening interval (sometimes sung to "Here comes the bride"), "Here - comes" is a perfect fourth. So, if you're designing a website for someone's bridal shower or wedding, choosing a scale based on the perfect fourth (3:4, or 1.333) might be a fun and meaningful choice.

Using a 4:3 scale (1.333) for size values based on an `18px` base font size will result in a typographic scale with these values:

```
18
23.994 (18 × 1.333)
31.984 (23.994 × 1.333)
42.635 (31.984 × 1.333)
```

The scale's pixel values can then be used to set heading sizes in CSS, in em units:

```
h1 {
  font-size: 2.369em;
    /* 42.635px / 18px = 2.369 */
}
h2 {
  font-size: 1.777em;
    /* 31.984px / 18px = 1.777em */
}
h3 {
  font-size: 1.333em;
    /* 23.994px / 18px = 1.333em */
}
/* h4 same size as page type; h5 and h6 not used */
```

However, the 2.369em size is probably too large for mobile-first design, so a more robust design might move down the scale for the mobile-first site, and tuck the larger sizes in a media query (see Chapter 14):

```
h1 {
  font-size: 1.777em;
    /* 31.984px / 18px = 1.777em */
}
h2 {
  font-size: 1.333em;
    /* 23.994px / 18px = 1.333em */
}
/* h3, h4 same size as page type; h5 and h6
   not used */

@media screen and (min-width: 800px) {
  h1 {
    font-size: 2.369em;
      /* 42.635px / 18px = 2.369 */
  }
  h2 {
```

## OTHER SCALES AND INTERVALS

If making the leap from music to typeface sizes isn't your thing, you can also create rectangles based on ratios, and evaluate their appearance. Widescreen televisions are sized based on a 16:9 ratio (or 1.78:1). Laptops are often 16:10, which is why Netflix and other sites streaming 16:9 video display with black letterbox bands at the top and bottom of laptop screens.

16:9 is a pleasing ratio for displaying landscape images (16 units on the long side, 9 units on the short), and is also workable for creating a scale to set your type at. If you're creating a site that's geared around movies, you might use the classic ratio for widescreen films, 1.85:1. Or if you're big into math and irrational numbers, Phi, also known as the golden ratio, is 1.618:1.

Whatever scale you choose, the intent behind any typographic scale is to take some of the guesswork out of type sizes, and build on a system that has inherent predictable visual harmony.

```
  font-size: 1.777em;
    /* 31.984px / 18px = 1.777em */
}
h3 {
  font-size: 1.333em;
    /* 23.994px / 18px = 1.333em */
}
  /* h4 same size as page type */
}
```

An additional weight, color, or capitalization scheme might then be necessary to distinguish more minor headings, particularly at mobile scale. The next section of this chapter addresses a more pressing problem: the larger headings will appear broken on the page's 22-pixel baseline grid.

## WORKING WITH BASELINE GRIDS

Typographic scales offer a compelling and systematic way of setting type at different sizes, while maintaining an internal consistency based on a ratio. The variance among type size is contrasted against the constant, predictable rhythm of the baseline grid. Baseline grids use simple multiples and fractions of a page's base line height to ensure a comfortable amount of space for the lines of your headings, paragraphs, and lists, and for vertically offsetting headings from paragraphs, paragraphs from lists, and one list item from another. A pair of articles from Rutter (2006) and Miner (2007) are essential reading for working with baseline grids on the web, and I will synthesize those techniques here.

## Setting Headings

There's a problem with the headings set in the last section (see Figure 17.1). Because the baseline grid established on html is the em equivalent of 22 pixels, the larger heading text is clipped and broken in weird ways. (The figures in this chapter all display the baseline grid as a series of dashed lines down the page. See the book's companion site for instructions on adding a visible baseline grid to assist you as you work.)

A starter solution for this is to increase the line-height based on fractions and multiples of 22, the page's base line height. That will preserve a constant rhythm vertically down the page. Begin by working with the baselines in the mobile-first area of the stylesheet:

```
h1 {
    font-size: 1.777em;
        /* 31.984px / 18px = 1.777em */
    line-height: 1.376em;
        /* 44px / 31.984px = 1.376em; two gridlines */
}
h2 {
    font-size: 1.333em;
        /* 23.994px / 18px = 1.333em */
    line-height: 1.375em;
        /* 33px / 23.994px = 1.375em;
            one and a half gridlines */
}
/* h3, h4 same size as page type; h5, h6 not used */
```

A 33-pixel line height could conceivably work for both headings, given that h1 is sized at 31.984 pixels (1.777em). Depending on the length of text run in the major heading, that might be enough. Just to

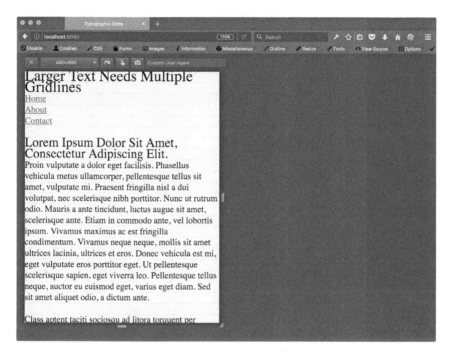

**Figure 17.1.** Type at larger sizes is clipped by the 22-pixel (1.222em) baseline grid.

ensure comfortable reading, I've here calculated a full two gridlines to accommodate h1. But because two gridlines would be almost twice the size of h2's 23.994-pixel font-size, a gridline and a half is better suited to it (see Figure 17.2).

Once the mobile-first styles are in place, headings in the media queries can be similarly adjusted. The book's companion site shows the full examples here, and offers additional guidance for setting headings using bold weights and color.

## Setting Paragraphs

Setting paragraphs for comfortable reading is essential for dense, text-heavy designs. Cyrus Highsmith (2012) wrote an entire book just on setting paragraph text.

Paragraphs are traditionally set one of two ways. The most traditional, space-conserving way is to leave no line of space between paragraphs, but instead indent the first line. Bringhurst (2012, 40) notes

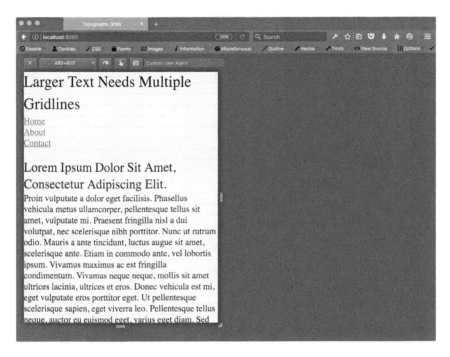

**Figure 17.2.** A more comfortable typographic setting for mobile-scale headings.

that paragraphs are commonly indented either by one em or by one *lead*, which in CSS terms would be one `line-height`. In the stylesheet from this chapter, one lead is 22 pixels or 1.222em. Bringhurst also suggests omitting the indentation on any paragraph that immediately follows a heading. So, the CSS style declarations for paragraphs indented according to Bringhurst's guidance look like this:

```
p {
  text-indent: 1.222em;
    /* One lead, or 22px (base line-height) */
}
h1 + p,
h2 + p,
h3 + p,
h4 + p {
  text-indent: 0; /* No indentation on
    paragraphs that follow headings */
}
```

## BLACK AND WHITE

Black text on a white background is a no-nonsense color scheme that's useful when setting up the typography for a page. Sometimes that minimal look remains for the life of the design.

True white (`color: #FFF`) and true black (`color: #000`) are often too stark, and can make **anti-aliased** text appear more jagged on lower-resolution screens. So when working with black and white, lighten the black and darken the white:

```
html {
  color: #F0F0F0; /* Very light shade of gray;
    text will appear white */
  background-color: #222; /* Very dark shade
    of gray; background will appear black */
}
```

Even for light on dark designs, it's always better to run the background color a little lighter than true black. On sites that have photographs, the darker shades of the photographs can look washed out on a completely black background. By contrast, no pun intended, a dark gray background gives photographs a greater look of depth.

If your site design aims for a more traditional, conservative look, an indented paragraph setting is probably the way to go. However, a more modern and web-friendly approach, where readers are used to quickly skimming content, is to omit any first-line indentation and instead drop a blank gridline between paragraphs. That setting would be written in CSS like this:

```
p {
  padding-bottom: 1.222em; /* One empty gridline
    (22px) */
}
```

If you opt to drop an empty gridline after each paragraph, do not also indent the first line, as that can make text harder to scan. Choose indents, or an empty line of space, but not both.

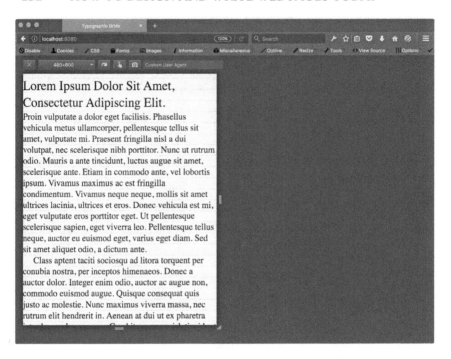

**Figure 17.3.**   In traditional paragraph settings, paragraphs are indented unless they immediately follow a heading.

## SPACING BETWEEN HEADINGS, PARAGRAPHS, AND LISTS

When setting a page, I tend to favor an empty gridline of space between all headings, paragraphs, and lists, which results in CSS something like this:

```
p,
ul,
ol,
dl {
  padding-bottom: 1.222em;
    /* One empty gridline (22px) */
}
h1 {
  font-size: 1.777em;
    /* 31.984px / 18px = 1.777em */
```

```
line-height: 1.376em;
  /* 44px / 31.984px = 1.376em; two gridlines */
padding-bottom: 0.688em;
  /* 22px / 31.984px = one gridline */
}
h2 {
font-size: 1.333em;
  /* 23.994px / 18px = 1.333em */
line-height: 1.375em;
  /* 33px / 23.994px = 1.375em;
     one and a half gridlines */
padding-bottom: 0.917em;
  /* 22px / 23.994px = 0.917em; one gridline */
}
```

Those styles can be tweaked further, especially on headings, where half a gridline might better spatially associate the heading and the

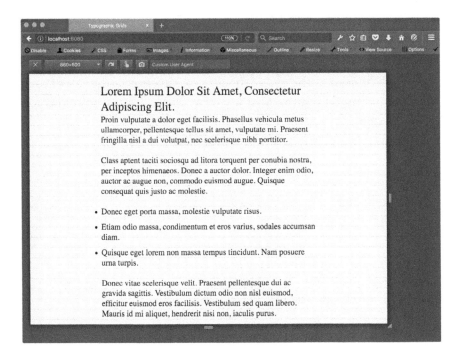

**Figure 17.4.** Whole and partial empty gridlines establish a page with structure and rhythm, while headings sized to a modular scale provide hierarchy.

paragraph that follows it. See the book's companion website for those and other possible gridline-based type settings.

## Setting Lists and List Items

An empty line of space works well for offsetting an entire list from the block that follows. Individual list items themselves are more readable when offset, but an entire line is too jarring. Half or even a third of a gridline is enough to make it clear that list items are associated with others in the same list, while making them easily scannable:

```
ul,
ol {
  padding-bottom: 1.222em;
    /* One empty gridline (22px) */
}
li {
  padding-bottom: 0.611em;
    /* One-half empty gridline (11px) */
}
```

The problem with that bit of CSS is that there will now be a line and a half of space at the end of the list: one line from either ul or ol, plus the half line from the final list item. There are two solutions to that problem.

The first is to use the :last-child pseudoclass:

```
ul,
ol {
  padding-bottom: 1.222em;
    /* One empty gridline (22px) */
}
li {
  padding-bottom: 0.611em;
    /* One-half empty gridline (11px) */
}
li:last-child {
  padding-bottom: 0;
}
```

That will ensure that the last child `li` inside of an unordered or ordered list has no bottom padding. However, there's a mathematical solution to the problem that I prefer:

```
ul,
ol {
  padding-bottom: 0.611em;
    /* One-half empty gridline (11px) */
}
li {
  padding-bottom: 0.611em;
    /* One-half empty gridline (11px) */
}
```

That approach simply reduces the bottom padding on `ul` and `ol` to a half gridline. The half gridline introduced by the final list item will add to that to make a full gridline following the completed list. Valid HTML permits only `<li>` as the child element of either list type, so this approach will always work for any valid list. The benefit to the CSS is that it is DRY: no need to repeat two different `padding-bottom` values for `li`. I have also found that this method makes it easier to consistently set nested lists. See the book's companion website for examples.

## STYLING OUTLIERS

Chapter 16 showed how branding and navigational content blocks are just headings, paragraphs, and lists nested inside the `<header>`, `<nav>`, and `<footer>` sectioning elements. But in those contexts, content blocks are often styled differently from elsewhere on the page.

One common outlier style is for page navigation, which in HTML is usually structured like this, which is similar to the Rapid Prototyping Kit:

```
<nav id="navigation">
  <ul class="navigation">
    <li class="accessibility">
      <a href="#content">Skip to page
      content</a></li>
    <li><a href="/">Home</a></li>
```

```
    <li><a href="/about/">About</a></li>
  </ul>
</nav>
```

The navigation class on the unordered list provides a structural hook in CSS to style it differently from the other unordered lists and their list items on the page:

```
.navigation,
.navigation li {
  padding: 0; /* Remove padding set on base
    ul and li styles */
}
.navigation li {
  display: inline-block;
    /* Display navigation items side-by-side */
  line-height: 1; /* Set line-height to 1;
    replace with padding on li a */
}
.navigation li a {
  display: block; /* Display links as
    blocks for larger clickable areas */
  padding: 0.722em; /* 13px / 18px = 0.722em */
}
```

That example sets the line-height on .navigation li to 1, so that all of the spacing of the individual navigation items can be set with padding. They will still align with the baseline grid, if set properly. Specifically, the em equivalent of 13px of padding is set on the .navigation li a selector. Padding is clickable or tappable on the <a> tag. The 13px value for the padding might seem strange, but it's arrived at within the baseline grid. If .navigation li is the em equivalent of 18px, then its line height is 18px with line-height: 1 set. The baseline grid is 22 pixels, so 22 − 18 = 4. Splitting those missing pixels in half (2px) and adding a half gridline (11px) to the top and bottom (and left and right) of each navigation item results in 13px of padding: 13 + 18 + 13 = 44px, meaning that the row of navigation items will fill two generous, tap-friendly gridlines (see Figure 17.5).

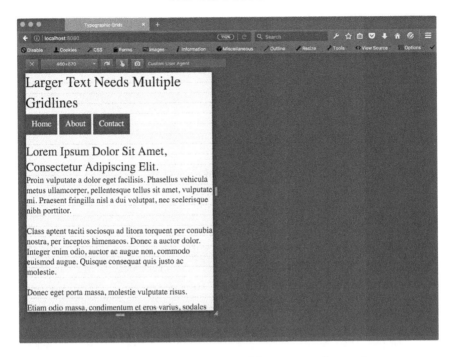

**Figure 17.5.** Controlling the outlier styling of the navigation list, resulting in a two-gridline clickable/tappable area.

## BUILDING A CSS FONT STACK: SYSTEM TYPEFACES

Setting a baseline grid and typographic scale before choosing a specific typeface can help you to think first about the rhythm and hierarchy of your page content. It can even be a useful design challenge to use a grid and typographic scale to make a page look good with a default typeface that you do not enjoy.

Even if you decide to include web-delivered typefaces in your design (see the book's companion website), your font-family declaration in CSS should include commonly available system typefaces, followed by a generic: serif, sans-serif, or monospace. The list of typefaces you specify on the CSS font-family property is called a **font stack**.

CSS Tricks maintains a list of excellent font stacks at `https://css-tricks.com/snippets/css/font-stacks/`. They are derived from an article by Michael Tuck (2009), who suggests this pattern for ordering font stacks:

- exact font
- nearest alternative
- platform-wide alternative(s)
- universal (cross-platform) choice(s)
- generic

System typefaces, the platform-wide and cross-platform component's of Tuck's pattern, are those that ship with specific operating systems. macOS, for example, ships with the Helvetica typeface. Windows does not, but Windows does ship with Arial (as does macOS). Scratch even a little bit at discussions of typography and you will find most type snobs come down hard on Arial as a lesser face than Helvetica. So, a very simple starting place for a sans-serif–based font stack organized around Helvetica would look like

```
html {
    font-family: Helvetica, Arial, sans-serif;
}
```

macOS and iOS, which also has Helvetica, will display Helvetica. So will any Windows or Linux-based operating system that has Helvetica installed. Otherwise, those machines with Arial will display Arial. Systems with neither Helvetica nor Arial will display whatever typeface the browser or operating system defaults to when displaying text in a sans-serif face.

You can specify very deep and complex stacks, such as this one from CSS Tricks based on Frutiger/Helvetica:

```
font-family: Frutiger, "Frutiger Linotype", Univers,
  Calibri, "Gill Sans", "Gill Sans MT", "Myriad Pro",
  Myriad, "DejaVu Sans Condensed", "Liberation Sans",
  "Nimbus Sans L", Tahoma, Geneva, "Helvetica Neue",
  Helvetica, Arial, sans-serif;
```

Of course, unless you've expended a great deal of money on purchasing typefaces for your computer, you might have no idea what Frutiger even looks like. Fortunately, sites like Fonts.com have Frutiger and many other typefaces for sale, and you can look at and even test samples of the faces. Here, for example, is Frutiger's page at Fonts.com: `http://www.fonts.com/font/linotype/frutiger`

Be sure to work with a given typeface for several days. See whether it grows on you or starts to contradict the content of your site. Be sure also to make any adjustments to your base font size and baseline grid to make text easily readable in your chosen typeface. For certain typefaces, you might want to include in your CSS classes introduced by a JavaScript-based web font loader, so that system fonts in your stack remain presented at the size and on the grid you specified originally. See the book's companion site for details.

## NEXT STEPS

Although web typography has matured rapidly, it is still in its early stages. With each new browser release, more and more users are able to enjoy the readability and unique look of web-delivered typefaces and the advanced OpenType features that some faces provide. But like any asset, rich web typography can come at the cost of page performance and user bandwidth, so web-delivered typefaces must be chosen carefully.

Once your baseline grid is established and your page has a consistent vertical rhythm, it's time to consider how your page is built horizontally with grid-based page layouts, the topic of the next chapter.

## REFERENCES

Bringhurst, Robert. 2012. *The Elements of Typographic Style*, 4th ed. Seattle: Hartley & Marks.

Highsmith, Cyrus. 2012. *Inside Paragraphs: Typographic Fundamentals*. Boston: Font Bureau.

Marcotte, Ethan. 2014. *Responsive Web Design*, 2nd ed. New York: A Book Apart.

MDN. 2016. "Text-rendering." https://developer.mozilla.org/en-US/docs/Web/CSS/text-rendering

Miner, Wilson. 2007. "Setting Type on the Web to a Baseline Grid." *A List Apart* (April 9). http://alistapart.com/article/settingtypeontheweb

Rutter, Richard. 2006. "Compose to a Vertical Rhythm." *24 Ways to Impress Your Friends.* https://24ways.org/2006/compose-to-a-vertical-rhythm

Tuck, Michael. 2009. "Eight Definitive Web Font Stacks." *SitePoint.* https://www.sitepoint.com/eight-definitive-font-stacks/

W3C. 2013. "CSS Fonts Module Level 3." https://www.w3.org/TR/2013/CR-css-fonts-3-20131003/

# CHAPTER 18

# Page Layout and the Grid

Text set to a repeated baseline, or some multiple or fraction of a baseline, establishes a regular, predictable vertical structure for your page. That's the purpose of a baseline grid. In mobile-first responsive design, it's an essential starting point.

But a single column of text sized much larger than mobile-scale screens becomes hard to read. Readers eyes can't reliably shift from the end of one line all the way to the beginning of the next line below. Navigation and other elements can start to look bulky, awkward, and intrusive if they remain sized to the entire viewport.

An existing baseline grid can be enhanced by a combination of grid-based layout and CSS media-queries to make more usable and inviting page designs across larger viewports. In the past, web designers relied on HTML tables for page layout, because that was the only reliable cross-browser technique available. That is no longer good practice, as tables for layout introduce accessibility problems and unnecessary markup with no semantic value. This chapter looks at some concepts behind grid-based design executed using only CSS and semantic HTML.

## ROUGH SKETCHES AND MOCKUPS

Rough sketches on paper will start you thinking about page design. They do not have to be works of art (see Figure 18.1). A rough sketch only needs to provide a rough representation of the content where you would like it to appear on your page at an approximate viewport size. Once you have done some sketching on paper, it may be helpful to create a mockup

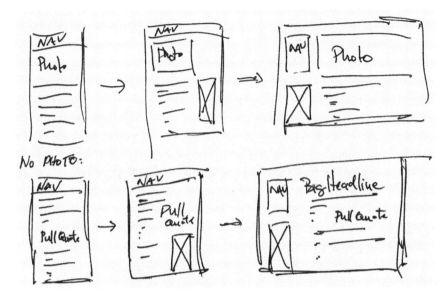

**Figure 18.1.** A few rough sketches of the author's, used only to think about page layout across a range of viewports.

of your page in an image editor, so that you can get a better sense of how big things will appear on screen in relation to one another. My preference is to get straight to building page layouts in CSS.

If you would rather spend more time prototyping on paper or in an image editor, there are additional books listed in the "Resources for the Future" section at the end of this book. Just be aware of the potential disconnect between the layout of a page in any fixed medium (paper, or an image editor at a specific size) and the actual responsive design across a wide and flexible range of viewports.

## Start with a Typical, Representative Content Page

Although it is tempting to begin page designs by starting with a site's home page, the home page is often markedly different from the other pages in a site. Designing by thinking first about a more representative content page, as suggested in Chapter 15, will help you develop a layout that works for most of your pages. From that general idea, you can work to build a home page that contrasts nicely with the typical pages of your site (see the sidebar "Modifying Designs for Special Pages").

As has been mentioned throughout this section of the book, you can almost never go wrong following this rule of web design: begin by building things that represent a typical page or feature on your site. Whether that's choosing a comfortable base size for your site's type or establishing a two-column layout that works well for the typical content on most of your site's pages, design to the general first and to the specific later.

For example, your site might include a portfolio that opens with an overview page. That overview links to individual projects. Each project will have its own page, one that is more representative of the content and design of most pages on the site. With a representative content page sketched, however roughly, and partially built in HTML and CSS, you will have a better reference to work from when designing your site's home page and any overviews. Adding identifying classes to your body tag, such as `class="home"` or `class="overview"` or even `class="portfolio-overview"`, is all the structure you need to make specific home- and overview-page adjustments in your CSS later (see the "Modifying Designs for Special Pages" sidebar). Do not create additional, separate stylesheets for the sake of unusual pages. One stylesheet should be responsible for the entire design of your site. (See Chapter 21 for guidance in other matters of site architecture.)

## DESIGNING WITH A COLUMN GRID

Grids provide a solid foundation for page design, even if some page elements violate the rigid columns on the grid to add visual interest. I often urge web design students to focus on the rough, geographic areas of a page first, placing elements like the header, navigation, content, and footer areas in some kind of organized spatial relationship. Having the spatial relationships established by a column grid provides an organizing structure to experiment with other aspects of a design, such as typefaces and colors or the size and scale of media elements.

### Grid Terminology

At its most basic, a grid is made up of at least one column of content. *Content* can be text, media, or both. **Margins** offset the column from

## MODIFYING DESIGNS FOR SPECIAL PAGES

Chapter 16 suggested writing a class on the body tag of each page to make it easier to target the designs of specific pages. If your home page opens with `<body class="home">`, you can use that class as a hook in your CSS to create special home-page styles. For example, if your site name in the page header is `1.777em` on most of your pages, but you want it to run larger, at `2.369em` on home, your CSS might read:

```
#header h1 { font-size: 1.777em; } /* 31.984px
 all pages */
.home #header h1 { font-size: 2.369em; } /*
 42.635px on home page*/
```

There's no need to create a separate style sheet for the home page, or to diverge greatly from the structure that it shares with other pages. All style declarations are stored in a single CSS file, referencing the body class as a hook in a descendant selector to set divergent styles on pages that need them.

the edges of the browser viewport. Here, *margins* refer to the space between the grid and the edge of the viewport, not necessarily the CSS `margin` property. In this chapter, grid margins are established using the `padding` property. When working with two or more columns, a **gutter** refers to the space between columns (see Figure 18.2).

More complex grids can be derived from **grid systems**, in which a page is divided into multiple columns separated by gutters. **Spatial zones** that occupy multiple columns give order and hierarchy to the page, and horizontal breaks result in **flow lines** (see Figure 18.3).

In responsive web design, it is common and often necessary to employ different grid systems across a page's natural breakpoints. At mobile scale, a page might be a single-column grid that eventually becomes a two-column grid, which then becomes a grid system of multiple columns. A multicolumn grid system that works well at smaller sizes might need to be reconfigured at larger sizes. That is how this chapter will proceed in demonstrating the principles behind grid-based layout. The book's companion site showcases additional examples of different modular scales and grid systems at work.

**Figure 18.2.** A two-column grid illustrating the concept of columns, gutter, and margins. The larger column is twice the size of the smaller, which is a traditional 2:1 ratio for basic two-column grids.

## Return of the Modular Scale

If you've chosen and carefully set the type of your page to a modular scale (see Chapter 17), you can continue your use of the scale to establish a harmonious grid for your page, rather than choose arbitrary numbers. For example, a page's typographic scale might be set to a 16:9 (1.778) ratio to establish text sizes larger and smaller than the page's base font size. Ratios can also guide the size relationships of columns in a two-column grid. If the main column of text should be roughly 320 pixels wide, then the smaller column in a 16:9 ratio will be approximately 180 pixels wide (320 ÷ 1.778 = 179.977). The next section will look at converting pixels to relative, percentage-based units for fully responsive designs in CSS.

Once the columns have been sized in proportion to each other, a gutter should separate them. Without a gutter, the text in one column will be claustrophobically close to the text in the other. When setting a

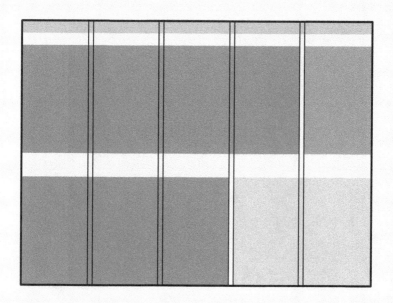

**Figure 18.3.** A five-column grid system illustrating a page layout made up of different spatial zones, which establish a hierarchy of content areas and guide readers' eyes over the page.

## GRID SYSTEMS

Do a Google search for *web design grid system* and you will find links to the work of many different web designers who have released their own grid systems that others may use. Some systems are rigid, modernist groups of columns, while others are more experimental and apparently free form.

You may also encounter CSS-based grid systems. Be careful of those, especially if they require introducing nonsemantic classes like `column-1` or `col-1` into your HTML. Those are presentational classes. Semantic classes and IDs, such as those in the RPK, are equally suited to use in grids and grid systems, as is demonstrated later in this chapter.

gutter, I usually begin with the size of one gridline from the baseline grid on a page (see Chapter 17), and test a few different gutters based on it.

For example, if a page has its type set on a 22-pixel baseline grid, it's convenient to begin by setting the gutter at 22px, too. The modular scale can be used to generate additional gutter sizes. A 22px baseline grid on a page with a 16:9 (1.778) scale could have a more generous 39.116px gutter ($22 \times 1.778 = 39.116$) or a tighter 12.373px gutter ($22 \div 1.778 = 12.373$). There is a noticeable size difference between 39 and 12 pixels, however, so it might be worth plugging in a half gridline to the ratio, too: $11 \times 1.778 = 19.558$ pixels. Numbers like those are only a starting point, of course. What matters most is how they look as part of your entire design. Look for column and gutter sizes that make reading comfortable, while maintaining visual harmony with your baseline grid.

A page's baseline grid can also be used to establish a grid design's top and bottom margins. A few gridlines at the top and bottom of the page is a strong starting point. It's generally better to set a grid's top and bottom margins only once your header and footer areas are complete and it's clear how much space is needed to offset them from the page content areas. Particularly at mobile scales, it is common practice to set the navigation flush against the very top of the viewport, in which case the navigation occupies space in the grid's margin (Figure 18.4). That is similar to how page numbers and running chapter titles are positioned within the top and bottom margins of a printed book.

## Grid Systems

The modular scale can also guide the design of harmonious multicolumn grid systems, in a similar fashion to the basic two-column grid described above. To create a multicolum grid system, I will often start with the size of the gutter, and determine the width of the columns based on some value derived from the gutter. Starting with a 22px gutter for mathematical simplicity, again with a 16:9 (1.778) modular scale, provides some potential widths for a grid system's columns:

```
22px
39.116px  (22 × 1.778)
69.548px  (39.116 × 1.778)
123.656px  (69.548 × 1.778)
219.860px  (123.656 × 1.778)
```

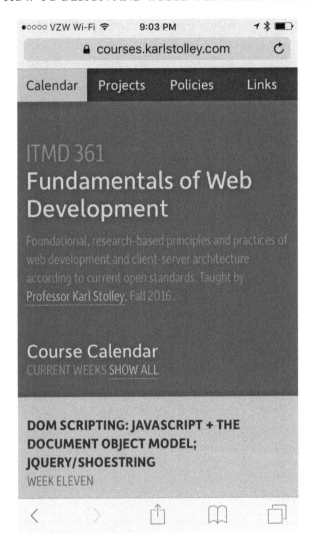

**Figure 18.4.**    Navigation runs flush with the top of the viewport in this design, in the page grid's margin.

If that stack of numbers looks familiar, that's because it is the same as the approach from Chapter 17 (except with a different ratio) to determine type sizes based on a modular scale. For creating a column grid, the numbers here suggest how wide each column can be within the grid system, with 22px as a constant gutter size.

To create a five-column grid system for use on a screen of roughly 400 pixels, I might opt to set the columns at 39.116 pixels. Modifying that five-column system for a 700-pixel wide screen, a 123.656px column might make more sense. As with the em units calculated in the last chapter, I am rounding the pixel units to three decimal places. Of course, a computer cannot display a fraction of a pixel; those are preserved rather than rounded to a whole number for the sake of building **fluid grids** in CSS, using percentage widths.

## GRID EXECUTION IN CSS: DIMENSIONS AND OFFSETS

The pixel dimensions in the previous section, much like the pixel-based font sizes in Chapter 17, are not meant to be written in CSS directly. The formula `target ÷ context = result`, used to calculate em units for text sizing and the baseline grid, can also be used to calculate widths in percentages. The challenge is knowing what value to use for `context`.

Initially, the context is the width of the browser viewport or the containing element of the page. That element is `<div id="page">` in the RPK, which by default is 100 percent of the viewport, as is any other block and sectioning element that does not have a `width` or `margin` property set in CSS.

A single-column, mobile-first layout requires only enough CSS styles to set the grid margin around the column, which keeps text from running into the edges of the viewport. Again, *margin* is the grid term. The CSS `padding` property can be used to set grid margins. In addition to preserving an element's background color, padding also avoids situations where multiple CSS `margin` properties collapse (MDN 2016a).

A starting point for determining the grid margin at mobile scales is to set the left and right padding on a containing element to the same value as a full baseline. Assuming a 22px baseline grid:

```
#page {
  padding-left: 22px;
  padding-right: 22px;
  /* Pixel units for testing purposes */
}
```

With those styles set, preview the page in a browser using its responsive design mode. Gradually pull the viewport open (Figure 18.5). Based on the typeface and size, look for the point at which the lines of text become too long to read comfortably. Bringhurst (2012, 26) notes a range of optimum readability between 45 and 75 characters per line. The lines in Figure 18.5 break at about 60–65 characters per line. But the actual experience of reading is the deciding factor in line length: If you notice a major shift in how far your eyes must travel from the end of one line to the beginning of the next, the line is likely getting too long. In extreme cases, you may actually feel your eyes moving. It's not comfortable. Depending on the typeface, how large it is, and how dense your content is, a viewport of anywhere from 450 to 800 pixels might reveal the limitations of a single-column layout with a 22px margin (or whatever value your baseline grid is) on either side.

Note the width of the viewport where reading becomes difficult. That will be the value for your first `min-width` media query. In this

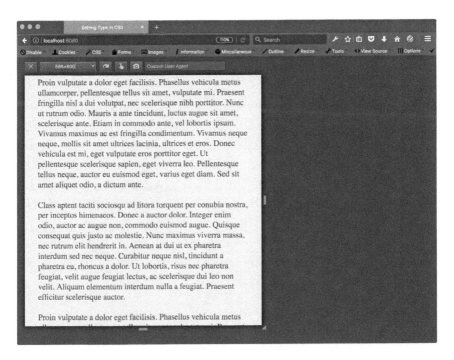

**Figure 18.5.** At a 585-pixel-wide viewport, the lines of text become too long to read comfortably for the chosen font, given the column's 22px margins.

example, text becomes difficult to read in a single column on a 585px viewport. Write the media query and add a note to yourself as a CSS comment:

```
@media screen and (min-width: 585px) {
  /* New column grid will be defined here... */
}
```

To set responsive margins on the mobile-first grid, go back to your mobile-first selector, #page if using the RPK, and add half again the gridline value (22px + 11px). Then, calculate the padding values as a percentage of the viewport width, which is the context value for #page:

```
#page {
  padding-left: 5.641025641%;
    /* 33px / 585px = 0.05641025641 */
  padding-right: 5.641025641%;
    /* 33px / 585px = 0.05641025641 */
}
```

You may have to make some further adjustments, but with this in place, your mobile-first styles should have a comfortable margin from the edge of the screen. Adding the half gridline is just to ensure comfortable grid margins at even smaller scales, given that the padding values in this example have been calculated according to the largest possible mobile-first viewport: the width of the first breakpoint, 585px.

Returning to the breakpoint's media query, at 585 pixels in this example. That viewport size is a candidate for the two-column grid described above with the primary and supporting areas in a 16:9 (1.778) ratio with each other, with a gridline-derived 22px gutter between them.

But the padding set on the grid margins set a new context value. Some basic math is necessary to calculate the two columns' widths. At the first media query, the viewport is 585 pixels wide, but 66px of that is taken up by the combined left and right padding on #page. So the space for the grid to occupy is 519 pixels (585 − 66 = 519). Subtracting from that space a 22px gutter, there is a total of 497 pixels of space for the two columns to occupy (519 − 22 = 497).

The remaining mathematics challenge is to divide that 497 pixels into two parts, in a 16:9 (1.778) ratio. (I know, this is a ton of math, but the visual result will be worth it.) The most straightforward way to figure this out is to add the numbers in your ratio together (16 + 9 for a 16:9 ratio = 25). Then divide the remaining column space, 497 pixels in this example, by that number: 497 / 25 = 19.88. Multiply that value, 19.88 pixels in this example, by the two components of the ratio. In this case:

```
16 * 19.88 = 318.08px
9 * 19.88 = 178.92px
```

Adding up 381.08 and 178.92, just as a check on all of this math, returns the number 497. The values of the columns' widths are correct and in the expected 16:9 ratio with each other. With these three values (318.08px and 178.92px for the columns, and 22px for the gutter that separates them), it's possible to build up the media query for 585px specified earlier. This can be done in percentages, using the padding-corrected content width of #page that was calculated above (519 pixels, in this example):

```
@media screen and (min-width: 585px) {
  #primary {
    width: 61.28709056%;
      /* 318.08px / 519px = 0.6128709056 */
  }
  #supporting {
    width: 34.47398844%;
      /* 178.92px / 519px = 0.3447398844 */
  }
}
```

As you can probably see, the CSS above specifies widths for the primary and supporting columns (matching two semantically structured sectioning elements marked with the IDs primary and supporting in the RPK). It does so in percentage units, which are calculated based on 519 pixels, the total width that the grid occupies at the 585px breakpoint. Don't forget to multiply that result by 100 to arrive at a percentage value (e.g., 0.6128709056 × 100 = 61.28709056%). Previewing the work at this point (Figure 18.6), the columns' widths have

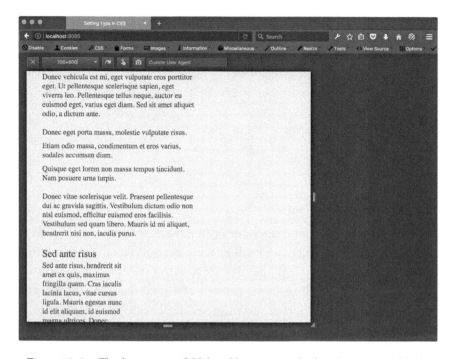

**Figure 18.6.** The first step in a CSS-based layout is to calculate the proper widths for the columns. But without some kind of CSS to position the elements, they appear stacked on top of each other.

been adjusted. Additional CSS is required to position them side by side.

But before moving on to position the primary and supporting columns, it is good practice to keep in your CSS a record of all of the calculations used to arrive at a grid's dimensions and ratios. Those values can be written in a CSS comment, just before the media query that will set the layout:

```
/*
  Baseline grid: 22px
  Viewport: 585px
  Modular scale: 16:9 -> 1.778 (minor seventh)

  585px - 66px grid margin = 519px of available
    space
  2-Column Grid:
```

```
Margin: 33px
Grid width: 519px (2 columns + 1 gutter)
Gutter: 22px
Primary Column: 318.08px
Left-hand Offset: 340.08px (Primary column +
  gutter)
Supporting Column: 178.92px
*/
```

## CSS Layout with Floats

There are two traditional methods of handling layouts in CSS: positioning and floats. Positioning will be used later in the chapter, but for setting columns whose lengths may vary, with one sometimes longer than the other depending on the content of a page, floats are the better method currently. Another, superior method called CSS Flexbox, which is not yet widely supported enough in browsers to be used on its own, is implemented using JavaScript-based feature detection in Chapter 20. The book's companion website describes still another method, CSS Grids, which has yet to be released in its final specification by the W3C (2016).

CSS floats are created using the float property (MDN 2016b). The float property can be set to left, right, or none. Setting float: left on an element pulls it out of the normal document flow, allowing other elements that follow to sit to the floated element's right. float: right would do the same, but allow elements that follow to sit to the left. float: none disallows any elements to sit to the right or left, and is usually used to reset an element that would had been floated left or right.

For the two-column layout in this example, the primary column (#primary) can be set to float to the left. The supporting column (#supporting) must then offset the width of the primary column plus the gutter. That pixel value is noted in the CSS comments for the left-hand offset two-column grid above: 340.08px (318.08px for the column plus 22px for the gutter). The offset will be set using the CSS margin property, which does not add to the width of an element the way that padding does.

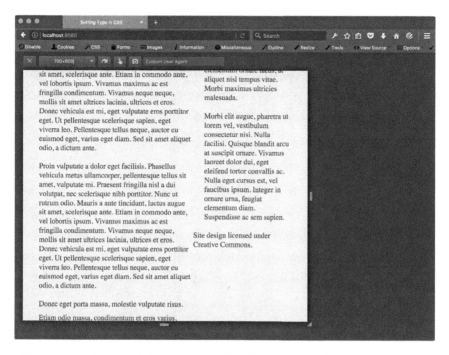

**Figure 18.7.** This page's footer appears below the secondary column and floated next to the primary column. The CSS `clear` property set on the footer will fix this problem.

When using floats, its useful to set another property called `clear` on elements that should not move to appear next to a floated element (MDN 2016c). Like `float`, `clear` can take a value of `left` or `right`, but it's more common and convenient to use `clear: both`, which disallows the element from sitting next to either left- or right-floated elements. In the case of the RPK, the footer element could potentially float next to `#primary` (see Figure 18.7). So it's a candidate for `clear: both`.

Adding the correct float and left-hand margin values, plus setting the footer to clear any floated elements so it appears at the bottom of the page, the completed media query for the two-column grid looks like this:

```
@media screen and (min-width: 585px) {
  #primary {
    width: 61.28709056%;
      /* 318.08px / 519px = 0.6128709056 */
```

```
    float: left;
  }
  #supporting {
    width: 34.47398844%;
      /* 178.92px / 519 = 0.3447398844 */
    margin-left: 65.52601156%;
      /* 340.08px / 519px = 0.6552601156 */
  }
  #footer {
    clear: both;
  }
}
```

Previewing the design in the browser, the two columns continue to expand to fill the width of the grid, because their values have been set as percentages. This is the phenomenon of fluid grids in responsive web design. The footer is now also clearing the floated column, as expected (Figure 18.8).

## BUILDING GRIDS FOR
## EVER-LARGER VIEWPORTS

Building larger grids repeats the process presented so far. Open the viewport wider and watch for lines of text, particularly in the larger #primary column, that get too long to read. The styles set in the 585px media-query show that the new two-column design's larger column becomes uncomfortable to read at around 945 pixels. That's the same 60-odd character line-length where the original single-column design became too difficult to read. So it's time to create a new media query, this one at 945 pixels.

The important thing to note, before going any further, is that the page content and design dictate the breakpoints for each media query. Many designers mistakenly set their breakpoints based on the screen sizes of the latest must-have smartphone or tablet, but those sizes are moving targets. If you always set your breakpoints based on the viewport size at which your design looks best for the content it contains, your design will always look fantastic, regardless of the screen size on the next killer, must-have device.

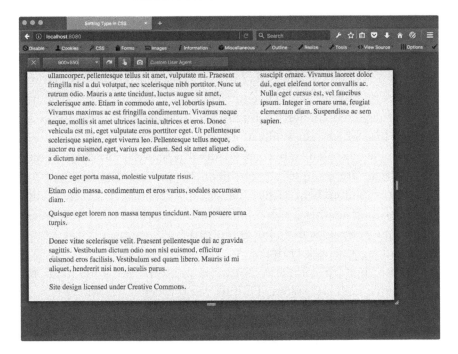

**Figure 18.8.** Percentage units allow the grid-based design to fill the allotted space. The CSS `clear` property keeps the footer where it belongs, below the primary column.

## FIXED VERSUS FLUID GUTTERS

The examples in this chapter include gutters in the calculations for the page's spatial zones and offsets. That will result in fluid gutters, which might not be desirable given that the baseline grid from which they are derived remains constant as the viewport expands and contracts. The gutters, in other words, might look better if they remain constant, with only the sizes of the columns themselves expanding. The mathematical trade-off there is that the columns will no longer remain in mathematical proportion to the gutters. The book's companion site includes examples showing how to use fixed gutters. Test your design with both forms and see which one looks better across a range of viewport sizes.

With more space to work with on a 945px viewport, a grid system can take the place of the simple two-column grid: in this case, I have chosen a five-column grid system. That choice is not wholly arbitrary. 16 + 9 = 25, so a 5-column grid (25 ÷ 5 = 5) is implied in the 16:9 ratio. Think of it as five groups of five tiny columns, if you like. Grid systems of odd-numbered columns naturally avoid perfect symmetry across a page. Although certain applications of symmetrical grids make sense, for example to a calendar of events or other repeated information, most page designs are going to support hierarchies of information. An odd number of columns helps ensure that one multicolumn spatial zone will be larger than another. From a simple aesthetic standpoint, symmetrical designs seem appealing, but asymmetry holds stronger visual interest over longer periods of time.

Here is the CSS comment that contains all the sizing information for a five-column grid system. I'll walk you through it below:

```
/*
  Baseline grid: 22px
  Viewport: 945px
  Modular scale: 16:9 -> 1.778 (minor seventh)

  5-Column Grid System
  Margin: 119.36 (238.72 / 2)
  Grid width: 706.28px (5 columns + 4 gutters)
  Gutter: 22px
  Column: 123.656px

  Spatial Zones:   Offsets:
  1 col: 123.656   1 col: 145.656
  2 col: 269.312   2 col: 291.312
  3 col: 414.968   3 col: 436.968
  4 col: 560.624   4 col: 582.624
  5 col: 706.280   5 col: -
*/
```

In the comment, I refresh my memory about the baseline grid and the viewport for which a grid is designed, as well the modular scale. It's possible that at larger screen sizes, a typeface might need to run large enough that it becomes necessary to adjust the baseline grid. But for now, this grid system is sticking with the 22px baseline grid.

The comment then notes the number of columns, plus their gutters and widths. The 123.656px width is derived from the 1.778 modular scale, and I chose it because columns of that size would fit within the 945 pixels of the viewport at the point the media query is introduced. The grid system's margin is arrived at by subtracting the total grid width from the size of the media query (945px − 706.28px), and dividing the remaining space in half for a centered page. An alternative would be to set uneven margins based on the 16:9 ratio, using the same method for arriving at the two-column grid above: Divide the total margin by 25, and then multiply by 16 to get the width of one margin, perhaps the right, and multiply by 9 to arrive at the smaller margin, which would have the design sitting a little more closely to the left-hand side of the viewport.

Finally, still within the CSS comment above, I created a reference table of spatial zones (columns plus inner gutters) and offsets (spatial zones plus another gutter). There's no five-column offset because that would be off the grid, obviously.

Compared to the first two-column grid, the grid-system styles in the 945px media query are not a whole lot more complex:

```
@media screen and (min-width: 945px) {
  #page {
    padding-left: 12.63068783%;
      /* 119.36px / 945px = 0.1263068783 */
    padding-right: 12.63068783%;
      /* 119.36px / 945px = 0.1263068783 */
  }
  #primary {
    width: 58.75403523%; /* 3-column zone */
      /* 414.968px / 706.28px = 0.5875403523 */
  }
  #supporting {
    margin-left: 61.86894716%; /* 3-column offset */
      /* 436.968px / 706.28px = 0.6186894716 */
    width: 38.13105284%; /* 2-column zone */
      /* 269.312px / 706.28px = 0.3813105284 */
  }
}
```

## CSS BOX SIZING

On all modern browsers, CSS sizes boxes according to the content-box model. In the content-box model, padding and border are added to width (and height) of the boxes content. Consider this CSS:

```
#navigation {
  width: 200px;
  padding: 20px;
}
```

The actual displayed width of #navigation in a browser will be 240px: 200 pixels of width plus 20 pixels of padding on the right and left. The same behavior occurs with percentages and other units.

For mathematical convenience, web designers sometimes alter that behavior by setting the box-sizing property in CSS to border-box. In border-box sizing, padding and border effectively *subtracts* from the width allotted to content as set on the width property.

```
#navigation {
  box-sizing: border-box;
  width: 200px;
  padding: 20px;
}
```

In that case, #navigation will display as 200px, with the padding appearing to push the content away from the edges of the box by 20px on a side. box-sizing is useful for page layout when combining a fixed gutter with a fluid grid column or spatial zone. Regardless of the box model, the CSS margin property has no effect on an element's width, which is why it is used to execute offsets in grid-based layout.

See the MDN on box-sizing for more information: https://developer.mozilla.org/en-US/docs/Web/CSS/box-sizing

Unlike the two-column grid, which preserved the same 33px-derived grid margins as the single-column design, at 945 pixels the grid margins reflect the remaining space left over from the grid system. Those percentage units are derived from the entire viewport, 945 pixels. Having established that, the rest of the design relies on setting the new three-column

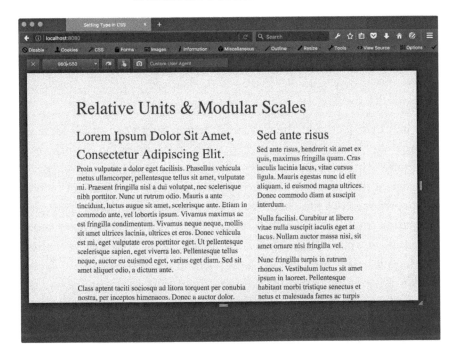

**Figure 18.9.**    The page's layout is now set to a five-column grid system.

spatial zone for the `#primary` element, plus the two-column spatial zone of the `#supporting` element. Because the media queries in this chapter's examples query for `min-width`, there is no need to repeat any of the float properties from the two-column grid. That adheres to the DRY principle (Don't Repeat Yourself): as with the baseline styles, styles set in `min-width` media queries carry forward to ever-larger screens.

Figure 18.9 shows the completed grid-based layout. The process of establishing and setting the content to new and size-adjusted grid systems could continue indefinitely for ever-larger screens. But because a new site often needs lots of other work, it's possible to look once again at where the primary column's text becomes difficult to read, and freeze the design at that point, even as screens get larger. A media query where this five-column grid breaks down, at around 1170 pixels, is all that it takes:

```
@media screen and (min-width: 1170px) {
  #page {
    max-width: 875px;
```

```
    margin: 0 auto;
    padding-left: 0;
    padding-right: 0;
  }
}
```

First, that query sets the max-width property to 875 pixels for the #page container. All of the percentage-based units set on the primary and supporting columns' widths and offsets will remain locked as a percentage of that number. The max-width property itself cannot be set as a percentage, or the page layout will continue to expand. A simple centering trick, margin: 0 auto, ensures that the grid remains centered in viewports larger than 1170 pixels. With that in place, this media query sets the left and right padding for #page to zero. That padding is no longer needed, because the margin property now sets the grid system's margin.

Just remember to come back and build the larger media queries as your site matures.

## APPLYING THE GRID TO THE HEADER

This chapter has applied the different grids only to the example's content area. By way of concluding, let's look at an example of applying the grid to the page header and the navigation area that the header contains. Figure 18.10 shows that the navigation is sitting basically unstyled beneath the page's major heading, although both the heading and the navigation are set to the page's baseline grid.

To make the navigation easier to find visually, it could run flush with the very top of the page, with the page's major heading below it. Both the navigation and the heading will remain consistent with the page's baseline grid, however. The three navigation elements will be arranged horizontally and occupy the entire width of the viewport, to keep their clickable/tappable areas as large as possible on smaller screens.

Rather than use floats, this part of the grid can be executed with CSS positioning. The MDN pages (2016c) for the position property have complete details for all of its values. But in summary, by default all HTML elements are positioned statically (position: static).

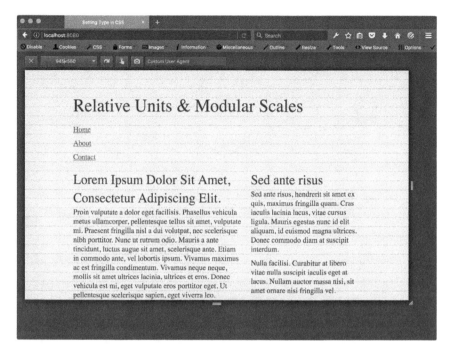

**Figure 18.10.** The header area and navigation are set to a baseline grid, but not positioned to conform with the rest of the page layout.

When making a significant change to the layout using positioning, the element that needs to move the farthest away from its static position is given `position: absolute`. Other elements on the page will behave as though the absolutely positioned element no longer exists. Figure 18.11 shows a rendering that includes the following CSS for positioning the navigation absolutely, setting it to occupy 100 percent of the viewport, and aligning it to the very top left corner of the page using the `top` and `left` positioning properties:

```
#navigation {
  position: absolute;
  width: 100%; /* Prevent from collapsing
    to content's size */
  top: 0;
  left: 0;
}
```

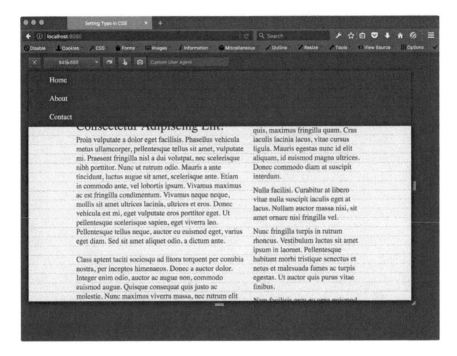

**Figure 18.11.**   Once positioned absolutely, the navigation area appears to run over the top of the page's major heading.

With this simple layout, `position: absolute` positions the navigation absolutely relative to the viewport. In more complex layouts, it's sometimes necessary to position an element absolutely relative to a parent element, rather than the viewport. The parent element is set with `position: relative`. For examples of that, see the book's companion website.

All that is necessary to add here, however, are the styles to display the navigation list as a horizontal navigation bar. Those styles follow a rule to push the page's major heading down below the space occupied by the navigation. This is accomplished by setting the em equivalent of three gridlines of padding (66 pixels for a 22px baseline grid) to the top of #header:

```
#header {
  padding-top: 3.667em;
    /* 66px (button + gridline) / 18px = 3.667 */
}
```

```
.navigation li, .navigation li:last-child {
  display: inline-block;
  padding: 0;
}
.navigation {
  line-height: 1;
  padding: 0;
}
.navigation li a {
  display: block;
  background-color: #222;
  color: #EFE5BE;
  text-decoration: none;
  padding: 1.222em; /* 22px / 18px = 1.222em */
  padding-top: 0.722em; /* 13px / 18px = 0.722em */
  padding-bottom: 0.722em;
}
```

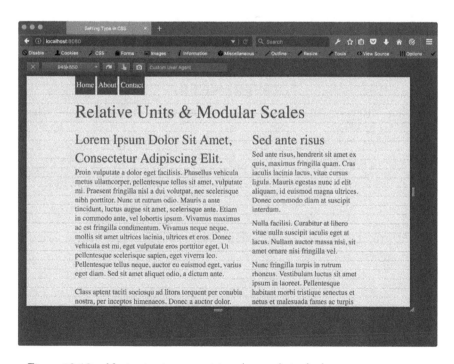

**Figure 18.12.**   Navigation is now positioned properly in the layout.

See the book's companion site to see how the navigation in this example is adjusted to conform to the two-column 16:9 grid and the five-column grid system.

## NEXT STEPS

This has been a dense and challenging chapter. The fluid, percentage-width grids that form the foundation of responsive design must be calculated precisely to keep a design from falling apart within a given media query's breakpoint. If positioning techniques prove challenging for you, there is nothing wrong with setting your grid's width values to pixels first and getting the positioning right before calculating widths as percentage values. If you are using Git, create a branch to isolate that work, preserving the rest of your CSS until your grid is set just right.

Unlike lines of text, which automatically expand and contract to fit different fluid layouts, images and video require special preparation and treatment to behave responsively. The next chapter looks at responsive media that integrates seamlessly with grid-based responsive page design.

## REFERENCES

Bringhurst, Robert. 2012. *The Elements of Typographic Style*, 4th ed. Seattle: Hartley & Marks.

MDN. 2016a. "Mastering Margin Collapsing." https://developer.mozilla.org/en-US/docs/Web/CSS/CSS_Box_Model/Mastering_margin_collapsing

MDN. 2016b. "Float." https://developer.mozilla.org/en-US/docs/Web/CSS/float

MDN. 2016c. "Position." https://developer.mozilla.org/en-US/docs/Web/CSS/position

W3C. 2016. "CSS Grid Layout Module Level 1." September 29. https://www.w3.org/TR/css-grid-1/

# CHAPTER 19

# Responsive Media

Chapter 3 provided an overview of gathering and preparing multimedia content, including images, audio, and video. This chapter looks at the most accessible and sustainable methods for displaying media elements and integrating them with the design of your page. HTML5 introduced new methods to load audio and video elements without the need for plugins, but because the precise details of those methods continue to change and are in some cases too complex to go into here, additional information and updated source code examples are available at the book's companion website, http://webpg.es/.

The Rapid Prototyping Kit (RPK) includes a media folder with subfolders for images, audio, and video. If you decide to host media content on your own server (versus, for example, using YouTube for video hosting), take advantage of the RPK's folders or a structure like them to keep your media content organized and manageable (see Chapter 21). As the examples in this chapter show, it's essential to keep your media files organized, because your site must make available different formats and versions of each media file.

## CONTENT IMAGES: BASIC HTML AND CSS

Content images are an essential part of many web pages. They make content more attractive and add visual interest to pages for sighted users. All content images—that is, all images that appear on your pages as content, not decoration—should be loaded in the HTML image tag, <img />, which requires two attributes:

- `src`: the path to your image file, from the page referencing it. Remember from Chapter 3 that web-friendly formats include JPEG files (`.jpg`, `.jpeg`), PNG files (`.png`), and GIF files (`.gif`). Never use HTML to load TIFF files or the authoring files from your image editor (e.g., the `.psd` files from Adobe Photoshop). They cannot be displayed in most web browsers.
- `alt`: the short alternate text for your image. `alt` attributes can include text like "A photo of . . . " or "An illustration of . . . " or even "A pie chart showing . . ." to describe the media in the image, followed by the fewest possible words to describe its content. `alt` attributes must be kept brief. Older browsers render only the first 100 characters or so of `alt` text. I have also found that some newer browsers, particularly Safari, will not display `alt` text that runs longer than the width of an image, which is of course completely arbitrary, especially in responsive design.

A complete, basic well-formed `<img>` tag looks like this:

```
<img src="/media/img/woods.jpg" alt="Photo of a road
 in the woods." />
```

The rest of this chapter will look at improving on the form of the basic image tag for greater accessibility.

Note that the `<img />` tag should no longer include `height` and `width` attributes. While that was once considered good practice, responsive images rely on CSS, not HTML attributes, to specify the size of an image. The RPK's CSS file includes this style declaration for handling responsive images:

```
img {
  display: block;
  max-width: 100%;
}
```

By default, browsers display images inline, so that declaration sets them to display as blocks, which is necessary for having better control over how images are positioned and conform to a layout. Images are also given a `max-width: 100%` style, which sizes them no larger than

**Figure 19.1.** Responsive images assume the size of their parent element.

their containing element (Figures 19.1 and 19.2). The next section looks at the semantic `<figure>` element, which is a new tag introduced in HTML5 to semantically structure images and other media. Any decorative or background images should be loaded using the CSS `background-image` property; see the book's companion site for examples.

## New HTML5 Figure Elements

HTML5 introduced the `<figure>` element "to annotate illustrations, diagrams, photos, code listings, etc." Content inside of `<figure>` is "self-contained (like a complete sentence) and is typically referenced as a single unit from the main flow of the document" (W3C 2014a, under the section "Grouping Content"). An individual image, or a gallery of images, can function as "self-contained" content. `<figure>` can optionally contain a `<figcaption>` element, although *optionally* is

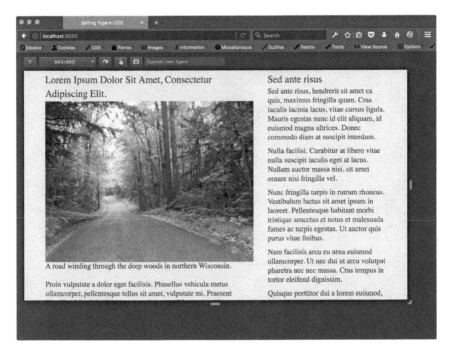

**Figure 19.2.** Same page as shown in Figure 19.1, but at a larger viewport. In this case, the image is set within the two-column grid from Chapter 18.

only from a validator standpoint. A `<figcaption>` element *must* be present to make media more accessible and meaningful to all users:

```
<figure id="photo-woods">
  <img src="/media/img/woods.jpg"
    alt="Photo of a road in the woods." />
  <figcaption>
    A road winding through the deep woods in
    northern Wisconsin.
  </figcaption>
</figure>
```

It is useful to include a unique ID on figure elements, so that they can be referenced from elsewhere on the page. In responsive web design, where layouts change to conform to the space of the browser viewport, it would be a bad idea to reference an image from the main text of a page by writing *The photo above* or *The photo at left*, because its position may change in response to the layout, or a future design. It may also change if someone switches to a readability mode in their browser, or reads your content in one of the many available apps that save web content for reading later or offline.

But by referencing the figure element's fragment identifier in a hyperlink (see Chapter 7), page text can reference images and other media in a way that takes advantage of HTML semantics and browser behavior of scrolling to URL fragments:

```
<p>
  I snapped <a href="#photo-woods">the photo
  on this page</a> while on a walk in the
  woods last summer.
</p>
```

By prefixing all figure element IDs with `photo-`, a simple attribute selector can style anchor elements that point to photos: `a[href*="#photo-"]` will style any anchor tags that reference a photo, even if the referenced photo is on another page within your site (see Chapter 12 for more on attribute selectors). A more generic ID prefixed with `#figure-` might be useful on pages or sites with many different kinds of figure elements, while a class such as `photo` or `video` on the figure element can provide a useful style hook for any figure styles unique to a specific type of media.

## Improved Accessibility with ARIA

Chapter 7 mentioned ARIA attributes for enhancing the accessibility of the page. Two attributes that every figure element should have are `aria-labelled-by` and `aria-described-by`. Note the British spelling of `labelled`, with two Ls.

The W3C (2014b) notes that "The aria-labelled-by attribute is similar to aria-described-by in that both reference other elements to calculate a text alternative, but a label should be concise, where a description is intended to provide more verbose information."

Both attributes take as their value a unique ID that labels or describes the media marked by the figure element. `aria-labelled-by` is a natural pointer to the `<figcaption>` element with the unique ID of `caption-woods` in this example:

```
<figure id="photo-woods"
  aria-labelled-by="caption-woods"
  aria-described-by="description-woods">
  <img src="/media/img/woods.jpg"
    alt="Photo of a road in the woods." />
  <figcaption id="caption-woods">
    A road winding through the deep woods in
    northern Wisconsin.
    <a href="#description-woods">Full
      description</a>.
  </figcaption>
</figure>
```

The ID `description-woods` would reference some element or section within the page that talks about the photo in greater detail, perhaps the paragraph in the example above that used a fragment identifier to reference the photo. In addition to referencing that ID from an ARIA attribute, an anchor tag points all users to the relevant section of the page that describes the media. That's universal design in action: an enhanced experience for all users.

Consistently prefixing IDs with `caption-` and `description-` makes it possible to write a similar attribute-selector shorthand as described above. Additionally, combined with the CSS `:target` pseudoclass (MDN 2016a), elements targeted by a URL fragment that includes `#description-` can also be styled:

```
*[id^="description-"]:target {
  color: red;
}
```

The earlier example used attribute selectors to style anchor tags pointing to URL fragments. This selector styles any element (`*`) whose unique ID begins with *description-* `[id^="description-"]` when that element is targeted in a URL fragment. A URL pointing to `http://example.com/#description-woods` would, with that CSS, color the description's text red. That is useful for layouts that require no scrolling. The book's companion site at `http://webpg.es/` has examples of this that also include CSS transitions for a smoother, more noticeable presentation of content referenced by a fragment identifier.

# RESPONSIVE IMAGES

The text-based enhancements and fallbacks provided by `<figure>`, `<figcaption>`, and ARIA attributes significantly increase the accessibility of images beyond the humble `alt` attribute on the image tag. But there is still a critical accessibility problem with the original image tag: the `src` attribute.

`src` can only take a single value, meaning it can only point to one image. That comes with significant trade-offs in responsive design, where one page should be as accessible to a small, low-resolution phone on a slow internet connection as it is to a 5K desktop display with blazing connection speeds. If `src` points to a low-resolution photo, it will look dinky on the 5K. But if the 5K-friendly image is loaded, phones and other smaller devices will download far more image information than they can display, gobbling up precious amounts of expensive mobile data in the process.

That limitation of `src` motivated the work of the Responsive Issues Community Group (formerly the Responsive Images Community Group, W3C 2016a), which pushed forward on two new HTML features for handling responsive images: the `srcset` attribute and the `<picture>` element. Those features have been a part of HTML: The Living Standard since 2012 (WHATWG 2016) and are set to be included in the HTML 5.1 specification being finalized by the W3C (2016b). Browser support is strong for `srcset` and `<picture>`, but nowhere near universal. Chapter 20 describes a JavaScript-based polyfill that delivers responsive images to less-capable browsers.

## srcset

In its simplest usage, `srcset` complements the existing `src` attribute on the image tag by providing browsers a list of multiple candidate image files to select from. That information is contextualized by a second attribute, `sizes`, that lists media query breakpoints and the approximate width of the viewport an image will occupy, using the viewport width (vw) unit.

Revisiting the design from Chapter 18, and assuming that content images will run the width of the primary column, this range of image sizes would be required:

## SIZING IMAGES FOR THE WEB

In the old days, meaning up until a few years ago, images were best saved to the  exact dimensions as they would be displayed on the web. The first edition of this book gave that same advice.

Responsive images change that, and both `srcset` and `<picture>` provide a simple but powerful mechanism to deliver the right image to the right screen. Once a grid is in place (see Chapter 18) and you have figured out your breakpoints, you can quickly calculate a set of image sizes across your different layouts.

Images must be sized in pixel dimensions. High-density/retina displays re-quire a pixel-doubled or even pixel-tripled version of the image. When preparing images, I create a simple table like this:

```
Pixels
    300 / 150 @2x / 100 @3x
    600 / 300 @2x / 200 @3x
    750 / 375 @2x / 250 @3x
   1200 / 600 @2x / 400 @3x
   1500 / 750 @2x / 500 @3x
```

That lists the widths of images across a design's breakpoints, and notes their doubled (@2x) and tripled (@3x) sizes. Using the techniques in this chap-ter, the 600px image might be delivered to a standard screen needing an image about 600px wide, or to a high-density @2x display needing an image smaller than 300px wide.

Sizing images should be one of the last tasks completed before a site goes live. It's unwise to spend a lot of time resizing images in an image editor and experimenting with compression rates when a grid and layout are still in flux.

```
mobile: -> 519px max. (100% width of #page @ 585px)
min-width: 585px -> 317-580px
   (61.28709056% width of #page @ 945px)
min-width: 945px -> 415-687px
   (58.75403523% width of #page @ 1170px)
min-width: 1170px -> 514px max.
   (58.75403523% max-width of #page @ 1170px)
```

## IMAGE ASPECT RATIOS

Responsive image sizes are calculated by widths, and browsers will respect the aspect ratios inherent in the pixel dimensions of image files.

A modular scale used to set your type sizes and column grids can also help determine the aspect ratios for your images: 4:3, 16:9, and so on. For example, a 700px-wide image in a 4:3 aspect ratio will be 525 pixels tall (700 #db 1.333 = 525.131; image files must always be rounded to the nearest whole pixel).

Examples of the actual calculations are on the book's companion site, but in brief summary, the width ranges of the images are calculable by determining the width of #page and then taking the percentage value of #primary, at both the smallest and largest possible size at the upper and lower bounds of a specific media query. From largest to smallest, a basic set of @1x images for this design might have widths of 520, 580, and 690. Those are the largest possible widths at each breakpoint, rounded up to an even number.

A few other widths can be determined with the minimum sizes: at mobile scale, 260 is a simple half of 520 for smaller screens. There is a 263px difference (580px − 317px) between the smallest and largest possible images within the 585px breakpoint, and a 272px difference (687px − 415px) at the 945px breakpoint. 448 (132 + 317) and 551 (136 + 415) are the respective half sizes, but those are close enough to the 520 and 580 values already in the initial list of sizes.

With the list of images now at 260, 520, 580, and 690, the image dimensions for use on pixel-doubled (@2x) and pixel-tripled (@3x) displays can be calculated:

```
--- @1x
  260 / 130 @2x / 86 @3x
  520 / 260 @2x / 173 @3x
  580 / 290 @2x / 193 @3x
  690 / 345 @2x / 230 @3x
--- @2x
  1040 / 520 @2x / 346 @3x
  1160 / 580 @2x / 386 @3x
  1380 / 690 @2x / 460 @3x
```

```
--- @3x
   780 /  390 @2x /  260 @3x
  1560 /  780 @2x /  520 @3x
  1740 /  870 @2x /  580 @3x
  2070 / 1035 @2x /  690 @3x
```

Not all of those sizes will need to be generated from your source image. The @1x image sizes (260, 520, 580, and 690) probably should be. 520 @1x is the same image as 260 @2x, so that size is already covered. The 1040 @2x image should be included, however. 260, 520, 580, 690, and 1024 are good starter sizes. For the images larger than 1040 (the two larger @2x images and the three larger @3x images), let your image editor be your guide, particularly in the file sizes it outputs.

One benefit of the extraordinarily large images, like the 1740px image required for 580 @3x, is that it is often possible to use an image editor to compress the image far beyond what would look acceptable for a @1x image of comparable display size. Image dimensions are always in hardware pixels, but they are rendered as virtual or reference pixels on high-density displays. An image that displays as 400 × 300 on a @2x HDD requires an image file with 800 × 600 pixels. For a @3x HDD, the image file would have 1200 × 900 pixels.

In certain cases, a highly compressed @2x or @3x image may have a smaller file size than a @1x image with fewer pixels. But because @1x images are usually displayed on lower resolution devices, they should be compressed as little as possible while still maintaining a reasonable file size. For examples, see the book's companion site.

When saving files to be used as responsive images, I use a file-naming scheme that lists the image width in pixels, and the compression rate that I used in my image editor. So the file woods-580-60.jpg indicates that the image file is 580 pixels wide, compressed at 60 percent (a number that is arbitrary to the program used to do compression; on some programs, higher numbers means higher compression, while others use lower numbers for higher compression, usually with a reference to the quality of the image).

The width is a useful piece of information to have in the file name, because srcset requires that each candidate image be followed by a width value of the file's pixel dimensions:

```
<img
  srcset="/media/img/1024-20-woods.jpg 1024w,
    /media/img/woods-690-60.jpg 690w,
    /media/img/woods-580-60.jpg 580w,
    /media/img/woods-520-80.jpg 520w,
    /media/img/woods-260-80.jpg 260w"
  sizes="(min-width: 945px) 44vw,
    (min-width: 585px) 54vw,
    100vw"
  src="/media/img/woods-260-80.jpg"
  alt="Photo of a road in the woods." />
```

Having the width in the file name makes it easy to write those w values. The `sizes` attribute provides instructions to browsers as to how large an image will be relative to the size of the viewport. That is calculated by taking the minimum image size and dividing it by the size of the viewport in the media query. Recall this line from above:

```
min-width: 585px -> 317-580px
  (61.28709056% width of #page @ 945px)
```

For that size, $317 \div 585 = 0.542$, or `54vw`. That means that images within that breakpoint are sized `54vw`, or roughly 54 percent of the viewport's width (vw).

As you can see in the example above, images and the range of sizes are listed largest to smallest in `srcset`. A browser will first look at the size ranges and calculate how wide the image will be, factoring in whether the display is @1x, @2x, or @3x. It then looks through the images and width values in `srcset` until it finds a match. Listing images and especially sizes from largest to smallest prevents a too-small image being loaded on a large screen. The browser, in other words, stops when it finds an image that fits. Small images fit on large screens, obviously, so a browser would find a match prematurely among images listed smallest to largest.

## <picture>

The images listed in an `srcset` attribute should all contain the same image, differing only in dimensions and compression rates. But simply resizing an image is often not enough to keep its content accessible. The same image displayed at 1000px across and 200px across will not reveal the same level of detail. Cropping and perhaps even a different orientation (portrait or landscape) may better convey the content of an image across a range of viewports.

To accommodate that scenario, the RICG developed a spec for the <picture> element. <picture> takes a set of <source> elements. Each <source> element matches a particular media query, using a special media attribute, but has its own srcset. Each <source> element might correspond to a cropped version of the image, or to an image prepared in a specific orientation (portrait or landscape).

The source code for <picture> is beyond the limits of what is easy to run in this book, but the book's companion website contains numerous examples and full explanation of the source code.

The remainder of this chapter will look at the HTML <audio> and <video> tags. Those, too, are presented in additional detail, and with actual audio and video content, on the book's companion site.

## HTML5 AUDIO

Sound must be treated with care if you're not going to drive your audience away with it. There are three common mistakes that sites make in misusing audio:

- **Sound that plays automatically when someone loads a page.** People view websites at work, in their offices, and other places where sound would be embarrassing or unwelcome if it started playing unannounced. Other people prefer to have music playing on their devices while browsing the web. Don't create sonic embarrassment or chaos with your site. The HTML <audio> element has an autoplay attribute. Never use it.

- **Sound that cannot be stopped once it begins playing.** If the only way to stop sound on a website is to close it or go to another site, that is exactly what site visitors will do. And they will be very wary of listening to any sound on your site in the future, should they ever return. The HTML <audio> element has a `controls` attribute that instructs browsers to provide playback controls. Always use it.

- **Sound that is recorded at very low levels.** Sound that is recorded at low levels (that is, sound that is very quiet relative to other sounds, including music and system sounds) will force visitors to turn up their speakers or headphones as high as they can. Such an adjustment can just about send people out of their minds with fright when music or operating-system sounds—like a new email alert—play at considerably higher levels. Refer to the book's companion website at `http://webpg.es/` to learn more about ensuring proper sound levels when you record and edit sound files.

The HTML `<audio>` element instructs capable browsers to play audio files. A basic `<audio>` tag should be prepared like this:

```
<audio controls="controls">
  <source src="/media/audio/interview.mp3"
    type="audio/mpeg" />
  <p>Download <a href="/media/audio/interview.mp3">
    the audio file</a>.</p>
</audio>
```

The `controls` attribute, prepared in well-formed style as `controls="controls"`, will display basic playback controls for users to play, pause, and otherwise interact with the audio. An audio tag can include multiple `<source>` tags for providing audio in multiple formats. Each source tag has an `src` that refers to the path to an audio file, as well as a MIME type indicating the type of audio file. See MDN (2016b) for a full list of supported audio formats across different browsers.

To keep audio accessible to users of browsers that do not support the `<audio>` element, a simple paragraph contains a link to download the audio file for listening in a program or device that supports MP3 files. While many examples of `<audio>` use on the web show a fallback that reads something like *Your browser does not support audio*, it's better practice to provide an alternative means of access.

Audio files that contain speech, including spoken word and singing, should be accompanied by transcripts. Those can be as simple as a separate HTML file, but see the book's companion site for up-to-date information on using the `<track>` element to provide timed transcripts for speech in web audio and video.

## HTML5 VIDEO

HTML5 also introduced the `<video>` element for native video playback (MDN 2016c). Unlike the nearly universally supported MP3 format for HTML audio, video must be presented in a few different formats in order to be maximally accessible across different browsers and devices (MDN 2016b).

A `<video>` tag is prepared similarly to the audio example above:

```
<video controls="controls">
  <source src="/media/video/virtual-tour.mp4"
    type="video/mp4">
  <source src="/media/video/virtual-tour.webm"
    type="video/webm">
  <p>
    Download this video as
    <a href="/media/video/virtual-tour.mp4">
      MP4</a>
    or <a href="/media/video/virtual-tour.webm">
      WebM</a>.
  </p>
</video>
```

Unlike `<source>` tags used with the picture element, there is no way at present to offer native HTML video at different sizes. Be judicious about file sizes when preparing videos. The book's companion site has information about working with hosted video services, which are somewhat better at handling video for slower connections and smaller screen sizes. However, most video-hosting services require users to embed their videos using an `<iframe>` tag instead of the native `<video>` tag.

The book's companion site also has examples of native HTML video. As with images, CSS can ensure that audio controls and videos are responsive. This is the full responsive media style from the RPK:

```
img,audio,video {
  display: block;
  max-width: 100%;
}
```

All media will be sized no larger than its parent element, including controls for audio playback.

## NEXT STEPS

This chapter has covered some of the core concepts and challenges of loading responsive media content into your web pages. The next chapter will look at interactive elements to enhance your pages.

## REFERENCES

MDN. 2016a. "Audio." https://developer.mozilla.org/en-US/docs/Web/HTML/Element/audio

MDN. 2016b. "Media Formats Supported by the HTML Audio and Video Elements." https://developer.mozilla.org/en-US/docs/Web/HTML/Supported_media_formats

MDN. 2016c. "Video." https://developer.mozilla.org/en-US/docs/Web/HTML/Element/video

W3C. 2014a. "HTML5: A Vocabulary and Associated APIs for HTML and XHTML." https://www.w3.org/TR/html5/

W3C. 2014b. "Accessible Rich Internet Applications (WAI-ARIA) 1.0." https://www.w3.org/TR/wai-aria/

W3C. 2016a. "Responsive Issues Community Group." https://www.w3.org/community/respimg/

W3C. 2016b. "HTML 5.1." https://www.w3.org/TR/html51/

WHATWG. "HTML: The Living Standard." https://html.spec.whatwg.org/

# CHAPTER 20

# Interactive Elements

There are two possible accessibility-minded responses to the question, "Does the site I am building need JavaScript?" The first is *No*: all of a site's content and basic functionality (following links, viewing images, and so on) should be available in the absence of JavaScript. For some sites, JavaScript is simply not necessary. The second accessibility-minded response is *No, but the site is better with it*. That is the attitude of progressive enhancement: JavaScript, when available, improves a site on capable devices, without punishing less-capable devices.

This chapter looks at two approaches to progressively enhancing HTML via the Document Object Model (DOM): one based on browser detection and enhancement, and one based on user interaction. Both approaches demonstrate improved page display and interactivity made possible by careful use of JavaScript.

## PROGRESSIVELY ENHANCING BROWSERS

Standards support across the latest releases of major browsers has never been better or more uniform. But there will always be browsers in use that are many versions behind the latest release. Browsers can be progressively enhanced first by checking for support for a given web standard, and second by loading a script known generally as a **polyfill** that adds the feature to less capable browsers, when such a script exists.

## Feature Detection for Better Browsers

Feature detection scripts run a small test in a browser. The Modernizr project (2016a) is a popular, actively developed feature-detection library that allows web designers to select detection scripts for only the features that a site actually uses.

One of the feature detections I use most is for CSS Flexbox (MDN 2016a), which offers layout methods that overcome many of the short-comings of floats and traditional CSS positioning (see Chapter 18). The book's companion site walks through selecting feature detection scripts. Modernizr adds two lines of comments to the top of its minified scripts. For detecting flexbox support, those lines look like this:

```
/*! modernizr 3.3.1 (Custom Build) | MIT *
  * https://modernizr.com/download/?-flexbox-
    setclasses !*/
```

Those are important points of reference for both the version of Modernizr (3.3.1 in that example), as well as the detection scripts (flexbox). The URL to Modernizr can be revisited, should you need to update or add additional detection scripts.

Once downloaded, a reference to the saved Modernizr script must be added to the very bottom of every HTML page on a site:

```
  <script src="/js/modernizr.min.js"></script>
</body>
</html>
```

In a browser that supports JavaScript and, in this case, flexbox, the <html> tag will have a class added to it:

```
<html class="flexbox" lang="en">
```

That class, in turn, can be used with descendant selectors in CSS (see Chapter 12). Here, the navigation layout from CSS is prepared using flexbox on browsers that support it:

```
.flexbox #header {
  display: flex;
  flex-direction: column;
  padding-top: 0;
}
```

```
.flexbox #header h1 {
  order: 2;
}
.flexbox #navigation {
  position: static;
  order: 1;
}
```

A full description and multiple examples of flexbox are available on the book's companion site, but what this example does is get rid of the trickery involved with `position: absolute` that was used in Chapter 18. Note that the `.flexbox #navigation` selector in this example restores `position: static`, the browser default, and instead uses the flexbox `order` property so that the navigation (`order: 1`) displays above the major heading `<h1>` (`order: 2`).

Importantly, the older float and position styles should remain in the CSS. That preserves the layout for older, less capable browsers while providing the newer flexbox layout method for browsers that support it, as determined by the Modernizr detection script.

## Polyfills for Less-Capable Browsers

Modernizr only detects whether a browser supports a feature. It does not extend the feature's functionality to less-capable browsers. Certain features can be added to older browsers through polyfills, provided that the browsers are running JavaScript. Scott Jehl's Picturefill (`https://github.com/scottjehl/picturefill`), for example, is an essential polyfill for pages designed to deliver responsive images (see Chapter 19). In other words, feature detection provides only hooks for use in CSS or JavaScript to capitalize on a browser's existing support for a feature, as with the `.flexbox` descendant selectors above. A polyfill introduces functionality to browsers that otherwise would not support a given feature.

Most polyfills can be added simply by downloading the script and loading it into each page of a site, just like a feature-detection script. Picturefill can be loaded in much the same way as Modernizr was above, with a few differences:

```
<head>
  <!-- Other <head> elements here -->
```

```
<script>
  // Create a <picture> element for older IE
  document.createElement('picture');
</script>
<script src="/js/picturefill.min.js"
  async="async"></script>
</head>
```

First, a `script` tag uses the `document.createElement()` method from JavaScript's Document Object Model (DOM) API (MDN 2016b) to create a `<picture>` element that older Internet Explorer browsers can interact with and style. Second, the minified Picturefill script is loaded, using the `async` attribute introduced in HTML5 (MDN 2016c), which allows the HTML page to continue to load while the `picturefill.min.js` script downloads in the background before running.

Polyfills like Picturefill require no adjustments to the source code. `<picture>` elements and `srcset` attributes, as described in Chapter 19, can be written in a standards-compliant way, and Picturefill will enable them to work in less-capable browsers running JavaScript.

To keep a page accessible to people with browsers that support neither native responsive images nor JavaScript, it is essential to provide a vanilla `<img>` tag and simple `src` attribute. See the examples in Chapter 19.

The Modernizr project community maintains a frequently updated wiki listing polyfills (Modernizr 2016b). But before loading up your site's pages with a dozen different polyfill scripts, be sure that the feature is worth including. Responsive images have the potential to drastically reduce the bandwidth a given device consumes, which is especially important on mobile data plans. But an excessive glut of JavaScript can also bog down the performance of a page.

## PROGRESSIVELY ENHANCING CONTENT

Browser-based progressive enhancement through feature detection and polyfills happens automatically. Users with capable devices may never be aware of such enhancement. By contrast, content-based progressive enhancement routinely requires some kind of user interaction. The

## JAVASCRIPT LIBRARIES

A key benefit of using a JavaScript library (sometimes also called a framework) is that it does the heavy lifting for the scripting of your site, leaving you to write leaner, higher-level code. Libraries that are updated frequently can also improve the performance of your site over time.

Also, you can elect to host your own copy of your library at your site, or you can use a service like the Google Libraries API and pull in the copy of the library that the service hosts. While it is usually beneficial to have your own copy of the library while you're doing web development on your computer (if only because you can work without an internet connection), using the Google Libraries copy may make your live site load faster if someone has already visited another site that also loads the library. And depending on how you load the script from Google, they can manage updates to the library for you, too.

For an up-to-date list of JavaScript libraries and third-party hosts, see this book's companion site.

remainder of this chapter will look at JavaScript used to progressively enhance page content via the Document Object Model (DOM).

Some books, like Jeremy Keith's (2005) classic book *DOM Scripting*, will teach you to write unobtrusive JavaScript completely from scratch. That is becoming an ever-more-viable technique as browsers align to the latest ECMAScript specifications. However, many sites still benefit from using a JavaScript library such as jQuery, whose CSS-like API is friendlier for beginners. jQuery also works out some of the idiosyncrasies among older browsers still in active use.

While writing JavaScript entirely from scratch is a useful skill, the rest of this chapter features examples that are built using a JavaScript library called jQuery (jQuery Foundation 2016). Libraries like jQuery simplify DOM scripting because they are developed and tested extensively on many different browsers. That usually makes cross-browser compatibility much easier to achieve in your scripts.

Additionally, JavaScript libraries simplify DOM scripting by offering an **application programming interface** (API) to extend the library through your own custom scripts. You can think of a library's API as being something like the controls on a video player: you probably don't need to know how, for example, the play or pause buttons on the player work, but you know what they should do when you press them. You also know that buttons only work in certain situations or under certain conditions: if a video is stopped, for example, the pause button will not do anything.

Programming library APIs are vastly more complex than the controls on a video player, though. Fortunately, most good libraries have extensive documentation. The jQuery library's general documentation, for example, is at `http://learn.jquery.com/` and its API is thoroughly documented at `http://api.jquery.com/`.

## ANATOMY OF DOM SCRIPTING

The DOM is how a web browser represents the structure and contents of an HTML document once the HTML has finished loading. Java-Script can then manipulate the browser's representation, or model. Take a familiar example: when you write CSS styles, particularly more complex selectors like `header#header h1`, you rely on the browser to have a model or representation of `<h1>` inside of `<header id="header">` so that the style you write in the CSS appears correctly when the browser displays the page.

jQuery scripts work best when run as soon as the DOM has finished loading. jQuery provides a method for doing that called `ready()`, or the ready event, which is attached to the document object (for more on JavaScript objects, see Chapter 13). Versions 1 and 2 of jQuery require `ready()` to be called directly, but as of version 3, the ready event is implicit. jQuery itself is just an object, aliased to the dollar sign (`$`):

```
// JavaScript
$(
  function() {
    // Scripts written here will run
    // once the DOM has loaded.
  }
);
```

jQuery calls an anonymous function (`function(){}`) that should contain all references to any JavaScript that must run once the DOM has loaded. The book's companion site includes example code for accessing the `ready()` event in older versions of jQuery, which are required for sites that target legacy browsers.

Translated to plainer English, "When the document object is ready, do all of the things listed here." Relying on the ready event and keeping JavaScript out of your HTML are the most important factors in keeping your JavaScript unobtrusive. If JavaScript isn't available in a visitor's browser, the script never runs, but the site must still be accessible to the JavaScript-less site visitor.

## Avoiding Conflicts with $

On a page calling many different JavaScript libraries, it's possible that more than one library might try to claim the variable $. So a safer way to handle jQuery is to use the `jQuery.noConflict();` method with the `jQuery` object directly and reference $ in the ready event's anonymous function:

```
// release $ from jQuery's control:
jQuery.noConflict();
// call the jQuery object directly:
jQuery(
  // jQuery passed in as a reference using $:
  function($) {
    // Scripts written here will use $
    // and run once the DOM has loaded.
  }
);
```

jQuery gets passed as a reference to the anonymous function, using its own local dollar sign variable: `(function($) {});`. Everything that's tucked inside the anonymous function can continue to use $ as in any other jQuery script, but without running into conflicts with other JavaScript libraries. The book's companion website details additional methods for avoiding collisions and naming conflicts.

## MANIPULATING THE DOM

jQuery makes most DOM manipulation possible using selectors that are basically identical to CSS. If, for example, you wanted to use DOM scripting to put the text *DOM Scripting Is Awesome* in the `<h1>` tag inside of `<header id="header">`, you could use jQuery and write a line of JavaScript inside the anonymous ready function:

```
jQuery(
  function($) {
    $('#header h1').html('DOM Scripting Is \
      Awesome');
  });
```

What that would do in the browser is first select all matching elements from the document by passing the selector #header   h1 to jQuery, locally aliased as $. jQuery completes the match using a descendant selector that you know from CSS (#header h1), which will find all of the `<h1>` elements inside of `<header   id="header">`. There should be only one match for `<h1>` on pages constructed according to the guidance in this book. Once the match is found, jQuery will use its .html() method to set the `<h1>` tag's text to *DOM Scripting Is Awesome*, regardless of what text the tag contained before. As the example shows, JavaScript requires a backslash when a string breaks over multiple lines.

Under most circumstances, it's better not to use DOM scripting to set the text of HTML elements. Write the text as you'd want it to appear directly in the HTML itself. In the more practical examples that follow, DOM scripting will manipulate classes on HTML elements, which are then styled according to rules in the CSS.

## Is JavaScript Available?

Whenever I build sites that use DOM scripting, I write a simple function that adds a class of hasjs (short for *has JavaScript*) to the `<html>` tag. My HTML itself contains a class of nojs (short for *no JavaScript*), so the HTML looks like `<html class="nojs">`. I then use jQuery or another framework to make the switch. Here is how to do that with jQuery, inside the anonymous ready function. In this and the remaining examples, the ready function has been removed for brevity. Full examples are on the book's companion site:

```
// remove the nojs class on the <html> tag:
$('html').removeClass('nojs');
```

```
// add a hasjs class on <html>:
$('html').addClass('hasjs');
```

Those lines use the jQuery to select the <html> tag on the page. The script then uses jQuery's `.removeClass()` and `.addClass()` methods to make the switch. Because most of jQuery's methods are chainable, it's possible to combine those methods into one line:

```
$('html').removeClass('nojs').addClass('hasjs');
```

Whether written in the one- or two-line style, which is arguably more readable, if JavaScript is available and a user's browser understands the DOM (which jQuery checks for automatically), the <html> tag of that document will have added to it the hasjs class once the script has run. (You can check that the class has been added by choosing the View Generated Source menu from the Pederick Web Developer Add-on for Firefox.)

## Reveal Hidden Attribute Data

Used alone, that line of JavaScript is not very exciting. Because it's only adding a class, you'd not even notice that the script has done anything, unless the class then becomes a hook for CSS styles that are dependent on JavaScript being available, similar to the Modernizr detection script for flexbox described above. For example, to assist JavaScript-enabled touchscreen devices, I usually write special styles for <abbr> (abbreviation) tags that have a title="" attribute (see Chapter 12 for more about attribute selectors in CSS). To style those differently in CSS when JavaScript is present, my stylesheet will have a section something like this:

```
/* CSS */

.nojs *[title] {
  /*
    Default styles for elements
    that have a title attribute
  */
}
.hasjs *[title] {
```

```
/*
   Styles for elements with title attributes
   when JavaScript is active.
*/
}
```

But because the contents of title attributes are only shown under certain conditions, JavaScript can make the contents more accessible to all users.

First, I use jQuery to find all of the abbreviation tags that have title attributes. It will capture the text marked by each abbreviation, and add a data-expanded attribute containing both the contents of the title attribute and the abbreviation itself, in parentheses. Finally, the tabindex attribute will be set to 0, allowing keyboard users to tab through the abbreviations, which normally do not receive focus via the keyboard:

```
$('abbr[title]').each(function() {
  var abbr, title, expandedText;
  abbr = $(this).text();
  title = $(this).attr('title');
  expandedText = title + ' (' + abbr + ')';
  $(this).attr('data-expanded', expandedText);
  $(this).attr('tabindex', '0');
});
```

Once that portion of the script runs, HTML like this:

```
<abbr title="Cascading Style Sheets">CSS</abbr>
```

will be transformed to:

```
<abbr title="Cascading Style Sheets"
  data-expanded="Cascading Style Sheets (CSS)"
  tabindex="0">CSS</abbr>
```

With that in place, a little more jQuery will be used to add an event listener for either clicks or keypresses (again, in deference to keyboard users). When an <abbr> tag is clicked, tapped, or highlighted with the Tab key and activated with Return, the <abbr> contents will be replaced with the contents of the data-expanded attribute, and the data-expanded, title, and tabindex attributes will be removed. They are no longer necessary once the expanded abbreviation is visible:

```
$('abbr[title]').on('click keypress', function() {
  $(this).html($(this).attr('data-expanded'))
    .addClass('expanded')
    .removeAttr('data-expanded title tabindex');
});
```

So, after a click, the HTML above is transformed to:

```
<abbr class="expanded">Cascading Style Sheets
  (CSS)</abbr>
```

The .expanded class might be used in CSS to override any styles attached to the abbr selector. But more importantly, users on touch devices can now access the expansion of any abbreviations. This is a perfect example of progressive enhancement: the original HTML contained both the abbreviation (CSS) and the expansion, in the title attribute (Cascading Style Sheets). A little DOM scripting puts that existent information to use for everyone. You can see this full example in action, with additional improvements, at the book's companion website, http://webpg.es/.

## Increasing the Base Font Size

One of the advantages of using em units to size text, line heights, and other vertical spacing (see Chapter 17) is that an entire page can be scaled up just by setting a new base font-size on the html selector. Handling that kind of adjustment is simple in JavaScript, especially with jQuery, which provides a css() method to both get and set the value of a particular CSS property.

In this function, a control (a.textsizer) will increase the text size of a page by 10 percent every time it is clicked. It does this first by setting up a variable size, which gets the current size (in pixels, even if the stylesheet sets the font-size in em or another relative unit). It then sets the new, larger font-size property using an anonymous function:

```
$('a.textsizer').on('click keypress', function() {
  var size = $('html').css('font-size');
  $('html').css('font-size', function() {
    var newsize = size.split('px')[0] * 1.10;
    return (newsize / 16) + 'em';
  });
});
```

That anonymous function creates a `newsize` variable, which uses the `split()` method to separate the `size` string, which might be something like 24px, into an array and immediately calls the [0] element in the array, which will be the number 24 without the px unit. That number is then multiplied by 1.10, the equivalent of adding 10 percent (26.4). The anonymous function then returns `newsize` in ems (dividing by the default of 16px per em), and uses concatenation to convert the value to a string with the em unit, which for 26.4px will be 1.65em. Clicking the control for text sizing will repeat the process, multiplying 26.4 by 1.10, and so on. Be sure to go to the book's companion site to see this example in action, including the JavaScript required to add a `textsizer` control to the HTML.

## Handling External Links

One final example to round out this chapter: So far we have looked at DOM scripting to manipulate HTML (the `<abbr>` example) and CSS (the text-sizing example). This example uses JavaScript to manipulate the `window` object to open external links in new windows. Beginning HTML writers discover that they can add `target="_blank"` to their anchor tags, which will cause browsers to open the link in a new page:

```
<a href="http://getfirefox.com" target="_blank">Get
Firefox</a>
```

That is poor practice for two reasons. First is that it makes a decision for users where a link ought to open. Users who really like to open links in new windows/tabs probably know how to do so. `target="_blank"` disallows any choice but to have the link open in a new window. But second, `target="_blank"` introduces behavior into a page's HTML, which should be purely about structure.

So if after careful reflection and intense soul-searching you conclude it truly is in all users' best interests to open external links in a new window, JavaScript should be used to handle the behavior.

The HTML should first be simplified to remove the `target` attribute:

```
<a href="http://getfirefox.com">Get Firefox</a>
```

jQuery and JavaScript can then work in tandem to create the new window. Again, these lines would appear inside the jQuery anonymous ready function:

```
$('a[href^="http"]').on('click', function(e) {
  // open window with the window object:
  window.open(this.href,'_blank');
  // prevent the default link-clicking behavior
  e.preventDefault();
});
```

That uses jQuery to select all anchor tags whose `href` attribute begins with `http`, using a CSS-style attribute selector. The jQuery `.on()` method, as in the previous examples, listens for the `click` event (which includes both mice clicks as well as finger taps on touchscreens), and executes an anonymous function that's passed the `click` event (`e`). Whenever a matching link is activated, it opens a new `window` object pointed at the anchor tag's `href` attribute value. Finally, the click event `e` calls its `.preventDefault()` method, which stops the browser from both opening a new window *and* following the link in the active window.

Again, forcing links of any kind to open in a new window is a dubious practice. I've included it here because it is a good example of changing browser behavior by adding events to elements of the DOM, but also because it's a pattern that many beginning web designers want to use. I suggest you leave opening new windows/tabs up to your users.

## NEXT STEPS

This chapter has only scratched the surface of how pages can be progressively enhanced with JavaScript. The book's companion site includes additional examples, including for working with dates and times, creating slideshows and lightbox effects, as well as loading remote data.

The next part of the book looks at common problems and typical solutions to the architecture and construction of whole websites and their deployment to the open web.

## REFERENCES

jQuery Foundation. 2016. *jQuery*. https://jquery.org/

Keith, Jeremy. 2005. *DOM Scripting: Web Design with JavaScript and the Document Object Model*. Berkeley, CA: Friends of Ed/Apress.

MDN. 2016a. "Using CSS Flexible Boxes." https://developer.mozilla.org/en-US/docs/Web/CSS/CSS_Flexible_Box_Layout/Using_CSS_flexible_boxes

MDN. 2016b. "Document.createElement()." https://developer.mozilla.org/en-US/docs/Web/API/Document/createElement

MDN. 2016c. "Script." https://developer.mozilla.org/en-US/docs/Web/HTML/Element/script

Modernizr. 2016a. *Modernizr: The Feature Detection Library for HTML5/CSS3*. https://modernizr.com/

Modernizr. 2016b. "HTML5 Cross Browser Polyfills." https://github.com/Modernizr/Modernizr/wiki/HTML5-Cross-Browser-Polyfills

# PART IV

## PROBLEMS AND SOLUTIONS

This section of the book examines problems and common solutions that impact the architecture and launch of your live site. It also introduces some of the dynamic approaches and systems that you can use to help build and maintain your website, including preprocessors that streamline custom source-code generation and maintenance. The section concludes with a chapter on participating in the social web, highlighting Open Graph metadata to make your content easily shareable so that you can extend your reputation further across the web, beyond the borders of your own site.

# CHAPTER 21

# Site Architecture

The architecture of a website is the organization of all its pages and assets, and how its pages relate to one another within the site's root directory and subdirectories. In the RPK, `site/` is the root directory. A good site architecture matters to you as a site's designer, because it helps you to easily locate and edit your media elements and pages, and link them to one another.

Site architecture is equally important to your site's visitors. A predictable, consistent URL structure and a site navigation that reveals the general contents of your site increase the likelihood that users will understand your site: what's on it, how to find it, and where they are in relation to the rest of your site. Simple, memorable URLs also aid users who wish to share your content with others (see Chapter 25).

A thoughtful, scalable architecture should be a part of your site's plan in its earliest stages. Be sure to test it in a web-like local development environment (see Chapter 5). This chapter looks at some of the choices you will have to make in developing your site's architecture.

The Rapid Prototyping Kit (RPK) provides a directory structure for organizing the design and media components of your site. Remember that *directory* is basically synonymous with *folder*; this chapter will use the word *directory* to describe site organization. The architecture of your site will help to determine how you set up the navigation for your pages, too.

The root directory of your website must contain every file that is associated with your site—every HTML, CSS, and JavaScript file as well as every image and media file. If you store images and other media elsewhere on your computer, you need to make copies of those files and store them in your site root, probably in a subdirectory.

## ARCHITECTURE TYPES

There are three types of architecture that are commonly used on websites:

- **File-oriented architecture,** which places all of the HTML pages of a site in the root web directory
- **Directory-oriented architecture,** which places individual or related pages into separate subdirectories in the root web directory
- **Data-driven architecture,** which typically relies on databases or other dynamic data stores and a server-side web application to mimic file and directory references in site URLs (see Chapter 23)

Each type of architecture has its benefits and appropriate applications, depending on the size and type of site that uses them.

### Basic: File-Oriented Architecture

The most basic site architecture is created by saving all of your HTML files right in your root web directory (the directory called site/ in the RPK, for example). This keeps your URLs short and relatively simple, in a pattern like http://example.com/mypage.html. A root site/ directory would contain the mypage.html file.

Having all of your HTML files located in the root of a site may not be a problem for small sites. But if a site grows to dozens of pages or more, having a massive list of all of the .html files may make it difficult to find the page you want to edit. And when passing URLs around outside of the web, such as in a verbal exchange, the file extension can cause confusion (*Was it resume-dot-htm, or resume-dot-html?*).

Site organization presents another problem for a designer who dumps all pages into the root of a site, regardless of the site's size. Pages that are related to one another, such as pages for individual portfolio items, will not necessarily be grouped together in the usual alphabetical list of files shown by an operating system.

With a file-oriented architecture, users may become disoriented, too. If all of a site's pages are kept in the root web directory, but the site has several distinct areas, a file-only URL does not reveal anything about the user's location or the context of a given page. Consider the difference between the URLs `http://example.com/fruit.html` and `http://example.com/paintings/fruit.html`. Which page can you better guess the contents of? The latter provides more than a hint and is the product of a directory-oriented architecture. A site's navigation might help suggest context, but a navigation area quickly becomes challenging to use if it offers users too many options.

## Complex and Scalable: Directory-Oriented Architecture

Using directories, rather than files, is the primary method for controlling the clutter of individual files in the root web directory. It also helps users orient themselves within your site, by creating directories for each of your pages and major site areas, just as the `paintings/fruit.html` URL did above.

For example, rather than having a portfolio overview located at `http://example.com/portfolio.html`, your portfolio can be located at `http://example.com/portfolio/`, thanks to the default behavior of the index file on most web servers (see "The Index File" sidebar). A directory-oriented architecture would store all of your portfolio items in a `portfolio/` directory. Individual items, such as a company newsletter that you designed, would be accessed at URLs like `http://example.com/portfolio/company-newsletter.html`. Or you can go completely directory based and put the contents of `company-newsletter.html` into its own `index.html` file in a `/company-newsletter/` subdirectory inside of `/portfolio/`, which would create a URL like `http://example.com/portfolio/company-newsletter/`.

Provided that each directory and subdirectory contains an `index.html` file, visitors to your site can modify your URLs in their browser's address bar. Removing the file or final directory name off of the end of the

## THE INDEX FILE

Most web servers are configured to serve the contents of `index.html` when either the root of a site or a directory is requested (e.g., `http://example.com/` or `http://example.com/contact/`). If you save a file named `index.html` in your root, but still see a listing of files, you may need to configure your web server to serve `index.html` by default.

To keep people from snooping the contents of directories in your website that contain media files or other site assets, an empty `index.html` file will prevent your web server from listing a directory's contents. However, a more sustainable solution would be to read the documentation for your web server and web host to determine how to configure your web server to disallow directory listings.

URL will take visitors to an overview page such as `http://example.com/portfolio/`.

And that is what is meant by a shallow architecture and navigation: a long URL like `http://example.com/portfolio/design/newsletters/` represents a deep architecture. Users should expect overviews or landing pages at each level of `portfolio`, `design`, and `newsletters`. Representing those in navigation or promotional links becomes a challenge—as does sharing long URLs in email and on social media. A careful selection of materials to showcase on a site will lend itself to a shallow architecture and help prevent a site from becoming needlessly complex.

A directory-oriented architecture is useful even for areas of your site that might have only one page. You might save your résumé, for example, as `index.html` and place it in a `resume` directory, resulting in a URL for the résumé like `http://example.com/resume/`.

Directory-based URLs also allow you to change up how your pages are constructed, particularly if in the future you move to some kind of a dynamically generated site that uses data-driven architecture. To Google and to your users, a URL is a URL, whether it points to actual files and directories, or later to an abstract reference in a database.

## Dynamic: Data-Driven Architecture

If you decide to build a site using WordPress or another blogging or content management system (CMS), your site's architecture with that system will likely be entirely dynamic. For example, `http://example.com/resume/` on a WordPress site would not necessarily point to a résumé directory containing an `index.html` file. Instead, WordPress uses the `resume/` part of the URL to pull your résumé out of its database.

Some dynamic systems use query-string style URLs like `http://example.com/?q=resume`. But any modern dynamic system will have some means of rewriting URLs, so that while a user sees `http://example.com/resume/` in the browser's address bar, the server extracts the `resume` part and plugs it into the uglier query string behind the scenes.

Even a static site generator, such as Jekyll (see Chapter 23), can be configured to create directories out of sets of Markdown files. So to prepare the way for a more sophisticated means of organizing and maintaining your site, directory-oriented architecture is again preferable.

# ARCHITECTURE, PATHS, AND NAVIGATION

Site architecture matters also when it comes time to start loading images and other media, linking your pages together in the navigation, or creating contextual links in your site's content. To link to resources within your site requires an understanding of file paths, which instruct the browser to load different resources from your site onto an HTML page (images, media, and CSS and JavaScript files) or to take visitors to different pages within your site.

When you link to pages in your own site, you need not include the full URL. Only the path to the page is required. The path is everything that comes after the domain name; so, for example, if your domain is `http://example.com/`, the path is everything that comes after `.com`. The initial trailing slash in that URL points to the site's root web directory.

There are three types of paths that you can write for your links: absolute, relative, and root-relative. To keep websites portable and to make their development easier (especially when using a development

## TROUBLESHOOTING PATHS

At some point, you will run into trouble when linking to a CSS or JavaScript file, or trying to load an image on your page. One of the easiest ways to trouble-shoot those kinds of links is to go to the source view of your browser. All modern browsers automatically create hyperlinks out of linked files and other paths. Click on the link and see what happens. If you're using the RPK, it has a custom 404.html file that will display if you follow a broken link or asset path when testing in a local development server.

The contents of that broken path suggest a laundry list of things to check. First, are your paths and file names spelled correctly? Spelling mistakes and typos, where the file name does not match what's in the path, are common sources of errors. Capitalization is a problem, too, especially on images. Your camera or smartphone might create capitalized .JPG or .JPEG extensions. But because web servers are usually case-sensitive, photo.jpg and photo.JPG are references to two different files. Be sure that your files are always lowercase, and adjust your paths accordingly.

server's http://localhost/ URL), it's generally preferable to use relative or root-relative links.

## Absolute Paths

Absolute paths (sometimes called absolute URLs or absolute links) include your full domain name and the name of the page/resource. For example, the absolute path to your résumé might be http://example.com/resume.html. Absolute URLs are what people share in email and what must be used to link one website to another.

Apart from an absolute link to your website's home page in the header area of your pages, which is included in the RPK, it's usually not a good idea to use absolute paths to pages within your own site. Not only are absolute paths longer, but if you should switch domain names or set up archives of your site at a subdomain, for example, http://archive.example.com/resume.html, any absolute http://example.com/ URLs in your links will no longer refer to items within the same version of the site.

However, when linking to an external site, you must use the `http:` or `https:` prefix found in absolute URLs. The following link will not work properly:

```
<a href="www.google.com">Search Google</a>
```

Following that link on `example.com` will result in this from the browser: `http://example.com/www.google.com`. Without the `http:` or `https:` prefix, a web server will try to find a file called `www.google.com`. So to rewrite the link correctly in that example, it's:

```
<a href="https://www.google.com">Search Google</a>
```

The `http:` and `https:` prefixes tell the browser to initiate contact with a resource on a completely different domain.

## Relative Paths

To make sites maximally portable, you should use relative paths, which are paths created relative to the current document's place in the site architecture.

In a site with a file-oriented architecture, where all files exist directly in the root web directory, relative paths are very easy to write: to link from any page in the site to, for example, your résumé, you would just write `<a href="resume.html">view my resume</a>`.

But if your portfolio were in one directory and your resume in another, to link to your résumé from a page in your `portfolio/` directory, you would have to write `<a href="../resume/">`. The `../` tells the server to move up one directory (out of `portfolio/` and up to the web root) and then down into the résumé directory. To move up two directories would be `../../`, three would be `../../../` and so on. It gets confusing pretty quickly; so let relative links serve as another argument against a deep architecture.

## Root-Relative Paths

I prefer to write root-relative paths for simple sites that will appear on a domain that I own. Root-relative paths always begin with a slash (`/`), representing the root web directory, and proceed to the full

## THE TREE COMMAND

Most operating systems have or can install a command called `tree`, which can be run from within any directory to output the paths to different files. For example, running `tree --dirsfirst ./` inside of the RPK's default `site/` directory outputs:

```
.
├── ./css
│   ├── ./css/gfx
│   │   └── ./css/gfx/.keep
│   ├── ./css/_reset.css
│   ├── ./css/css-readme.md
│   ├── ./css/print.css
│   └── ./css/screen.css
├── ./js
│   ├── ./js/js-readme.md
│   └── ./js/site.js
├── ./media
│   ├── ./media/audio
│   │   └── ./media/audio/.keep
│   ├── ./media/img
│   │   └── ./media/img/.keep
│   ├── ./media/video
│   │   └── ./media/video/.keep
│   └── ./media/media-readme.md
├── ./404.html
├── ./index.html
├── ./prototype-with-comments.html
└── ./prototype.html
```

If you're writing root-relative links, copy all but the `.` portion of the path listed for each of your files and directories.

path relative to the root of the site. Root-relative paths will work from anywhere in a site whose root directory you control, even if you have a very complex architecture: `<a href="/resume/">` can be used anywhere; because it starts from the root, it can always be found—provided that `resume/` is in the root web directory.

However, root-relative paths will only work during the development and testing of your site if you use something like `http-server` to run a web server on your local computer. If you open your files directly in the browser, with `File > Open`, lots of things will be broken, because `/` in a file URL represents the root of your hard drive. But, you should be using a development server, rather than a file-system view (ugly paths in your browser that start with something like `file:///`). See Chapter 15 and the book's companion site for getting set up with a development server that runs on your computer.

There is one case where you cannot write root-relative paths beginning with a slash, though. If you are using a web account like you might get through your school or business and it has a URL structure like `http://example.edu/~yourusername/`, you'd need to prefix all of your paths with `/~yourusername/` to make them root-relative—otherwise, the root-relative paths will point to (nonexistent) files and directories off of `example.edu/`. The same is true for GitHub Pages and other repository-hosting services (see the companion site for details). And, of course, once you have added something like `/~yourusername/` to your links, they will no longer be portable if you decide to purchase your own domain name. So add the root-relative path issue to the list of reasons why Chapter 5 urged you to buy your own domain name, rather than relying on hosting from your school or employer. For maximum portability across any hosting service or URL structure, it's probably better to use relative links.

## NEXT STEPS

As you begin to build a site architecture and test your pages with a local development server, you move closer to creating a site that is ready for posting to the open web. Proceed to Chapter 24 if that's the next step for you. The next two chapters will look at preprocessors for simplifying some aspects of generating the markup and CSS for a site, followed by a conceptual overview of dynamic sites and how to approach designing custom HTML and CSS themes for them.

# CHAPTER 22

# Preprocessors

There's no question that writing HTML and CSS by hand can be tedious sometimes, not to mention error-prone. You will become more skillful at it over time, and learn to catch your mistakes with the help of linters and validators. But once you have mastered those languages, you can introduce preprocessors into your workflow.

There are HTML, CSS, and even JavaScript preprocessors (and postprocessors) written in or inspired by many different programming languages. This chapter will introduce the concepts behind two preprocessors that emerged from the Ruby language (Haml and Sass), and one postproceessor for CSS (PostCSS) that was written by members of the Node.js community. Although all of the processors in this chapter can be compiled under Node.js, serious users of Haml and Sass will want to set up a Ruby installation. Updated details on both the installation and usage of the processors covered in this chapter are at this book's companion site.

## HTML PREPROCESSING WITH HAML

Haml, or the HTML Abstraction Markup Language, is shorthand for describing HTML (Haml Team 2016). It is often used in conjunction with web applications, including the Ruby on Rails framework. Rather than using angle brackets, tags in Haml are opened with a percentage sign, %. Haml markup does not include closing tags. Nesting is achieved through levels of indentation, and when compiled as HTML, Haml closes all open tags automatically and in a well-formed, standards-compliant way.

The following is a small snippet of Haml:

```
!!! 5
%html
  %head
  %body
```

It gets compiled by adding the `haml-coffee` command in Node.js, or the `haml` command in Ruby, to the following HTML:

```
<!DOCTYPE html>
<html>
  <head></head>
  <body></body>
</html>
```

The HTML5 DOCTYPE declaration is produced with the string `!!! 5`, while tags need only be opened, prefixed with `%`.

Indentation matters in Haml. It knows, for example, to nest `%head` and `%body` inside of HTML because each is indented two spaces. Provided your indentation is correct, Haml will close all of your tags for you, in the proper order.

## Attributes and Values in Haml

Here is an example of Haml that nests the character set and viewport meta elements, with their attributes and values, inside of `<head>`:

```
!!! 5
%html
  %head
    %meta{charset: "utf-8"}
    %meta{name: "viewport",
      content: "width=device-width"}
    %body
```

That compiles, as expected, to:

```
<!DOCTYPE html>
<html>
  <head>
```

```
    <meta charset="utf-8" />
    <meta content="width=device-width"
      name="viewport" />
  </head>
  <body></body>
</html>
```

Beyond indenting the two %meta lines, that example shows how to set attributes and values: by opening a curly brace, writing the attribute name (e.g., charset) followed by a colon, followed by its value in quotes: %meta{charset: "utf-8"}.

Text content can follow the Haml tag on the same line:

```
%title Compiled from Haml
```

which compiles to:

```
<title>Compiled from Haml</title>
```

More complex content can be written on the lines immediate below the Haml tag, but indented two spaces:

```
%p
  Here is a paragraph in Haml, written
  across multiple different lines in
  the source code.
```

That compiles to the following HTML, which has preserved the line breaks written in the HAML:

```
<p>
  Here is a paragraph in Haml, written
  across multiple different lines in
  the source code.
</p>
```

## Classes and IDs

While it is possible to create a class in Haml with the syntax above, such as %html{class: "nojs"}, Haml provides shorthand for classes and IDs that are borrowed from CSS notation:

```
!!! 5
%html.nojs
  %head
  %body#home
```

That compiles to:

```
<!DOCTYPE html>
<html class="nojs">
  <head></head>
  <body id="home"></body>
</html>
```

## Markdown in Haml

Haml that is installed under Ruby with the necessary dependencies also provides the means to process Markdown (Gruber 2004; see the book's companion site for additional details about Markdown processing in Haml). All that is required is :markdown, indented inside the tag where you wish to render Markdown, and the content written in Markdown, indented one level further:

```
%div
  :markdown
    ## I Am a Second-Level Heading

    I will be a paragraph. And here is an
    unordered list:

    * Red
    * Green
    * Blue
```

That is compiled to this HTML:

```
<div>
  <h2 id="i-am-a-second-level-heading">I Am
  a Second-Level Heading</h2>
  <p>I will be a paragraph. And here is
  an unordered list:</p>
```

```
<ul>
  <li>Red</li>
  <li>Green</li>
  <li>Blue</li>
</ul>
</div>
```

Note that the Markdown processor that Haml loads has created a unique ID based on the text content in the <h2> tag.

## CSS PREPROCESSING WITH SASS

Sass (2016), or Syntactically Awesome Style Sheets, works a bit differently from Haml. Haml looks nothing like HTML, and only takes care of things like properly closing and nesting HTML elements. Outside of a more complex system, like a web application, Haml is essentially a shorthand for HTML. By contrast, Sass provides a syntax that looks almost identical to CSS. The syntax is called Sassy CSS, or simply SCSS for short. Much of an SCSS file is actually vanilla CSS (Catlin, Weizenbaum, and Eppstein 2016).

But while the syntax is very similar to CSS, Sass adds some useful features that simplify some of the trickier aspects of writing CSS.

### Variables

Stylesheets quickly fill up with repeated values: a color that's used over and over again, for example, or a particular border style. Sass allows any CSS value to be declared in a variable. All Sass variables begin with a dollar sign, $. Here is an example:

```
$primaryColor: #6054FF;
$serifFontStack: Georgia, Palatino,
  "Times New Roman", serif;
html {
  color: $primaryColor;
  font-family: $serifFontStack;
}
```

When processed through Sass, that will output the following CSS:

```
html {
  color: #6054FF;
  font-family: Georgia, Palatino,
    "Time New Roman", serif;
}
```

The power of variables is more obvious when spread across a stylesheet. But the ability to change a repeated color or other value from a single variable declaration makes it much easier to fine-tune a design once a stylesheet increases in complexity. SCSS leads to DRYer stylesheets (Don't Repeat Yourself).

## Nesting

SCSS syntax allows you to group and nest descendant selectors. For example:

```
header {
  color: red;
  background: #222;
  h1 {
    color: #EEE;
  }
}
```

Notice that the h1 selector opens inside of the header selector. In CSS, that would cause an error. But as SCSS, it compiles neatly to CSS with a descendant selector for header h1:

```
header {
  color: red;
  background: #222; }
header h1 {
  color: #EEE; }
```

## Built-In Functions

Sass contains dozens of built-in functions. You can find them listed in the Sass documentation (Catlin, Weizenbaum, and Eppstein 2016). For example, there are functions to either lighten or darken a color, which can be useful on something like a :hover/:active state:

```scss
$linkColor: #900;
a {
  color: $linkColor;
  &:hover,
  &:active {
    color: lighten($linkColor, 40%);
  }
  &:visited {
    color: darken($linkColor, 20%);
  }
}
```

That will lighten the link color by 40 percent on hover or active states, and darken the link color by 20 percent if the link has been visited. The resulting CSS is:

```css
a {
  color: #900;
}
a:hover, a:active {
  color: #ff6666;
}
a:visited {
  color: #330000;
}
```

And because the link color is specified as a variable, any changes to the color declared by the variable will be lightened and darkened accordingly when the SCSS is recompiled to CSS.

## Custom Functions

Sass also allows you to write your own functions. For example, it's possible to write a function that does all of the target ÷ context = result conversions from pixel units to ems:

```scss
@function toEms($target,$context) {
  // Multiply by 1em to return em units
  @return $target/$context * 1em;
}
```

That function can be used in SCSS like this:

```
html {
  font-size: toEms(19px,16px);
}
```

Of course, since 16px is the default font size in most browsers, we can modify the function slightly to default to 16px unless another value is specified:

```
@function toEms($target,$context: 16px) {
  // Multiply by 1em to return em units
  @return $target/$context * 1em;
}
```

Provided that the context is 16px, the function can be used like this:

```
html {
  font-size: toEms(19px);
}
h1 {
  font-size: toEms(27px,19px);
}
```

In the case of h1's font-size, it's necessary to pass the 19px context, established on html, to properly size h1 at 27px. The resulting CSS that that SCSS outputs is this:

```
html {
  font-size: 1.1875em;
}
h1 {
  font-size: 1.42105em;
}
```

It's necessary to cross-reference a site's compiled CSS with its SCSS file as you're designing, since all of the mathematical relationships are in the SCSS file. Working with relative units becomes much easier when a simple function like toEms() can eliminate mathematical errors. See the book's companion website at http://webpg.es/ for additional useful custom SCSS functions.

# CSS POSTPROCESSING

A preprocessor like Sass or Haml takes a modified or shorthand syntax and compiles it into the full, expected syntax and rules of the target language. A postprocessor, by contrast, takes completed HTML, CSS, or JavaScript and outputs it in additional styles or with additional features that would be tedious or time consuming to write by hand.

PostCSS (2016) is a postprocessor for CSS maintained by an active group of developers working in Node.js. PostCSS has an expansive and growing library of plugins, but two of them are useful for all kinds of projects.

## Vendor Prefixing

Certain CSS features, such as CSS Flexbox (see Chapter 20), can work on slightly older browsers if the CSS properties and values are listed with vendor prefixes, such as -webkit- for WebKit-based browsers or -moz- for Mozilla Firefox.

However, those vendor prefixes can get very complex. Ideally, for example, the container element of a flexbox would be set as it was in Chapter 20, relying on a detection script to add a flexbox class to HTML in supported browsers:

```
.flexbox #header {
  display: flex;
}
```

Run through the PostCSS autoprefixer, that simple CSS becomes:

```
.flexbox #header {
  display: -webkit-box;
  display: -webkit-flex;
  display: -ms-flexbox;
  display: flex;
}
```

The autoprefixer plugin steps in to add those prefixes automatically. When working with a postprocessor, it's good practice to keep your prefix-free stylesheet named something like screen.src.css or _screen.css, and have the postprocessor output the screen.css file that you actually use on your site. I prefer to use the underscore style, to remind myself that any file with an underscore appears for reference only, such as the _reset.css file in the RPK.

## Minification

The reason that the RPK includes the _reset.css file is that a minified version of its contents appears in the screen.css file. PostCSS has several different minification plugins, although I prefer an all-purpose Node.js program called Minify (Coderaiser 2016), which will minify HTML, CSS, and JavaScript. A minifier program removes all of the unnecessary whitespace from a file, and in the case of JavaScript, will substitute and shorten certain variables and other components of the script.

Minifying the autoprefixed CSS from above results in:

```
.flexbox #header{display:-webkit-box;display:-webkit
-flex;display:-ms-flexbox;display:flex}
```

All of the spaces have been removed, except for the descendant-selector space between .flexbox and #header, and outside the bounds of a printed book, all of the content would appear on a single line.

Minification can help save the amount of time and bandwidth that it takes to download assets for your site. But it is no substitute for lean source code to begin with. If you use a detection script that looks only for the most compliant implementations of something like flexbox, which was the case in Chapter 20, there's no reason to add in the vendor prefixes for older browsers that will fail the detection script anyway.

To help others who might want to study your work, you might want to post a nonminified version of your CSS to your website, or on a source-code hosting service like GitHub, and put a pointer to it in a comment in the minified source file.

## NEXT STEPS

This chapter gave a very brief overview of some of the many tools used to enhance the writing of HTML and CSS. Such tools are not a substitute for expertise with HTML and CSS, however. If you do select some kind of processor to assist your work, make sure that your level of skill with HTML, CSS, and JavaScript is high enough that you can evaluate the source the processor outputs for its compliance with web standards and accessible, sustainable development practices like those outlined in this book.

The next chapter provides a broad overview and general approaches to working with more complex systems that can generate entire websites.

# REFERENCES

Catlin, Hampton, Natalie Weizenbaum, and Chris Eppstein. 2016. *Sass.* http://sass-lang.com/

Coderaiser. 2016. "Minify." https://github.com/coderaiser/minify

Gruber, John. 2004. "Markdown." https://daringfireball.net/projects/markdown/

The Haml Team. 2016. *Haml.* http://haml.info/

PostCSS. 2016. *PostCSS.* https://github.com/postcss/postcss

# CHAPTER 23

# Building Dynamic Sites

Websites that consist of HTML, CSS, and JavaScript files are often called **static sites**. The same HTML, CSS, and JavaScript files that someone writes locally on their own computer and puts on a live web server are the same files that users access when visiting a site. **Dynamic sites**, by contrast, do some degree of assembling components of a page upon request. That can be as little as adding repeated elements, such as headers and footers, or as much as generating the entire contents of a page. Additionally, in the case of web applications, a dynamic site might support user logins and authentication, editable content, commenting functions, and all of the other features that are commonplace across many kinds of sites.

The emphasis of this book is on static sites. For smaller websites or even larger websites whose content does not change all that often, a static site can still be a wise choice. Dynamic sites generally require a more powerful hosting server and consume more computing resources. Static sites use no more server resources than what is required to keep the server's operating system and web server running smoothly. Dynamic sites that connect to databases or accept user input present a number of security issues that static sites simply do not have, such as SQL injection attacks (Menegaz 2012).

A static site can be posted to a server and left more or less alone. Assuming that access to the server itself is kept secure (for example, by requiring key-based authentication over SSH as described on the book's companion site), a static site requires little ongoing maintenance beyond whatever improvements you make to the design or content. That is in stark contrast to dynamic sites, which require frequent updates just to keep security vulnerabilities patched. A compromised site can wreak havoc on the rest of the internet, and Google (2016) and other search engines may start to warn potential visitors that your site may be hacked. So while a dynamic site will do a lot of amazing things, it requires a substantial, ongoing time commitment to remain secure.

This chapter distills advice that I give to students who complete my web design courses and ask what they should learn next. It looks at how to go about choosing a platform for building dynamic sites, as well as some important questions to ask about the needs of the site you plan to build. A section toward the end of the chapter briefly describes static site generators, which are a compromise between fully static and fully dynamic sites. The book's companion site provides supporting starter code for a few different frameworks as well as a bonus chapter on developing custom themes for certain hosted blogging services, which handle all of the hosting and security matters while providing users a certain degree of freedom to develop their own HTML, CSS, and JavaScript.

## CHOOSE A DEVELOPMENT-FRIENDLY PLATFORM

One of the first things to consider before experimenting with a platform is whether it supports local development. It should be possible to set up and run the platform on your own computer, just like `http-server` makes it possible to test a website at your `http://localhost:8080/` URL. Here are some features to look for that suggest a platform fits that description:

- **A command-line based package manager.** It is much easier to keep a dynamic site platform updated if it has a package manager. For example, Ruby on Rails uses a package manager called Bundler, which relies on a file that keeps track of all of the dependencies (what other platforms call *plugins* or *addons*) for the application. There are many benefits to a system like Bundler, not the least of which is that the dependencies are stored apart from your own application. WordPress and Drupal have traditionally required plugins to be downloaded manually from a website and then uploaded to a site's hosting server. Keeping plugins as well as the platform itself updated is similarly manual and therefore time-consuming and error prone. Although package managers can be plagued with their own problems (Williams 2016), they are generally reliable and improving all the time. A platform that requires manual uploads and downloads will always be fraught with the potential for error.

- **A console or REPL.** A REPL, an acronym for Read-Eval-Print Loop, is an interactive way of writing and testing code line by line. If you have Node.js installed, for example, you can type `node` in your command-line shell to access the Node.js REPL. From there, you can write JavaScript line by line, and each time you hit the Return key, the REPL will read what you've written, evaluate or run the code, and print the output before returning (looping) to accept your next line of code (Figure 23.1). REPLs are great for testing small snippets of code, especially when learning a language (see the "Learn the Language" section below). Some frameworks provide an additional REPL-like console that will load up the entirety of your website's code and allow you to interact with it from the command line, which is the case with the Ruby on Rails `rails console` command. REPLs and consoles help isolate problems in application code, but they also suggest a given platform's supportive attitude toward its developers.

- **File-based configuration.** Bonus points for side-by-side configuration for different environments. Rails, for example, supports different configurations for development, testing, and production environments. Development environments are for work on your own local computer, as are test environments for running automated tests on your application's code. A production environment refers to the world-facing server where your application is hosted and accessible via the open web. But even if a particular platform has only a single configuration, a file-based configuration is arguably better than configuration stored in a database. WordPress, for example, has

```
● ● ●                        /bin/bash — /bin/bash — node
$ node
> currentTime = new Date();
2016-09-13T02:47:52.090Z
>
```

**Figure 23.1.**    The Node.js REPL, showing a single line of JavaScript that has created a new Date object.

a configuration file. Unfortunately, its contents are limited to information on how to connect to the database, which is where the bulk of the custom site configuration information resides. While database-backed configuration is convenient from a certain perspective, a corrupted or compromised database will chew up your site's configuration information in ways that rarely affect simple flat files. Flat files can also be tracked easily in a version control system, making it possible not only to experiment with different configurations, but also to use branches to manage configurations for different environments.

- **Fully customizable HTML output.** Some platforms make heavy-handed decisions about HTML structures for a given page and its components. For example, if a particular platform has a function for loading images into a template like `get _image()`, it's important to inspect the HTML source that it generates, and whether it can be modified in any way to use `srcset`, `<picture>`, and other components of responsive images (see Chapter 19). Look to see if there are lighter-weight functions, something like `get_image_path()`, which might return something like `img/some-image.jpg` that you can then insert into your own custom `<img>` or `<source>` tags.

- **Thorough, well-written, and up-to-date documentation.** Thorough documentation is essential. It is probably the best way to answer whether a system does any of the things listed above: providing a REPL, for example, or methods for storing configuration information. Before learning any new platform, spend some time with its documentation, and see whether there are message boards and other forms of community support for people developing sites with the platform.

## DOES YOUR SITE REALLY NEED A DATABASE?

This is an important question to ask, especially before opting for a web development platform that requires the use of a database. I often find that people have opted to use WordPress or Drupal just for the ability to do global themes for their entire site. But that one feature comes with the price of maintaining a database, which as mentioned above becomes a source of security headaches.

My own preference is to use a database-backed system only under one or more of the following conditions:

- Handling a very large number of new write operations. If you are hosting a site that gets updated frequently, for example a collaborative blog or a site with its own commenting system, a database might be the better way to store the content.
- Handling a very larger number of records. For example, a site that handles membership records to an organization. Of course, storing that kind of information puts people's privacy at risk, not just the integrity of your site itself.
- Doing database-like things with site content. Sorting or creating unusual associations between chunks of data typically warrants a database. Simple read and write operations do not.

If site-wide templating is all that a site needs, without the firepower and headaches of a database, a system like Jekyll is often the better way to go (see the "Static Site Generators" section at the end of the chapter).

## Learn the Language

Whichever platform you decide to learn, learn the language it's written in. If you choose WordPress, it's essential to learn PHP. If you opt for Rails or Sinatra, learning Ruby is a must, just as learning JavaScript is essential to building on top of Node.js and web-development platforms for it such as Express.js.

When I teach courses on web application development, one of the primary struggles that students have is understanding which components of the application's code are native to the language it is written in, and which components belong to the application itself. While I used to dive right in and start students building in Rails or Node.js from the very first week, I now schedule at least two weeks just for students to spend time with the language of the platform or framework of the course.

At the very least, before diving in to work with a framework, learn the basic syntax of the language it's written in, something similar to the contents of the JavaScript chapter of this book (see Chapter 13). Understanding how variables are assigned, how functions are called, and the different types of input and output (strings, numbers, Booleans, and so on) will provide at least some foundation for you to better understand the platform's source code.

## Learn the Documentation and API

Build a mental map for yourself of how the documentation is organized. Learn to understand how code examples and pseudocode are listed under different aspects of the API. Becoming familiar with an existing documentation set, such as the Mozilla Developer Network's references to HTML, CSS, and especially JavaScript, will help anyone tackling the documentation for server-side languages and the frameworks and platforms written in them.

Learn to use your search engine of choice to help narrow your focus to the official documentation for a given platform. When I'm building a project using Express.js, my search strings usually get appended with Google's `site:` syntax to limit myself only to the official API documentation. If I need to refresh myself on the parameters for `app .listen()`, for example, my search string will look like `app.listen site:expressjs.com`.

Documentation can also be complemented by reading a good book-length reference. If a platform is large and mature enough, there is probably at least one book that has been written about it. Some communities also have a more or less official book about the platform. Sam Ruby's (2016) *Agile Development with Rails 5* has long been the gold standard in the Rails community, as evidenced by the contributions to the book by Rails's creator, David Heinemeier Hansson.

Platforms evolve over time, of course, so before investing in a book or trying to track one down from your local library, be sure to find out what the current version is for the platform that you wish to learn. And while written and video tutorials can provide a good sense of how a platform is used and constructed, a book-length work by a seasoned professional generally provides a larger philosophical worldview that informs how to tackle developing your own application.

### Version Control Is a Learning Tool

Version control is also an excellent learning tool. I try to teach myself one new language or platform every year, just to remind myself of what it feels like to be a beginner all over again. The experience of learning a new language is greatly enhanced by version control. Making frequent commits to a repository of example code based on the examples in a book or other resource is an invitation to reflect, in the form of a commit message, on what you are learning. And commits become points to create a new branch to engage in additional experimentation beyond guided examples.

And obviously by using version control in that way, you also get better at commanding and understanding the version control system you've opted to use.

## STATIC SITE GENERATORS

Over the past several years, a class of development platforms called **static site generators** has emerged to bridge the gap between entirely static handwritten sites and dynamic server-side sites. Fully dynamic sites generate a site's pages each time a user requests them, querying a database and arranging different template files to produce what looks to the end user to be a static HTML page.

A static site generator compiles all of the components of a site into a collection of static HTML, CSS, and JavaScript files, which can then be posted to a live web server (see Chapter 24). Depending on the complexity of the generator and the site created with it, deploying a generated site to the web might be no different from uploading a collection of handwritten site files.

In many ways, static site generators are the best of both the static and dynamic methods of web design and development. Static site generators all generally have some kind of templating system built in, making it easier to have DRY (Don't Repeat Yourself) HTML for components repeated over multiple pages, such as headers, navigation, and footers. Some generators also render page content written in Markdown, making it easier to write and maintain content written using a simple syntax that is then generated into common HTML blocks (headings, paragraphs, and lists; see Chapter 16) that structure the unique content on each page.

Despite those and other advanced features, what a static generator produces is an ordinary set of HTML, CSS, and JavaScript files. So the security and maintenance concerns that can plague a typical dynamic site are not shared with a statically generated site.

See the book's companion website for an up-to-date curated list of static site generators, as well as a few select dynamic frameworks, written in a variety of different languages. The book's companion website, by the way, is built in a popular static site generator called Jekyll. I have provided instructions for downloading and compiling the entire site yourself, should you want to refer to it from somewhere that does not have a reliable internet connection.

## REMEMBER: IT'S ALL STILL HTML, CSS, AND JAVASCRIPT

Whether you work with WordPress or Rails, Drupal or Express.js, the end result is the same: any website, however created and generated, ultimately serves HTML, CSS, and JavaScript to a diversely abled and diversely equipped audience. Some platforms are more compliant than others with web standards, progressive enhancement, and newer development approaches like responsive web design. A framework's compliance with those standards and best practices may not be mentioned in the documentation. Even if it is, it is still up to you as the creator and maintainer of the site to routinely audit the source code that your framework of choice delivers to the browser. That is why I stress to my students and colleagues that it is important to learn the web's basic languages before diving into building a site with a framework or content management system.

That is especially the case with HTML. Few frameworks actively generate or manipulate CSS or JavaScript, although some will package and minify that code in clever ways. But all web development frameworks participate in the generation of HTML. As this book has argued, HTML is the foundation for an accessible and sustainable site. That rule does not change, no matter the server-side language or framework used to create a dynamic site.

## NEXT STEPS

Whatever method you choose to develop a site, once you have thoroughly tested it in a local development environment, you will likely want to post it to the open web. The next chapter looks at different ways to deploy your live site.

## REFERENCES

Google. 2016. "'This Site May Be Hacked' Message." https://support.google
    .com/websearch/answer/190597
Menegaz, Gery. 2012. "SQL Injection Attack: What Is It, and How to Prevent
    It." *ZDNet* (July 13). http://www.zdnet.com/article/sql-injection-attack
    -what-is-it-and-how-to-prevent-it/
Ruby, Sam. 2016. *Agile Development with Rails 5*. Dallas: Pragmatic Bookshelf.
Williams, Chris. 2016. "How One Developer Just Broke Node, Babel and
    Thousands of Projects in 11 Lines of JavaScript." *The Register* (March 23).
    http://www.theregister.co.uk/2016/03/23/npm_left_pad_chaos/

# CHAPTER 24

# Going Live

Once you have designed and tested your site locally and it's working to your satisfaction, it's time to publish your site to the web by deploying it to the server location provided by your web host. Assuming that you have been thoughtful in developing your site architecture by keeping everything in a single directory (see Chapter 21), such as in the `site/` directory of the RPK, going live should be a relatively painless task of transferring the files and directories inside of `site/` to the root web directory provided by your host. This chapter offers some checklists to run through before and after you transfer your site to your host, and some common methods for transferring your site files.

## BEFORE YOU UPLOAD: A CHECKLIST

Before you upload your site to your web server, here is a list of things to check in all of the files that make up your site:

- Check that you haven't written any links that refer to your testing URL, `http://localhost:8080/`. Make sure that you have no domain names in links that point to your own pages, excluding the link to your home page in the `<header>` area of your document, which should be your actual domain name and not `http://localhost:8080/`, if you have been using that for testing purposes.

- Likewise, check that you haven't written any file URLs, `file:///`.
- Check for links or paths to images loaded outside your website's root directory and its subdirectories. When you're working on your own computer, you can link to pages or images anywhere on your computer. Those links, however, will not work on the open web, so be sure that you have moved all of your images into a directory inside of your site root, and that links from your pages point there.

Also, if you have purchased your domain name from someone other than your web host (as was recommended in Chapter 5), you will need to go to your domain-name registrar's website and log in to the control panel the registrar provides for managing your domain. Once logged in, you will enter your web host's nameserver for your domain. Nameservers are usually in the form of `ns1.example.com` and `ns2.example.com`. Additionally, some registrars require each nameserver's IP address, which your host should have available for your reference. Those steps are required to ensure that your domain name points to your site at your hosted server space. Google for *nameservers* and the name of your domain provider to determine how to do this. Once you have changed the nameservers that your domain uses, it may take some time (around 24 hours) before your domain points to your hosting server.

## TRANSFERRING SITE FILES TO YOUR HOST

Your host will give you instructions, and possibly some web-based tools in the form of a control panel, to transfer your site's files. I recommend using FTP/SFTP, or Git hooks if your host supports them, to upload your site. They are generally more reliable and less error prone than web-based transfers, which may also have limits on how large a file you can upload. If you opt to use a command-line based file transfer, like the `scp` command, or a Git-based one, you will have a written log of your uploads in your command-line history. That can be very useful for tracking down problems, while also enabling you to automate uploads of your site as you make changes and improvements.

## Locating FTP/SFTP Instructions for Your Web Host

Every web host is a little different in terms of how you access your account to upload files. Make sure that you find, read, and follow the host's instructions carefully. Some require setting a "passive" FTP mode, for example, so you'll need to select an FTP client that supports passive mode. Do a Google search.

If you have a host that offers SFTP, use that rather than FTP. FTP transfers your password without any encryption, which makes it easy for someone to break into your site. Make sure, also, that you select a client that supports SFTP (see the "Selecting an FTP/SFTP Client" sidebar).

---

### SELECTING AN FTP/SFTP CLIENT

It is essential to select an FTP/SFTP client that meets the requirements of your web host. Here are some flexible clients that you might try to use. They are all free and open source and in active development as of the time of this writing:

- WinSCP (`http://winscp.net/`) is a solid choice for Windows users and can handle almost any kind of FTP/SFTP connection that your web host might require.
- CyberDuck (`https://cyberduck.io/`) is a versatile client for both Windows and macOS. It handles FTP/SFTP and a range of other transfer protocols. It behaves similarly to the file-browsing windows on Windows and macOS, so copying files from your computer to your server is no harder than copying files from directory to directory on your computer itself.
- FileZilla (`http://filezilla-project.org/`) offers a free and open-source FTP/SFTP client for Windows and Mac, as well as Linux.

If you have a Unix style command line, you probably also have access to command-line `ftp` and `sftp` tools, as well as `scp` (secure copy). Using `scp` to transfer a site to a host at `example.com` with a path to the web root at `/var/www/html` requires issuing a command like this:

```
$ scp -r ~/Projects/rpk/site/*
    username@example.com:/var/www/html
```

See the book's companion site for additional information on automating the process of transferring your site files.

---

Finally, you need to check the address where your host accepts file uploads. Sometimes this is a generic address for your host (such as webhost.example.com) that passes your files to your account based on your username. Sometimes you get an FTP address in the form of ftp.example.com that uses your own domain name. You will need to specify the correct address in your FTP/SFTP client, or via the command line if you go that route.

## GETTING YOUR FILES TO THE RIGHT PLACE

Every web host specifies a root web directory where you must place your site files. You'll need to check your host's documentation to determine where that directory is. Just like site/ is the root web directory in the RPK (see Chapter 15), different hosts may specify www/, httpdocs/, or even html/ as their root web directory. You want to make sure that you transfer your files from site/ to your host's root web directory. (But do not transfer the site/ directory itself, unless you want people

### FILE AND DIRECTORY PERMISSIONS

Early in the book, I suggested purchasing web hosting from a company that uses Linux servers and that grants you secure shell (SSH) access. Setting file and directory permissions is one area where SSH access is essential. It offers a straightforward mechanism for seeing and changing which users on a system, including the user the web server runs as, can read and write files.

There are two parts to permissions: the username of the file or directory's owner and the owner's group and what the file or directory's owner, associated group, and everyone with server access can do to the file (read, write, and/or execute). In order to enable browser uploads in WordPress, for example, you may have to change the permissions on your uploads directory to allow the web server to write files there. And sometimes, you also have to make sure that your own user, the one you access the server with to transfer files, can in turn download browser-uploaded files over FTP/SFTP.

Details on determining and setting file permissions are available at this book's companion site.

to access your website at `http://www.example.com/site/`. And nobody wants that.)

## USING GIT

If you've been faithfully using Git to track changes to your site, you have a number of better options available to you than moving files over SFTP.

Depending on your web host, Git may already be set up on your server. You can then use Git to transfer your files according to one of two basic methods. The simplest method is to SSH to your web server, and do a `git clone` of your page from a third-party Git host such as GitHub. A more complex method is to set up a bare repository on your web server, and push to that from your local computer. Using Git's post-hooks feature, or a more robust deployment system like Capistrano, publishing changes to your site is as simple as `git push live master`. Git deploys are much faster and more reliable than FTP-based transfers, as only the changed files will be transferred. You also don't need to remember which files were changed. Git handles all of that.

The book's companion site has up-to-date instructions and scripts for handling Git-based site transfers.

## AFTER YOU UPLOAD: A CHECKLIST

Depending on how large your site is, and how fast your internet connection speed is (even high-speed connections are often slower for uploads than downloads), it may take a little while to upload your site.

But once your FTP/SFTP client or command line indicates that your files have been uploaded, it's time to check out your live site for the first time by pointing your browser to your actual domain name's URL in the form of `www.example.com` or `example.com`, depending on whether you've elected to use `www.` or not (see the "WWW, or No WWW?" sidebar).

Check your live site for the following potential problems:

- **Do your pages load?** This is the most obvious check; you want to see your own work when you go to your domain name. If you

## WWW, OR NO WWW?

Some websites, like `https://www.google.com/`, force the use of `www.` in their URLs (if you try to go to `https://google.com`, Google's server will add `www.` onto the URL for you).

My attitude, shared with the people behind `http://no-www.org/` is that `www.` is superfluous for websites. It also gobbles up four unnecessary characters in social posts where character-count is at a premium. That's why my site forces `https://karlstolley.com`. Anyone using `www.` to access the site will be automatically sent to the www-less URL.

However, there is an alternate view, expressed by the community at `http://www.yes-www.org/` who urge the use of `www.` in web URLs.

Whether or not you use `www.`, or allow users to use both, is up to you; just make sure that, `www.` or not, people can access your site with either one. The book's companion site has links to instructions on how to configure your web server's use of `www.`

do not see your own work there, try reloading the page. Many web hosts will put a temporary `index.html` file in your root web directory, so you may need to use your FTP client to delete that if your files use the `.htm` file extension and your own `index.htm` file does not appear. Also, if you see a page that appears to be from your domain registrar, you will have to set up your domain to use your host's nameservers as described above. If you've done that already, try your site again in a few hours.

- **Do your images and CSS files load?** If you are seeing your HTML pages, but not your design, you need to first check that the files were uploaded. This can be as easy as pointing your browser to, for example, `http://example.com/css/screen.css` and seeing if your CSS file's source displays. If it doesn't, go back to your FTP client and upload it again. If the CSS file's source does display, you need to check the paths that reference the CSS file in your HTML (see Chapter 21).

- **Are your HTML pages and CSS files validating?** Particularly if you've included validation links in the footer, try them out and make sure that everything is validating. If they fail to validate, make the necessary corrections and re-upload any problem files.

# UPDATING FILES

Unless you do a major overhaul of your site, it's usually only necessary to upload your entire site once. Thereafter, you only need to upload files that you've changed. That should be as easy as finding your computer's copy of the file, and uploading it to the proper location on your web server with your SFTP client. Always keep both a local and a remote version of your site; backups on external storage media or cloud-based services are also smart to maintain in the event that both your own computer and your web server crash. You don't want to lose your work.

As noted above, Git makes it much easier to handle changes to your site. Just add and commit your changes as usual, and then transfer them to your site by whatever method you've chosen to work with Git, such as `git push live master`.

## Making Copies of Browser Uploads

If you use WordPress or another content management system (see Chapter 23), you likely also have the ability to upload files via your website. It is important to use your SFTP client regularly to download copies of those files. Be sure to preserve the same directory structure that stores the files on the server (WordPress, for example, will create its own set of subdirectories to keep things organized) so that you can restore your site if you change hosts or your hosting server crashes.

A more advanced method for backing up web-based uploads is to set up a crontab on your server that periodically transfers your uploaded files to another computer or server for safekeeping. Some hosts will also do automated backups for you for a monthly fee on top of the regular costs of your hosting.

# NEXT STEPS

Copying files or pushing commits is pretty yawn-worthy—though it should be exciting to see your site at your own URL that you can share with the rest of the world. You'll use these same steps into the future: edit and check files on your own computer, and then upload them before checking them again on the live site. If changes don't appear after you upload new files, try clearing your web browser's cache. The final chapter of the book will help you learn how to make it easier to share your content and build your identity across the social web.

# CHAPTER 25

# The Social Web

Websites all exist in relationship to one another. That is at the foundation of the anchor tag, `<a href="">`, which allows any one resource
on the web to link to any other. But those relationships, too, are built
within a nexus of social networks that exist offline as well as through
social media.

This chapter looks at problems and potential solutions for building
websites and pages whose content is easier to share on the social web.
It assumes that the advice in the rest of this book is already in place:
responsive standards-compliant HTML, CSS, and JavaScript that is
lightweight and transfers quickly.

## SHORT, DESCRIPTIVE, MEMORABLE URLS

As Chapter 21 noted, the directories and files of your website become
parts of the URL. A directory-based structure that leverages the automatically servered `index.html` file makes for short, memorable URLs:
`http://example.com/resume/` instead of `http://example`
`.com/resume.html`.

When you read the web (see Chapter 2), take note of repeated URL
structures that you see. About pages are often at `/about/`; contact
pages at `/contact/`. Those kinds of URLs are not only short and
memorable, but conventional as well.

If you are using a server-side platform to generate your site (see
Chapter 23), it may use query strings for URLs: `http://example`
`.com/?q=136`. Look into configuring the platform or your webserver

## LINK SHORTENERS

Some social platforms automatically shorten links that you post. For example, Twitter has its own `t.co` domain for pointing to links that it automatically shortens. My Twitter profile points to my website at `https://karlstol ley.com/` via its own short URL, `https://t.co/b2JpteDKIf`, for a savings of one whole character. And that comes at the cost of a URL that is not at all memorable.

Other standalone services, such as Bitlinks and its `bit.ly` domain, allow you to provide shortened links yourself. Often the link slugs are random, like the `t.co` one above, but some services permit users to choose their own link slug. The trouble with shortened links is that they are only good for as long as the service behind them continues to exist. Several years ago, when the Libyan government shut down internet access in the country, there were fears that the Libyan `.ly` domain itself would be taken offline (Watters 2011). While that did not happen, it serves as a reminder of how important it is to control your own domain.

I have registered a domain, `ks4.us`, where I run my own custom link shortener. I share `ks4.us` URLs primarily when I am speaking at conferences or sending course website URLs to students. In certain circumstances, it's probably worthwhile to build a site at its own short URL, as with `webpg.es`.

to create so-called pretty URLs, like `http://example.com/136/`. Better still, see if there is a way to *slugify* your URLs, where the page title becomes part of the URL. Instead of a numeric reference like `136`, a page titled "Project Members" might have a slugified URL such as `http://example.com/project-members/`. You might even be able to customize your URL slugs to the shorter, more memorable URL `http://example.com/members/`.

Shorter, descriptive URLs are easier to share on social platforms that limit the number of characters in a post (see the sidebar, "Link Shorteners"). And in cases where an important URL appears in print, shorter URLs require less time and effort to type, increasing the likelihood that someone may visit a URL at the top of your résumé or on a sign or a business card. I made a similar choice when I registered the `webpg.es` (*How to Design and Write* Web Pages *Today*) domain for this book's companion site.

# SHARING METADATA: OPEN GRAPH

Short, memorable URLs are important for social sharing. But Facebook and other social platforms sometimes provide previews to accompany shared links. Apple's iMessage platform introduced a similar link preview as of iOS 10. By default, those platforms might display the contents of the `<title>` tag, along with the opening text and the first image on a page, to create the preview. However, those platforms and many others accept metadata presented according to the Open Graph Protocol, which originated at Facebook. The Open Graph Protocol (OGP) is documented at `http://ogp.me`. The RPK includes the core OGP tags, which you can uncomment to use yourself.

A page can implement OGP using this set of meta tags, each of which is described below:

```
<meta property="og:type" content="website" />
<meta property="og:title" content="" />
<meta property="og:site_name" content="" />
<meta property="og:description" content="" />
<meta property="og:url" content="" />
<meta property="og:image" content="" />
<meta property="og:image:type" content="" />
```

## OGP Properties

The `og:` prefix in each property value refers to a namespace that should be established in the opening `<head>` tag, using the `prefix` attribute:

```
<head prefix="og: http://ogp.me/ns#">
```

That is required for your page to validate. Other prefixes might be necessary, in the event that your page implements additional RDFa vocabularies, such as Dublin Core. See the book's companion site. The `prefix` attribute can also be written on the opening `<html>` tag.

The individual OGP properties in the RPK are:

- **Type**: OGP supports many types of content. The default is *website*. There is also an *article* type that is descriptive of blog posts, as well as media-specific types for audio and video. But for basic pages, *website* is the preferred generic type. Consult the OGP documentation for the latest supported types.

- **Title**: This should have the unique title for the page. It might match the contents of the `<title>` tag, unless `<title>` includes the site name or other information, in which case the OGP Title property should match the major, unique heading for the page, perhaps the first `<h2>` inside of an `<article>` sectioning element (see Chapter 16).

- **Site Name**: The name of the site, obviously. For a company or organizational website, the company or organization name should appear here. Personal websites should reference the person's name.

- **Description**: This should be at most a one- or two-sentence summary or description of the page's content. It might repeat the contents of the site's tagline.

- **URL**: According to the OGP specification, the URL should be "the canonical URL of your object that will be used as its permanent ID in the graph." Be careful to avoid typos on this. Copying and pasting the live URL from a browser's address bar is the surest way to ensure the correctness of the URL.

- **Image**: This property should also be a URL that points to an image that will be associated with the page's ID. Social platforms may display this image in a preview when someone shares a link. The book's companion site has additional information on preparing images for use in social previews, as well as additional properties unique to preview images. One additional property worth mentioning here is `og:image:type`, which must reference the correct MIME type for the image itself: `image/jpeg` for JPEGs, or `image/png` for PNG. Some services will not render your preview image without the correct `og:image:type` value.

Once you have published your site or a new page, you can use Facebook's Sharing Debugger Tool at `https://developers.facebook.com/tools/debug/` to check that your OGP metadata conform to the specification.

# CREATIVE COMMONS LICENSING

Short, memorable URLs to content presented with additional sharing metadata, like OGP, provide a technological foundation to share content across the social web. An additional, legal step that you can take is to issue your content under a license that permits others to share, modify, and redistribute your work. What follows should not be construed as legal advice; any questions about copyright law and licensing should be directed to an attorney, which the author is not.

Creative Commons is an organization that has created a set of popular licenses for sharing content that others may use. Creative Commons licenses are an exercise of your copyrights, not a surrender of them. You can use the Creative Commons' tool for choosing a license at `https://creativecommons.org/choose/`. The most liberal license permits others to make adaptations of your work, and to use your work for commercial purposes, provided that you are given attribution. The latest version of the Creative Commons license tool will insert metadata into an HTML fragment that can be copied and pasted into your website. The RPK includes an improved version of the HTML generated by Creative Commons. See the book's companion website.

# TRACKING USERS (DON'T)

Here's one final opinionated section to conclude an opinionated book. Don't track users. Google Analytics is just one of many different suites of tools that allow you to insert JavaScript onto your pages to figure out what users are doing, and where else they've gone to and where they've come from. It's fun to look at that data, but on the level of an individual person, it's intrusive. It is arguably better to respect users' privacy while also limiting the amount of bandwidth that tracking scripts consume in addition to the files on your site, especially on mobile devices that are metered.

Social-sharing buttons also contain tracking code. If you are able to write your own custom buttons to open up a new post on a given social site, do that. But don't include sharing buttons, especially those offered up by third parties. They are invasive and they'll leave gaping holes in your page design for users who run blockers for ads and trackers.

If you do need access data, look into software that you can host on your own server. The Webalizer (`http://www.webalizer.org`) is a mature package that will analyze and provide visualizations based solely on the limited information transmitted in a typical request for a page from your site. Another user-friendlier way to track the spread of your content is to employ your own URL shortener, particularly if it is backed by shortening software that track clicks and sharing activity, in a more or less anonymous way. Finally, do not store your server logs for any longer than the time it takes to output anonymized visualizations and other analysis from them.

Stick with the advice in this chapter: Create useful, share-worthy content behind short, memorable URLs. Add meta tags for sharing according to Open Graph and other ad-hoc sharing protocols. And license everything you can under a permissive Creative Commons license. Build lightweight pages that are responsive and progressively enhanced, and adhere to the latest standards specifications while remaining backward compatible with older browsers to the greatest degree possible. That's the social web.

# Resources for the Future

There are so many books and resources on web design and development that it can be difficult to know which are worth your time to read. Below is a list of my favorites, many of which I consult regularly in my own web writing and design work. Most are written for advanced audiences, but the techniques and approaches in *How to Design and Write Web Pages Today* will prepare you to engage with these additional resources.

## WEB DESIGN MAGAZINES, BLOGS, AND PODCASTS

*The Big Web Show,* http://5by5.tv/bigwebshow/
An hour-long podcast hosted by web-standards veteran Jeffery Zeldman. New episodes released every month or so.

*Creative Bloq,* http://www.creativebloq.com/
A very active site with articles on a range of design matters.

*A List Apart,* http://www.alistapart.com/
*A List Apart* is one of the finest web magazines out there; several articles are published every month. Topics range from standards documents to design practices.

*Responsive Design Podcast,* https://responsivewebdesign.com/podcast/
A weekly podcast on responsive design matters, co-hosted by Karen McGrane and Ethan Marcotte, who coined the term *responsive web design.*

*ShopTalk,* http://shoptalkshow.com/
An engaging and often hilariously funny podcast, hosted by web developer Dave Rupert and web designer Chris Coyier.

*SitePoint,* https://www.sitepoint.com/
A sprawling site with dozens of new, peer-reviewed articles published each day on a number of different web design topics and languages.

*Signal v. Noise,* https://m.signalvnoise.com/
*Signal v. Noise* is an influential blog on work practices, industry, and the big picture of web design and development.

*24 Ways,* https://24ways.org/
A yearly, Advent-calendar blog that runs the month of December and covers some very inspiring, thought-provoking approaches to web design. Archives are well worth the read any time of year.

## ESSENTIAL REFERENCES

*HTML Dog,* http://htmldog.com/
A lean and lightweight set of references and tutorials. Makes a good companion to MDN, which tends to be more technical but also more detailed.

*Mozilla Developer Network,* https://developer.mozilla.org/
Hands down the most thorough reference on the web, with links to the full specification documents at the W3C. Maintained by an active community of contributors.

## CASCADING STYLE SHEETS

Cederholm, Dan. *CSS3 for Web Designers,* 2nd ed. New York: A Book Apart, 2015.
An important book on using some of the advanced features of CSS3 to progressively enhance a page at the user-experience level.

Snook, Jonathan. *Scalable and Modular Architecture for CSS,* https://shop.smacss.com
A thoughtful book on the organization of CSS files that inspired some of the advice in *How to Design and Write Web Pages Today.*

Takada, Mikito. *Learn CSS Layout the Pedantic Way*, http://book.mixu.net /css/
An open-access ebook that does an excellent job covering different layout techniques and oddities in CSS.


# JAVASCRIPT

Crockford, Douglas. *JavaScript: The Good Parts*. Sebastopol, CA: O'Reilly Media, 2008.
A solid companion to Haverbeke's book. Highly opinionated but with fascinating looks at the inner workings of JavaScript.

Haverbeke, Marijn. *Eloquent JavaScript: A Modern Introduction to Programming*, 2nd ed. San Francisco: No Starch Press, 2014.
An essential book on JavaScript. Probably the best there is, and an excellent introduction to programming concepts generally.


# HTML AND RESPONSIVE DESIGN

Jehl, Scott. *Responsible Responsive Design*. New York: A Book Apart, 2014.
Responsive web design read through a serious lens of progressive enhancement and device-neutral accessibility.

Keith, Jeremy. *Resilient Web Design*. 2016. https://resilientwebdesign.com/
A self-published ebook that is a beautiful example of web design and a sustainability-minded history of the web.

Keith, Jeremy, and Rachel Andrew. *HTML5 for Web Designers*, 2nd ed. New York: A Book Apart, 2016.
A compact introduction to HTML5, including its form elements.

Marcotte, Ethan. *Responsive Design: Patterns & Principles*. New York: A Book Apart, 2015.
Marcotte's follow-up to his original classic. Thoughtful treatment of RWD-based workflows.

Marcotte, Ethan. *Responsive Web Design*, 2nd ed. New York: A Book Apart, 2014.
The classic book on responsive design. Be wary of the use of `max-width` media queries in the examples, however.

Wroblewski, Luke. *Mobile First*. New York: A Book Apart, 2011.
A commerce-driven treatment of mobile-first design that is readily applicable to all kinds of sites.

## GENERAL DESIGN AND PROTOTYPING

Lidwell, William, Kritina Holden, and Jill Butler. *Universal Principles of Design*, rev ed. Beverly, MA: Rockport, 2010.
The title says it all: a treasure trove of different, essentially universal design principles. Covers design fields from print to industrial. An indispensable and inspirational reference.

Rothman, Julia. *Drawn In: A Peek Into the Inspiring Sketchbooks of 44 Fine Artists, Illustrators, Graphic Designers, and Cartoonists*. Beverly, MA: Quarry Books, 2011.
Prototyping by example. A fascinating look at how others use paper to work out a range of ideas to be executed in different media.

Snyder, Carolyn. *Paper Prototyping: The Fast and Easy Way to Design and Refine User Interfaces*. San Francisco: Morgan Kaufmann/Elsevier, 2003.
No better (or denser) coverage of prototyping than this book. If paper-based prototyping is your thing, that is.

## TYPOGRAPHY

Bringhurst, Robert. *The Elements of Typographic Style*, 4th ed. Seattle: Hartley & Marks, 2012.
The go-to professional manual on typography. Includes exhaustive guidance as well as appendices covering classic typefaces, foundries, and technical terminology.

Lupton, Ellen. *Thinking with Type: A Critical Guide for Designers, Writers, Editors, & Students*, 2nd ed. New York: Princeton Architectural Press, 2010.
The best all-in-one book on the topic of typography. While not necessarily screen-oriented, the principles still apply.

Lupton, Ellen, ed. *Type on Screen: A Critical Guide for Designers, Writers, Developers, & Students*. New York: Princeton Architectural Press, 2014.
A screen-based follow-up to Lupton's *Thinking with Type*.

# GRID-BASED DESIGN

Elam, Kimberly. *Grid Systems: Principles of Organizing Type*. New York: Princeton Architectural Press, 2004.

A treatment of grid design, specifically aimed at typography.

Samara, Timothy. *Making and Breaking the Grid: A Graphic Design Layout Workshop*. Gloucester, MA: Rockport, 2002.

A thorough investigation of grid-based design in print and digital media.

Tondreau, Beth. *Layout Essentials: 100 Design Principles for Using Grids*. Beverly, MA: Rockport, 2009.

Two-page spreads covering 100 different principles and techniques for using grids. A good place to start with grid-based design.

# Glossary

**absolute units**: CSS units such as pixel, inch, and point that have a fixed dimension.

**alpha channel**: A channel for setting transparency on a color; used with `rgba()` color notation in CSS.

**anti-aliasing**: In screen typography, anti-aliasing is a technique that displays use to smooth the curved edges of type.

**application programming interface (API)**: The set of functions that a code library or system can perform when accessed from a separate program.

**array (JavaScript)**: Collections of values that can be assigned to a single variable. Individual elements of an array are accessed by number, starting with 0.

**assignment (JavaScript)**: The equals sign, =, assigns a value to a variable. The equals sign is not a statement of equality.

**attribute**: In HTML, attributes provide metadata on tags; common attributes include `class` and `id`.

**attribute-value**: In HTML, values assigned to attributes can be called attribute-values; in `<nav id="navigation">`, *navigation* is the attribute-value.

**baseline grid**: A repeating value, often used the length of an entire page, for setting type. Text sits on the baseline. Similar to line spacing (single, double) in word processors, but more precise.

**block elements**: In HTML, block elements are headings, paragraphs, and lists, which would ordinarily appear vertically separated from other elements on a page.

**Booleans (JavaScript)**: Boolean values are `true` or `false` and are often used within loops and other program control structures.

**cache**: A storage mechanism used by browsers and other software to prevent redownloading assets on repeat requests. CSS and JavaScript files are often cached by browsers.

**case sensitivity**: Case sensitivity is a quality of operating systems, web servers, and other software. Case-sensitive software treats `FILE.txt` as a different file from `file.txt`. Most web servers are case sensitive.

**character entities**: Special codes used in HTML to write characters that are otherwise a part of HTML. The ampersand, &, is represented in HTML as the character entity `&amp;`.

**child**: The immediate descendant of an HTML tag. The `<head>` tag is always a child of `<html>`, for example.

**class**: An HTML attribute for adding additional structure that can be shared across a group of elements. Unlike unique IDs, classes can be used multiple times across a page.

**commit (Git)**: Commits are crafted markers in a project's history, written using the `git commit` command.

**console (JavaScript)**: A browser feature used for examining error output and testing JavaScript.

**declaration block (CSS)**: A set of style properties and values enclosed in curly braces. A declaration block is always associated with one or more CSS selectors.

**descendant**: Any tag nested inside of any other tag, no matter how deeply; a more generic relationship description than *child*.

**DOM scripting**: A method for interacting with the browser's representation of an HTML document (the Document Object Model, DOM) using JavaScript.

**DRY principle**: Don't Repeat Yourself. A piece of information about a system should only appear in one place. For example, using a single CSS file to style an entire site is a DRY practice.

**dynamic sites**: Websites that are generated by software, often running on a webserver, that may interact with databases and other data sources.

**element (HTML)**: An element in HTML refers to an opening and closing tag and the content they surround. The alphabetic contents of an HTML tag is an element selector in CSS.

**em**: A relative unit of measure used in CSS. Historically, an em was the length of a side of an imaginary square around a typeface's uppercase M. In most browsers, 1em is equal to 16px.

**file extensions**: The portion of a filename following a dot. The file extensions for HTML files are usually .html or .htm; CSS files are .css, and JavaScript files are .js. File extensions help certain pieces of software know how to open or process a file.

**flexible images**: A component of responsive web design; flexible images are sized and presented to conform to the size of their parent/containing element. They expand and contract with the viewport.

**flow lines**: In grid design, flow lines are horizontal lines that mark shared bottoms and tops of content within a grid.

**fluid grids**: A component of responsive web design; fluid grids are specified in percentage units, and when coupled with media queries, they enable content to remain readable while also conforming to the size of any viewport.

**font stack**: In CSS, a font stack is a list of typefaces that a browser may use to display a design. Font stacks are listed in order of preference and should always end with a generic name (serif, sans-serif).

**fragment identifier**: A portion of the URL, following a hash symbol (#), that references the unique ID of a page element. Browsers will often scroll to the top of an element referenced by a URL fragment identifier.

**functional notation (CSS)**: Notation used in certain CSS values, such as `rgba()` or `calc()`. Because the values are put inside parentheses, such values resemble functions in other languages, but may or may not be true functions.

**Git**: A popular free and open-source distributed version control system.

**graceful degradation**: The complementary effect of progressive enhancement, a page or feature gracefully degrades when there is a suitable fallback in content or design for less capable browsers, poor network conditions, and other challenging situations.

**grid system**: The use of two or more columns to design a page layout where content may span multiple columns.

**gutter**: The space between the columns of a grid.

**hexadecimal**: Numbers 0–9/A–F. F is equal to decimal 15. Hexadecimal numbers are used in CSS to specify colors.

**id**: An HTML attribute for adding additional structure to a unique element, once per page. An ID can also be reached through a URL's fragment identifier.

**infinite loop**: A condition where a loop in a program will run forever, because the condition tested in the loop will always be true. In JavaScript, an infinite loop may cause the browser to crash.

**inheritance (CSS)**: A quality of certain CSS style properties where the property's value transfers from a parent element to a child element. Most inherited CSS properties are related to text and fonts.

**inline elements**: HTML elements that are not free-standing blocks, but mark phrases of content. Examples include the bold/strong, italic/emphasis, and anchor tags.

**line endings**: The invisible character inserted by text editors when the Return/Enter key is used at the end of a line of text. For web purposes, line endings should be the Unix-style line feed (LF) character.

**margins (grid)**: The space between the edges of a grid and the viewport.

**media queries**: A component of responsive design, media queries are CSS notation for applying style rules under specific conditions, usually the minimum width of a screen. If the conditions are met, the CSS styles within the media query are applied.

**modular scale**: A set of mathematically derived, harmonious proportions. Used for specifying larger and smaller font sizes, as well as size ratios between grid columns.

**numbers (JavaScript)**: A data type in JavaScript. Numbers may be whole (6) or decimal (6.01). Unlike some programming languages, JavaScript does not distinguish between number types.

**objects (JavaScript)**: Objects in JavaScript may be simple primitives, which behave as collections of data similar to arrays, or more complex and include their own functions, called methods. There are numerous objects built into browser implementations of JavaScript, including the document object.

**package manager**: A piece of software used to download and install software and libraries for a particular operating system, language, or development platform. Package managers are used in lieu of manual downloads, such as from a website.

**parent**: The immediate ancestor of an HTML tag. The <html> tag is always the parent of <head> and <body>.

**pixel**: A common unit of measurement in digital design. A *hardware pixel* refers to an individual point of light on a display, while a *reference pixel* refers to a high-density display's effective pixel dimension, which may be four or more hardware pixels.

**point**: A traditional absolute unit from typography and typesetting. A point is equal to 1/72 of an inch. Point values are only used in CSS for creating print stylesheets.

**polyfill**: In web development, a polyfill is a piece of JavaScript that enables older browsers to render newer features that are not supported natively in the browser itself.

**progressive enhancement**: The gradual addition of more complex and sophisticated languages and behaviors on a web page, executed in a way that does not make a page nonfunctional or inaccessible to users with different devices or physical abilities.

**pseudocode**: Illustrative code that does not function, but rather to show how different parts of a language work or to suggest how a piece of a program would be written in full.

**quirks mode**: A legacy rendering method used to display old and incorrectly built web pages in modern, standards-compliant browsers. Quirks mode is triggered in the absence of a `<!DOCTYPE>` declaration on the first line of a page's HTML.

**read-evaluate-print loop (REPL)**: A program used to interactively write and return the results of programming language. Node.js provides a command-line REPL for JavaScript, for example.

**relative units**: CSS units such as em, rem, and percentage, whose dimensions are wholly dependent on context and user preferences.

**rem**: Similar to the em unit, the root em unit (`rem`) refers to the font size on the root element of an HTML document.

**root element**: In XML, the root element is a tag that contains all others in the document. In standards-compliant HTML, `<html>` is always the root element.

**root web directory**: The directory that contains all of a site's files and subdirectories. A file named `page.html` in the root web directory can be accessed at `http://example.com/page.html`.

**sectioning elements**: Sectioning elements are used to structure block elements into meaningful groups of related content. HTML5 introduced a number of useful sectioning elements for headers, footers, articles, sections, and asides, resulting in more semantically rich global page structures.

**Secure Shell (SSH)**: An internet communication protocol that allows one computer to access another from a distance. SSH is especially useful and important for interacting with a remote web server.

**selector (CSS)**: Notation that references some element, structure, or relationship in HTML. When a browser matches a CSS selector with a portion of the HTML, the selector's declaration block of styles is applied.

**semantic HTML**: HTML elements and attributes used to describe the structural meaning of a page's contents.

**SFTP**: Secure File Transfer Protocol, which transfers files over a secure connection (usually SSH).

**sibling**: HTML siblings are any adjacent tags that share a parent. The `<head>` and `<body>` tags are always siblings, sharing the same `<html>` parent.

**source formatting**: The use of line breaks, comments, and indentations to make source code easier to read.

**spatial zones**: In grid design, spatial zones are formed when content spans across multiple columns and their intermediate gutters.

**static site generators**: Software that assembles a set of HTML, CSS, and JavaScript files, independent of a user request, as in dynamic sites.

**static sites**: Websites whose HTML, CSS, and JavaScript files are either written by hand or stored on a server as such, as in the case of files produced from a static site generator.

**strings (JavaScript)**: Any collection of characters, including letters, numbers, and punctuation, contained between single or double quotation marks. `"cat"` is a string, and because of the quotation marks, so is `"42"`.

**style declaration**: The combination of a CSS style property and its value. Multiple style declarations can appear inside of a CSS declaration block.

**style property**: A particular design feature that can be specified using CSS. CSS offers properties that style text, set the dimensions of content boxes, and position HTML elements to create a page layout.

**style value**: Each style property is followed by one or more values that are unique to the design of a page. Colors, dimensions, and border styles are common CSS values.

**syntax highlighting**: A feature of text editors that color one language feature, such as HTML element names, differently from another, such as HTML attribute-value pairs. Syntax highlighting makes it easier to read and spot errors in source code.

**system fonts**: Fonts that are commonly installed on an operating system. The bulk of a CSS font stack should be comprised of system fonts used in different operating systems.

**type selectors**: Also called *element selectors*. The most basic form of CSS selector, which references only an individual tag's name.

**typographic scale**: A fixed set of font sizes for use within a given design. The traditional typographer's scale includes sizes such as 9, 10, 11, 12, 14, and 16, usually in points.

**Unicode**: An international standard written by the Unicode Consortium that maps particular glyphs to binary representations (0s and 1s).

**usability testing**: A method for determining the efficacy and ease of interacting with a designed object. In a usability test, trained professionals observe representative users interacting with a website or some other interface or product.

**validator**: A piece of software used to check a language's conformance to a specification. The W3C maintains web-based validators for HTML and CSS.

**vendor prefixes**: In CSS, newer properties and values are sometimes implemented by specific browser makers prior to the completed specification. Webkit browsers use the `-webkit-` prefix, while Mozilla/Firefox uses the `-moz-` prefix.

**version control system**: A specialized piece of software used to track the history of a project's development. Version control systems allow users to return to an earlier version of the project.

**viewport**: The area of a browser window or mobile device where web page content is rendered.

**viewport meta element**: A meta tag used to set certain display behaviors and properties of the viewport.

**void elements**: HTML tags that do not surround any content. Examples include the `<img>` and `<source>` tags.

**web standards**: An industry term for the specifications (not necessarily standards) issued by the ISO, W3C, WHATWG, Ecma International, and other groups who oversee the official definitions of the web's languages and protocols.

**well-formed**: In XML, well-formed documents follow a specific set of rules, including the order of closing nested tags and the quoting of attribute values. Well-formed style can also be practiced in HTML.

# Index

Page numbers in *italics* indicate sidebars in the book.

## About the Author

KARL STOLLEY is a faculty member of both the Department of Humanities and the Information Technology and Management Department at the Illinois Institute of Technology in Chicago. He holds a PhD in rhetoric from Purdue University and maintains a web presence at https://karlstolley.com/.